Current Issues in Alcohol/Drug Studies

Current Issues in Alcohol/Drug Studies

Edith S. Lisansky Gomberg, PhD
Editor

Routledge
Taylor & Francis Group
LONDON AND NEW YORK

First published 1989 by The Haworth Press

Published 2018 by Routledge
2 Park Square, Milton Park, Abingdon, Oxon OX14 4RN
52 Vanderbilt Avenue, New York, NY 10017

First issued in paperback 2018

Routledge is an imprint of the Taylor & Francis Group, an informa business

Current Issues in Alcohol/Drug Studies has also been published as *Drugs & Society*, Volume 3, Numbers 3/4 1989.

Library of Congress Cataloging-in-Publication Data

Current issues in alcohol/drug studies / Edith S. Lisansky Gomberg, guest editor.
p. cm.
"Also published as Drugs & Society, Volume 3, Numbers 3/4 1989" – t.p. verso.
Includes bibliographical references.
ISBN 0-86656-965-0
1. Alcoholism – Research. 2. Drug abuse – Research. I. Gomberg, Edith S., 1920-
HV5047.C87 1989
362.29 – dc20

89-24470
CIP

ISBN 13: 978-1-138-88181-5 (pbk)
ISBN 13: 978-0-86656-965-1 (hbk)

Current Issues in Alcohol/Drug Studies

CONTENTS

Foreword xi
Edith S. Lisansky Gomberg, PhD

The Perils of *Powell*: In Search of a Factual Foundation for the "Disease Concept of Alcoholism" 1
Herbert Fingarette

The Heritability of Alcoholism: Science and Social Policy 29
David Lester

Elements of Genetic Theory 29
Historical Development 32
Characteristic Methods 33
Boundaries of Genetic Theory 34
Research Results 36
Twin Studies 36
Half Sibling Studies 42
Adoption Studies 44
Genetic Markers and Alcoholism 51
Pharmacogenetics and Alcohol Metabolism 52
Practical Implications 57
Relations to Other Theories 61
Conclusion 62

Is Risk for Alcoholism Predictable? A Probabilistic Approach to a Developmental Problem 69
Robert A. Zucker

The Concept of Risk 70
Factors Necessary for the Anticipation of Risk: The Problem of Theory in Etiologic Research 71
Anticipating Risk for Alcoholism: Evidence for Continuity and Cumulation of Process 76

Specific vs. Nonspecific Etiology: A Cautionary Note 82
Anticipating Risk for Alcoholism and Alcohol Abuse: Evidence for Discontinuity and for the Operation of Mediational and Ameliorative Processes 84
A Probabilistic Framework for Risk and Outcome 86

The Problems of Nosology in Alcoholism Treatment and Research **95**
Thomas P. Beresford, MD
Frederic C. Blow, PhD
Kirk J. Brower, MD
Jack G. Modell, MD
Cindy Kracht, MSW

Purposes of Nosology in Alcoholism 96
Nosologic Systems 98
Conclusion 109

On Terms Used and Abused: The Concept of "Codependency" **113**
Edith S. Lisansky Gomberg, PhD

What Is "Codependency"? 115
Thesis 1 116
Thesis 2 118
Thesis 3 120
Recent Criticism of "Codependency" 123
A Note on the Term "Addiction" 125
From Alcoholic to Lottoholic 126
Discussion 128

Adult Children of Alcoholics: Is It Really a Separate Field for Study? **133**
Robert J. Beidler, DSW

Children of Alcoholics, Diagnostic Label or Category for Study? 134
Adult Children of Alcoholics and Individual Maladjustment 135
The Family Alcoholism and the Adult Child 136

General Theory on Adult Adjustment and Adult Children of Alcoholics 137
Sociopathy, Alcoholism, and Adult Children of Alcoholics 139
Conclusion 140

The New Temperance Movement: Through the Looking-Glass **143**
Dwight B. Heath, PhD

Antecedents in U.S. History 146
Empirical Evidence 151
Implications 163

Public Policy on Alcohol and Illicit Drugs **169**
Don Cahalan, PhD

Illicit Drug Issues 170
Alcoholism Prevention Programs 174
Issues Concerning Alcoholism Treatment 178
Organizational Issues 181

THE GREAT DRUG DEBATE

Taking Drugs Seriously **187**
John Kaplan

A Repeal of Drug Prohibition? 188
A Prescription System? 190
No Surrender? 192
The Case of Cocaine 194
The Dangers of Cocaine 195
Finding a Solution 198
Supply-Side Enforcement 201
Demand-Side Enforcement 203
The Prognosis 206

Don't Legalize Drugs **209**
Morton M. Kondracke

ABOUT THE EDITOR

Edith S. Lisansky Gomberg, PhD, has had a long and distinguished career in the field of alcohol and drug studies as a clinician, teacher, and researcher. She is currently Professor of Psychology in the Department of Psychiatry, School of Medicine, and Professor at the School of Social Work, both of the University of Michigan. She is also Research Consultant, Neuropsychiatry, Ann Arbor Veterans' Administration Hospital and Visiting Professor of Psychology at Rutgers University. Dr. Gomberg was a Mary E. Ives Fellow of Yale University, and an Elizabeth Avery Colton Fellow of the American Association of University Women. She has received numerous awards including the Pioneer Award of the National Council on Alcoholism Office on Women in 1977 and the gold medallion in 1986 by Rutgers Center of Alcohol Studies for her service to research and education in alcohol studies. Dr. Gomberg serves on the editorial boards of the leading journals in the drug and alcohol field. She earned her doctorate in psychology from Yale University and her masters' degree from Columbia University.

Foreword

In the early years of this century, the British Medical Research Council appointed a committee to study alcohol in order to, ". . . separate what is knowledge from what is surmise, conjecture or popular belief." In the final report of the committee, the chairman wrote,

> . . . Alcohol is an ungrateful subject. Most people who are interested in the subjects are already partisans . . . The majority of those who would give any attention to original work would do so less to gain knowledge than to find arms and argument to support their preconceived notion. (D'Abernon, 1918)

Seventy years later, alcohol is still an ungrateful subject, and this collection could not begin to deal with all the controversial issues which exist. To name a few disagreements: there is controversy about the "biological markers" and biochemical screening for alcoholism, about the "disinhibitory" effects of alcohol and the tension reduction hypothesis, about the motivation to drink and the etiology of alcoholism, and there are wars over the effectiveness of different treatment modalities: inpatient versus outpatient, long-term versus short-term, counseling, self-help, cognitive therapies, and so on. "Alcoholism" is much written about but we have yet to achieve universal agreement about definition/diagnosis.

We have selected here some current issues for discussion. Two aspects of these presentations are evident. First, there is more emphasis on alcohol-related issues than on problems of other drugs such as prescription medication, over-the-counter drugs, and banned substances. This is, in part, because there are simply more people writing, treating, researching, and thinking about alcohol-related problems. One may justify it in terms of sheer numbers, i.e., the number of people involved in alcohol-related problems.

Second, we have chosen not to present *debates* over the questions raised but to have various contributors present their points of view. But it is clear in this volume that there are significant differences among contributors in their perception of alcoholism as disease, in public policy issues like proposed legislative controls over alcoholic beverages.

Without premeditated attempt to make this a multidisciplinary collection, the invitation to participate produced contributions from a very wide variety of disciplines. Represented here are medicine and biochemistry, psychiatry and psychology, philosophy, anthropology, law, social work and journalism. That may be a commentary on the range of disciplines involved in drinking and alcohol-related problems in American society.

The collection opens with discussion of the disease concept of alcoholism and with a review of the literature on the genetics of alcoholism by Fingarette and Lester respectively. Zucker presents a developmental issue: what do we mean by "risk" and is the risk for alcoholism predictable? Beresford and his collaborators, a treatment and research team, analyze a number of current typologies in terms of different addiction models. Two challenges to widely held, well promoted, popularized ideas, "codependency" and the adult-children-of-alcoholics explanation of behavior, follow. I have examined the idea of "codependency" and the popularized extensions of "addiction," and Beidler critiques the adult-children-of-alcoholics explanation.

The last three contributions deal with social and policy issues. Heath calls attention to problems in the distribution-of-consumption model (the Ledermann hypothesis) and describes the pressure for stringent legislative controls on alcoholic beverages as the New Temperance Movement. Cahalan calls attention to the two-tiered drug problem in America and social class differentials in access to treatment and rehabilitation facilities. One suggestion to deal with "the drug problem" in America has been the legalization of banned substances and both Kaplan and Kondracke present very cogent arguments against this proposed solution of "the drug problem."

All of the issues raised in this volume are alive and well and are much debated. Alcohol and drugs may indeed be "ungrateful" subjects, and theory, treatment, research are the arenas in which the issues are central. Our knowledge is in a constant state of change: we add new facts and findings, discard the unworkable, generalize from our data, revise the accepted wisdoms, and continue on. We would hope that this volume sets out points of view on some of the critical issues.

Edith S. Lisansky Gomberg, PhD

REFERENCES

The Right Honourable Lord D'Abernon (1920). The scientific basis of drink control. *The British Journal of Inebriety*, 73-85.

Alcohol: Its Action on the Human Organism (1917). Report of the Advisory Committee: Lord D'Abernon, Chairman. London: H.M. Stationery Office, 1918.

Ledermann, S. (1956). *Alcool, alcoolisme, alcoolisation: donées scientifiques de caractére physiologique, economique et social*. Travaux et Documents de l'Institut d'Etudes Démographique 20. Paris: Institut d'Etudes Démographique.

The Perils of *Powell:* In Search of a Factual Foundation for the "Disease Concept of Alcoholism"

Herbert Fingarette

In *Powell v. Texas*[1] the United States Supreme Court addressed four opinions[2] to the significance of the "disease concept of alcoholism" for the criminal law. Leroy Powell had been convicted of public intoxication under the Texas penal code. The theory for reversal was that in light of *Robinson v. California*[3] it is "cruel and unusual" under the eighth amendment, and therefore a violation of due process, to punish a person suffering from the "disease" of alcoholism for manifesting an "involuntary" symptom of his disease by appearing drunk in public. In *Driver v. Hinnant*[4] and *Easter v. District of Columbia*,[5] landmark cases decided not long before *Powell*, the Fourth and District of Columbia Circuits accepted argument to the same effect. Contrary to the utterly confident expectations of a number of specialists in this area of law, the Court rejected Powell's appeal, five to four.[6]

The mere vote tally, however, does not show how precarious was the Court's refusal to adopt *Driver* and *Easter*. Four Justices both accepted the "disease concept" and, in a vigorous dissent by Jus-

---

Herbert Fingarette is Professor of Philosophy, University of California, Santa Barbara, CA 94106.

The author wishes to express his deep appreciation to Miss Ann Fingarette for her notable critiques of several drafts of this paper, and to the editors of the *Harvard Law Review* for their important help in final editing.

Reprinted with permission from the Harvard Law Review, 1970, 83, pp. 793-812.

tice Fortas, urged reversal. Justice White's was the swing vote for affirmance. In a separate opinion, Justice White appeared to accept, and surely expressed sympathy for, the theory of the defense, but felt that the theory did not fit the facts developed at trial. Even the four Justices who joined in the plurality opinion for affirmance found the "most troubling aspects"[7] of the case to be not the validity of the "disease concept" but the difficulties of containing within acceptable bounds a constitutional doctrine constructed upon it.

It is my aim in this paper to point out inadequacies in the structure of the *Powell* dissent and to document in some detail that "involuntariness" and "disease" are dangerously slippery concepts in this context. I wish neither to assert nor deny that courts may construct a sound constitutional rationale for withholding criminal punishment for the public drunkenness of alcoholics, but rather to contribute to a stronger foundation for future analysis. For this purpose, we need first a brief sketch of the kind of foundation such analysis might require.

I

One factual premise of the argument of *Driver*, *Easter*, and the *Powell* dissent is that alcoholism is a "disease" which is "involuntarily" and non-culpably caused and maintained.[8] This premise, which the courts seem to consider a unitary "concept,"[9] is of course analyzable—at least superficially and maybe also more fundamentally—into two approaches, one resting on the key word "disease" and the other on "involuntary."

The former approach relies on the purported "disease" status of the alcoholic, and on the holding of *Robinson* that the eighth amendment prohibits punishment for the status of being ill simpliciter. More specifically, the argument is that an alcoholic's public intoxication is a "condition" which is a constitutive part of the disease "status," within the meaning of *Robinson*.[10] On the face of this argument, nothing need be said concerning culpability or voluntariness.[11] The obvious difficulty with the *Robinson* analogy, however, is that *Robinson* emphatically limits its holding to the disease-status and excludes from its scope any anti-social "behavior'' associated with the disease.[12] This qualification raises prima facie doubts as to the propriety of applying *Robinson* to the *Powell* situation, since common sense at least would consider public drunkenness as partly ''behavior.'' In part to avoid this difficulty, the *Powell* dissent insists on labelling public intoxication as a ''condition'' and not conduct;[13] to accentuate the difficulty, Justice Marshall's plurality opinion for affirmance refers to public drunkenness as constituting ''behavior,''[14] ''acts,''[15] and ''conduct.''[16]

The prima facie applicability of *Robinson* may also be questioned on another score. In all the *Powell* opinions but Justice White's, public intoxication is at times conceived as a consequence of alcoholism.[17] The word ''symptomatic'' is sometimes used,[18] but this is an ambiguous term here; a symptom may be viewed with equal sense for various purposes as either a ''part'' of a disease or as an ''effect.''[19] At any rate, the question is whether Robinson applies if public intoxication somehow is a result of alcoholism but not ''part'' of it. *Robinson* does explicitly exclude antisocial acts which result from drug addiction from the scope of its holding[20] but says nothing of antisocial ''conditions'' which are results.[21]

These rather arid terminological difficulties with *Robinson* reflect the absence of any obvious rationale for that decision.[22] The *Powell* dissent escapes the necessity of resolving these difficulties by dealing with the problem of public drunkenness in terms of the second approach mentioned above, keyed on ''involuntariness.'' Such an extension of *Robinson* does not seem as inevitable and innocuous as the *Powell* dissent[23] and the courts which have accepted the ''disease concept of alcoholism'' apparently believe.[24] The extension of *Robinson* to public drunkenness under the rationale of ''involuntariness'' seems to compel us to apply the same rationale to the underlying condition of alcoholism. Thus, the defense in the *Powell* situation could be offered, quite independent of the *Robinson*-disease analogy, that public intoxication is an involuntary result of alcoholism, a condition itself non-culpably caused and maintained. This argument requires the intermediate finding, for the purpose of assessing culpability for public intoxication, that the alcoholic's excessive drinking is involuntary. The legal conclusion that resultant public intoxication cannot be made criminal then follows from a principle such as that adopted by the *Powell* dissent, that "[c]riminal penalties may not be inflicted upon a person for being in a condition he is powerless to change."[25]

I wish in the remainder of this paper to examine the factual content of the statements, central to the "disease concept of alcoholism," that alcoholism is a "disease" and that alcoholism, and the alcoholic's excessive drinking, are "involuntary." Specifically, I will first comment briefly on the *Powell* dissent's conception of those statements, and the factual support there offered, and then explore at greater length the relevant medical literature.

II

The dissent accepts, without evaluative comment,[26] the trial judge's "findings of fact":[27]

1. That chronic alcoholism is a disease which destroys the afflicted person's will power to resist the constant, excessive consumption of alcohol.
2. That a chronic alcoholic does not appear in public by his own volition but under a compulsion symptomatic of the disease of chronic alcoholism.
3. That Leroy Powell . . . is a chronic alcoholic who is afflicted with the disease of chronic alcoholism.

These "findings" constitute the "premises of a syllogism transparently designed to bring th[e] case within the scope of . . . *Robinson v. California*."[28]

Four of the Justices who reject Powell's appeal agree that these are not "'findings of fact'" in "any recognizable, traditional sense in which that term has been used in a court of law. . . ."[29] The first two[30] of the "findings" constitute sweepingly general assertions about a large class of alcoholics: it is asserted that chronic alcoholism is itself an involuntarily maintained status, and it is further asserted that medical science has demonstrated constant and inevitable relationships between this status and public drunkenness.

It is evident that no reasonable basis for such "findings" could appear either in the testimony of Powell himself or the testimony concerning his personal history. Conceivably the testimony of expert witnesses might justify the findings—yet in Powell's trial only one psychiatric expert testified. While this expert did in fact testify to the effect that a "chronic alcoholic" is an "involuntary drinker," his elaboration of this characterization obscures his meaning.[31] In any event, inconclusive testimony by a single expert witness could hardly justify even the findings as to involuntariness (the expert said nothing of alcoholism as a "disease") unless there were a background of theory so familiar, unambiguous, and unchallengeable as to render further elaboration otiose. A major portion of the dissent consists of an attempt to provide just such an appropriate medical background as a "context' which, as the dissenting opinion avers, an understanding of the case "requires."[32]

With respect to the medical background concerning "chronic alcoholism," the *Powell* dissent acknowledges that "there is a great deal that remains to be discovered," that "many aspects of the disease remain obscure," and that we are "woefully deficient in our medical, diagnostic, and therapeutic knowledge" in both this area and that of "mental disease."[33] Although this admission alone takes much of the ground from beneath the sweeping "findings of fact" of the trial judge, the dissent maintains that there are "some hard facts—medical and, especially, legal facts—that are accessible to us and that provide a context in which the instant case may be analyzed."[34]

One such "hard fact" appears to be that alcoholism is medically recognized as a disease.[35] The dissent also believes it to be a fact that the "core meaning" of the disease concept of alcoholism

> as agreed by authorities, is that alcoholism is caused and maintained by something other than the moral fault of the alcoholic, something that, to a greater or lesser extent depending upon the physiological or psychological makeup and history of the individual, cannot be controlled by him.[36]

It will be noted that neither of these "facts" mentions public intoxication. This is not because the "core meaning" merely happens to be formulated in the dissent as a very general statement, but because, as we shall see in detail later,[37] its statement can only be a very general one.

Though the "core meaning" is silent with respect to the symptoms or effects of alcoholism, or their voluntariness, it does raise the issue of voluntariness with respect to the causes of the status of chronic alcoholism and with respect to the persistence of that status. However, what it says is not that an alcoholic's condition is involuntary, but that an alcoholic's control over what causes his "disease" will be a matter of "greater or lesser degree"; the degree cannot be assessed in general for all "chronic alcoholics" but will depend upon the individual alcoholic's physiology, psychological makeup, and personal history. Such cautiousness contrasts sharply with the blunt conclusions of the trial judge and of the dissenters themselves that alcoholism is "involuntary."

Even more injudiciously blunt is the judgment that however alcoholism be caused, it is in any event not attributable to "the moral fault of the alcoholic."[38] The pontifical tone may be due in part to the fact that while medical men do have a certain expertise in studying causation, it is not, as medical scientists are themselves prone to insist, moral expertise. Expertise generates a sensitivity to the complexity of issues and a consequent cautiousness when generalizing on those issues; beyond the area of our expertise we tend to be freer with wholesale judgments. In fact, of course, moral exculpation is hardly a proper part of medical theory, and to offer it as medically established "fact" is on its face unjustifiable.

III

Such inconsistencies and logical difficulties indicate that there may be underlying, unacknowledged factors influencing the dissent's conclusions. We shall discuss some of these factors in section IV, when we examine the significance of the widespread medical acceptance of the proposition that "alcoholism is a disease." For the present, we shall focus on the "voluntariness" approach by looking to the medical literature.

Many of the leading health authorities view "loss of control" as the "hallmark" of alcoholism[39] The assertion is sufficiently widespread to give the impression of substantial agreement among many authorities on a basic fact having near self-evident moral-legal implications to men of goodwill. The *Powell* dissent is not unique in culminating its discussion of "loss of control" by quoting from a medical source:[40] "' ' . . . the main point for the non-professional is that alcoholism is not within the control of the person involved.' "

However, concepts which center around voluntariness, like those centering around intent and other questions of psychological fact, present some of the most complex issues in both law and ethics. A phrase like "I couldn't control myself" or "I had no choice" could report variously a strictly physical incapacity, unconsciousness, incapacity to conform due to mental illness, somnambulism,[41] involuntary intoxication,[42] extreme provocation, or the necessity to act to save life or to act with little time to reflect. Some of these circumstances could serve in some jurisdictions as a complete defense to criminal liability, others as complete defenses in certain factual contexts, or as "partial" defenses in some degree mitigating culpability; others would have no legal effect but might mitigate punishment. These very different senses of self-control by no means exhaust the range of meanings. In what sense, then, do the authorities on alcoholism speak of "loss of control" in connection with chronic alcoholism? The *Powell* dissent's categorical claim that alcoholism is not within the alcoholic's control dissolves when one discovers the very different things that authorities mean by the phrase, the different sorts of facts which purportedly justify it, the substantive qualifications ultimately appended, and the authoritative literature in which the phrase is conspicuously omitted or explicitly rejected.

In the first place, it is difficult to sustain *any* categorical statements about alcoholism in light of the multiplicity of diagnostic schemes.[43] Jellinek distinguishes and lists over one hundred hypotheses about the nature of alcoholism.[44] There is not even any substantial agreement about the region of knowledge from which the best understanding of alcoholism may be forthcoming. Hypotheses range from the genetic through the physiological and pharmacological to the psychological and sociological. More damaging to the "involuntariness" argument, probably no expert would dispute that "variations in the patterns of drinking [among alcoholics] are tremendous";[45] and most would also agree that what alcoholics have in common is simply "a heavy preoccupation with drinking"[46] which in *some* cultural groups often leads to serious disturbances in social adaptation.[47]

Thus it is not surprising that many authorities who use "loss of control" language ultimately introduce serious qualifications. It turns out, for example, that one of the leading authorities who holds "loss of control" to be the "pathognomonic symptom" of alcoholism does not mean by this phrase that the person cannot abstain or cannot stop once he has started drinking. Rather, we are told, the phrase means that "*it is not certain that* [the alcoholic] *will be able to stop at will*."[48] Another authority who uses "loss of control" as a "criterion" for diagnosing alcoholism tells us that in various "protected" situations (among them, incidentally, the prison) many alcoholics will with "little or no difficulty" abstain or stop.[49] Still other authorities characterize "loss of control" as "not an all-or-none phenomenon"[50] and "a relative and variable phenomenon."[51]

In short, we are told not that the alcoholic has *no* control of his drinking, but that he has greater or lesser control, *widely* varying in degree according to the circumstances and the individual. This consensus conforms with the "core meaning" of the "disease concept of alcoholism" summarized in the *Powell* dissent—that the alcoholic's inability to control his drinking can be of "greater or lesser extent depending on the physiological or psychological makeup and history of the individual"—but is inconsistent with the *Powell* dissent, *Driver*, and *Easter*, insofar as those opinions assume that chronic alcoholics as a group are, by virtue of their being such, without power to control their drinking.[52]

Thus far we have noted ways in which the notion of an alcoholic's "lack of control" must be qualified. We have not examined just which of the many possible senses of "control" is at issue. As my earlier remarks have recalled, there are a number of reasonable uses of the "loss of control" idiom which exclude neither conscious choice with awareness of the relevant consequences nor legal responsibility.

The frequent reference to alcoholism as an "addiction"[53] may seem to all but settle the volitional issue. Yet the World Health Organization's Expert Committee on Dependence-Producing Drugs recently abandoned the term "addiction,"[54] proposing instead a series of terms connoting various significantly different kinds and degrees of drug "dependence." The proposed terms range from mere "desire" through a "strong desire or need" to "overpowering desire or need."[55]

Since appeal to labels like "addiction" is not illuminating, we must ask in what way and in what degree an alcoholic is thought to be alcohol-dependent. Among those who incline to the "loss of control" characterization, a number hold for a "physical" or "physiological mechanism."[56] As to the nature of this mechanism, there is a wide variety of opinion. The most one can say by way of generalizing is that these theories postulate genetic, neurological, metabolic, or allergic abnormalities which create a peculiar vulnerability to alcohol. And while the word "physical" would appear at least to exclude meaningful choice, the specific hypotheses, as we have begun to see, are never that simple. Far from excluding volition, most consist of complex models which include volition, more or less explicitly, along with the physical causes.

In fact, there is universal agreement that alcohol is not as physiologically addictive as the morphine narcotics.[57] Beyond this threshold agreement, some theories postulate a physically induced craving for alcohol, while others speak of craving for the state of intoxication rather than for the liquor. More significant, some theories hypothesize a physically induced craving to begin drinking, whereas others assume control over the taking of a first drink, but with some loss of control over further drinking. Moreover, while some theorists view compulsion to keep drinking as due to a destruction of certain control centers in the brain, or as an involuntary, conditioned response to incipient withdrawal symptoms, others view this compulsion as only a learned, somewhat controllable preference for continued drinking. Finally, many of the "physical" hypotheses suppose a gradual physical change in an alcoholic caused by his habit, implying that the strength of the compulsion to drink varies over time.

Obviously the moral and legal implications of these various hypotheses may be quite different. If, for example, a physical craving for alcohol triggers a specific, automatic reflex of drinking alcohol, then we exclude by hypothesis any significant volition. To the extent such a reflex cannot be demonstrated, then we deal with volitional response to a desire, more or less strong. With respect to the many hypotheses which postulate no initial physical craving, but only a physical mechanism that compels continued drinking, a relevant question may be whether the alcoholic himself believes he can stop, and to what extent that belief is reasonable. The expert in *Powell* testified that many alcoholics have such a belief but that the reasonableness of that belief will vary with particular circumstances. Finally, some hypotheses find volition throughout the drinking pattern, conceiving both the initiation and continuance of drinking as volitional responses to a more or less compelling desire.

Hypotheses which stress involuntariness must contend with the fact that many alcoholics do choose to abstain or control their drinking—whether only occasionally, as is often true with chronic alcoholics,[58] or in some more permanent way, as by a personal decision to abstain, by seeking medical or psychological help, or by joining such groups as Alcoholics Anonymous or Synanon. Of course, capacity to resist the urge to drink on one occasion or for a period of time does not imply that the alcoholic will have such capacity at other times. However, it would at least be more difficult to find "cruel and unusual" the punishment of an alcoholic who enjoyed periods of abstinence or who could be supposed capable of voluntarily subjecting himself to a "cure."

It remains a central feature of most of the "physical" hypotheses that the alcoholic, though in some way peculiarly sensitive physically to alcohol, is one who faces a *very difficult and painful choice*. How one wishes to assess this for moral or legal purposes is a matter which I will not attempt to resolve here. Nor am I arguing that any of these hypotheses is false, though it is important to keep in mind that they often conflict with each other and that none has been confirmed.[59] My only purpose here is to indicate that "physical" hypotheses do not claim that there is no volition in the alcoholic's excess drinking but that, partly because of physical abnormality, the alcoholic is one who faces a choice which is (increasingly) more difficult than for most people.

Moreover, by no means do all the contemporary hypotheses

which are influential in the health professions claim that there is a critical physical factor at work. Many, though they may speak of "loss of control" (quite a number do not), ascribe this to psychological or social conditions rather than physical ones. Here the term "compulsive" or the like may again be used—though some authorities say improperly so[60]—but again we must look behind the metaphor.

One authority speaks of chronic drunkenness as "a means of adapting to life conditions which are otherwise harsh, insecure, unrewarding and unproductive of the essentials of human dignity."[61] Others refer to alcoholism as a "psychosocial behavior syndrome" and assert that the taking of alcohol is primarily a "central integrative symbol around which the person organizes his life."[62] Or, as another physician puts it: "[A]lcoholism is . . . only a 'common path' in the way of problem solving to a number of adaptational issues. . . . "[63] We should not be misled by the technical psychological and sociological language. This (large) group of authorities is simply saying that, on the whole, the alcoholic has chosen this way to handle his problems in life. On this view, it may be further supposed that the more he does so, the more he has a stake in this approach and a deep fear of or deep dislike for any other. To say "he can't control it" amounts in this context to saying that mere moralistic appeals of the usual kind by family and friends are no more likely to succeed than sub-vocal or vocal "resolutions" by the person himself. Excessive drinking has become his "way of life" in spite of such appeals and resolutions. But this view does not suppose that other kinds of appeal or a change in life-setting may not successfully lead him to self-control. A way of life is not easily or casually changed; on the other hand, it is not something beyond volition.

The most persuasive testimony in support of this view comes, unwittingly at times, from the very advocates of the various "loss of control" hypotheses. For when we look to the therapeutic techniques they propose or acknowledge as most effective, we see that these involve appeals for the alcoholic to adopt voluntarily one or another course of conduct. They appeal to him to enter voluntarily a "protective setting" such as a hospital and to abide voluntarily by its rules, or they appeal to him to enter voluntarily and cooperatively on a course of Antabuse, or of "reconditioning," or to join

Alcoholics Anonymous.[64] Thus the "psychological" and "sociological" hypotheses generally do not exclude volition but presume it both in their views of the "etiology" of alcoholism and in their attempts at therapy. Indeed, there are leading authorities who explicitly recommend coercive pressures to get the alcoholic to control his drinking.[65] The effectiveness of non-physical deterrent measures shows that drinking is to some degree volitional, and suggests that the threat of the criminal sanction may be a factor in controlling such drinking as is likely to lead to criminal offenses.

We may summarize, then, by saying that the *Powell* dissent's formulation of the "core meaning" of the disease concept of alcoholism, vague and cautious as it is with respect to voluntariness, is yet not unduly so. Indeed, quite the contrary. It errs on the "control" issue because it implies too much in the way of current medical knowledge. And it errs in implying that the phrase "loss of control," as used in the medical literature, implies absence of volition.

I have tried—translating the technical language and including the necessary qualifications—to formulate a statement in harmony with a large number of influential hypotheses about alcoholism:

> Possibly partly due to some abnormal physical condition, the chronic alcoholic is one who for any of a variety of other reasons has increasingly preferred drinking as a way of adapting to his life-problems; he has reached the point where the personal and social consequences of his drinking are such that abandoning heavy drinking and the life that goes with it would require him to make a choice which, though usually genuinely practicable, is so very distressing and so very difficult, both physically and mentally, that he is unlikely to make that choice and carry it out, although he may make it with the aid of special encouragement, professional guidance, or coercive influences.

It is in part because of ambiguities and confusion inherent in the "loss of control" phraseology that a good many authorities avoid such language altogether.[66]

IV

The second "medical fact" that we shall consider, and the one which probably has done most to foster the intuitive notion that alcoholism is an inappropriate object for criminal punishment, is the simple formula "alcoholism is a disease." The dissenting opinion notes at the very outset of its presentation of "hard facts" about alcoholism that

> [i]n 1956 the [AMA] for the first time designated alcoholism as a major medical problem. . . . This significant development marked the acceptance among the medical profession of the "disease concept of alcoholism."[67]

To anticipate, it is my conclusion that the widespread (but by no means universal) acceptance in the medical and health professions of the "disease concept of alcoholism" reflects a variety of considerations which are legitimate and important to the *health* professions, but that none of these considerations has any obvious bearing on the legal issue of punishability under the eighth amendment.

One such consideration is the underlying judgment, with which I certainly concur, that it is reasonable for the health professions to attempt to help with the problem of alcoholism. Another important consideration, suggested by the first, is the widespread *hope* and *expectation* that the medical profession will someday develop understanding of and remedies for alcoholism. While there is no doubt about the importance and inspirational efficacy of this expectation,[68] and while the reasonableness of the effort is apparent, these considerations are not obviously relevant to the propriety of punishing alcoholics.

There are certain ancillary practical considerations which also motivate acceptance among doctors of "the disease concept." In the first place, it is evidently in the interest of the medical attack on alcoholism that large sums of money be reliably accessible to researchers and therapists. Adherence within the profession to such formulas as "alcoholism is a disease" (or an "illness," or a "medical problem") does much to provide assurance to such fund-granting organizations as government agencies and foundations that the enterprise is legitimate. Such assurance was no doubt profoundly strengthened when the medical profession in 1956 formally and clearly expressed its concern to assume a responsibility in the area.[69] Similarly, the availability of hospitals for the medical effort against alcoholism was apparently facilitated by the official declaration of the AMA.[70] It is also necessary to the success of the medical effort to motivate more medical men to assume responsibility for treating alcoholics. Apparently this still has a long way to go.[71]

It is extremely important to concerned doctors that the general public support their efforts.[72] The official AMA announcement and the wide professional use—especially in public discussion—of such formulas as "alcoholism is a disease" have been vital to the growing public support of medical research in the area.[73] The doctors' public use of the phrase has been a powerful influence in combatting what many health professionals see as a major cultural obstacle to their efforts—the public's habitual allegiance to "moralistic" approaches. Many health authorities feel that moral, religious, and penal approaches have failed and are bound to fail, and tend to see public commitment to these approaches as a major diversion of effort, money, and resources from the medical effort.[74] There is also a profound but usually tacit moral judgment on the part of many health professionals that the condemnatory and penal approach is inhumane.

I recognize that one may grant that all these considerations have been important and relevant to medical acceptance of the "disease concept of alcoholism," yet retain a nagging wonder whether there is not in addition some more legally relevant factual content implicit in the phrase. This is not the place to discuss the concept of "disease" in general.[75] However, I do wish to direct attention to the well-known attempt by Jellinek to clarify the factual content of the disease concept of alcoholism,[76] an attempt which concludes almost as quickly as it begins. After noting the perfunctory circularity and unhelpful generality of the medical dictionary definitions of disease, Jellinek concludes:[77]

> [*A*] *disease is what the medical profession recognizes as such*. . . . [T]hrough this fact alone alcoholism becomes an illness, whether a part of the lay public likes it or not, and even if a minority of the medical profession is disinclined to accept the idea.

In general, I do not believe that anything I have said precludes in any way the many legislative options for establishing rational procedures and institutions, whether within penal or civil systems, for "detoxifying" the acutely intoxicated, for counselling, for treating, and for otherwise helping the alcoholic. Nor is there any support in anything I have said for the irrational, expensive, and inhumane harrassment of the alcoholic, especially the impoverished and alienated alcoholic, an approach today still so prevalent.[78] The burden of my remarks is, however, that one tempting road to reform—the building of new constitutional doctrine on the basis of purported medical knowledge of alcoholism—is also a very dangerous one.

NOTES

1. 392 U.S. 514 (1968).
2. Justice Marshall, joined by Chief Justice Warren and Justices Black and Harlan, held for affirming the conviction. Justice Black, joined by Justice Harlan, filed a separate concurrence. Justice White concurred in a separate opinion. Justice Fortas, joined by Justices Douglas, Brennan, and Stewart, dissented.
3. 370 U.S. 660 (1962).
4. 356 F.2d 761 (4th Cir. 1966).
5. 361 F.2d 50 (D.C. Cir. 1966).
6. *See* Hutt, *The Recent Court Decisions on Alcoholism: A Challenge to the North American Judges Association and Its Members*, in President's Comm'n on Law Enforcement and the Administration of Justice, Task Force Report: Drunkenness 110, 112 (1967) [hereinafter cited as Task Force Report]; Note, *Driver to Easter to Powell: Recognition of the Defense of Involuntary Intoxication?*, 22 Rutgers L. Rev. 103, 134 (1967). The preceding writers viewed it as "virtually certain" that the decision in *Powell* would accord with *Easter* and *Driver*, "the likelihood of the Supreme Court's rejection of the 'disease concept of alcoholism' being 'infinitesimal.'"

Prior to *Powell*, several other recent cases had presented the same or closely related issues. In one such case public intoxication was said by the court to be *malum prohibitum*, rendering pleas based on lack of *mens rea* irrelevant. City of Seattle v. Hill, 72 Wash. 2d 786, 794, 435 P.2d 692, 698 (1967), *cert. denied*, 393 U.S. 872 (1968). In a second case the court upheld a conviction for public intoxication, but there were three separate opinions. People v. Hoy, 380 Mich. 597, 158 N.W.2d 436 (1968). In a third case the court said that it would be unreasonable to require as a condition of probation that a person who is a chronic alcoholic refrain from drinking if expert testimony establishes that "alcoholism has destroyed [petitioner's] power of volition." Sweeney v. United States, 353 F.2d 10, 11 (7th Cir. 1965).

7. 392 U.S. at 534.

8. *Id.* at 560-61, 567-68; Driver v. Hinnant, 356 F.2d 761, 764 (4th Cir. 1966); Easter v. District of Columbia, 361 F.2d 50, 53 (D.C. Cir. 1966).

9. Though this attitude is most apparent from a reading of the entire argument of the *Powell* dissent, it appears quite explicitly in the concluding remarks:

> [T]he essential constitutional defect here is the same as in *Robinson*, for in both cases the particular defendant was accused of being in a condition which he had no capacity to change or avoid.

392 U.S. at 567-68.

10. Thus, the *Powell* dissent: "[T]he condition essential to constitute the defined crime is part of the pattern of his disease. . . . " 392 U.S. at 569.

11. On this issue there have been some differences in interpretations of *Robinson*, but there is no question that *Robinson* does not *say* that the disease must be involuntarily or innocently acquired or maintained. The only reference in the main text to this issue is the statement:

> In this Court counsel for the State recognized that narcotic addiction is an illness. Indeed, it is apparently an illness which may be contracted innocently or involuntarily.

370 U.S. at 667. In a footnote appended to this statement, it is noted that such innocent addiction may arise from use of medically prescribed narcotics or from the fact of having been born of a mother who is an addict. It seems plain to some, including myself, that this was merely designed to add to the force of the holding that it is unjust to punish for having a disease. Were this comment intended as defining the scope of the ruling, it would have involved drastic narrowing of *Robinson*. On this narrower view, *Robinson* would pertain only to that miniscule number of cases in which narcotics addiction is involuntarily and innocently acquired. It is difficult to believe that such a drastic restriction in scope was intended to be expressed by means of such an almost offhand and cryptic comment. *See* Starrs, *The Disease Concept of Alcoholism and Traditional Criminal Law Theory*, 19 S. Car. L. Rev. 349, 353 (1967); Note, *The Cruel and Unusual Punishment Clause and the Substantive Criminal Law*, 79 Harv. L. Rev. 635, 648-49 (1966). On the other hand, four of the judges of the District of Columbia Court of Appeals subscribe to that part of the *Easter* opinion in which it is stated flatly that in *Robinson* "[t]he Court said such [narcotics] addiction was a status involuntarily assumed. . . . " 361 F.2d at 54. *See also* Note, *supra* note 6, at 103, 121 n.100, 126, 127. Other cases in which the issue is touched upon but not clearly decided are People v. Davis, 27 Ill. 2d 57, 188 N.E.2d 225 (1963); State *ex rel*. Blouin v. Walker, 244 La. 699, 154 So. 2d 368 (1963), *cert. denied*, 375 U.S. 988 (1964).

One might initially suppose that the failure in *Robinson* to mention the question whether or not an addict voluntarily remains an addict is due to the obviousness of the answer that he does so involuntarily. Yet the answer is not self-evident. It is well known that a minority of addicts, but a growing one, voluntarily refrain from taking narcotics either under hospital supervision, or in such voluntary organizations as Synanon and others like it. Whether to call these "cures" continues to be a controversial question, *i.e.*, it is not clear whether addiction, once acquired, is beyond the addict's control. *See* note 54 *infra*.

12. 370 U.S. at 666.

13. In an earlier opinion in a case involving the same issue, Justice Fortas, in discussing public intoxication, referred to "certain aspects of *behavior* after he has been drinking." Budd v. California, 385 U.S. 909, 910 (1966) (dissenting opinion to denial of petition for writ of certiorari) (emphasis added). Thus it apparently is not obvious even to Justice Fortas that public intoxication is a "condition" and not "behavior."

14. 392 U.S. at 532.

15. *Id.* at 535.

16. *Id.* at 533.

17. *See id.* 530, 539, 568.

18. *Id.* at 569.

19. By way of aside, it is the small minority of chronic alcoholics, those who happen to be derelicts, who are arrested and charged with public drunkenness. Most chronic alcoholics can and do stay off the streets when drunk. It is thus possible to see public intoxication more as a "symptom" of homelessness and dereliction than of alcoholism. Yet there remains a tendency to view "alcoholism" itself—as well as public drunkenness—as a lower-class affliction. There is evidence that some physicians fail to recognize as alcoholics a very large proportion of chronic alcoholics who come to them with one or another specific complaint, but who do not fit the "derelict" stereotype. Blane, Overton & Chafetz, *Social Factors in the Diagnosis of Alcoholism*, 24 Q.J. Studies on Alcohol 640 (1963). This tendency, which may involve a kind of class, or even race prejudice, may well (and perhaps ironically) contribute to a court's willingness to see alcoholism as a "disease" and public drunkenness as an "involuntary" consequence.

20. 370 U.S. at 666.

21. *See* State v. Margo, 40 N.J. 188, 190, 191, A.2d 43, 45 (1963), holding that being under the influence of narcotics is "antisocial behavior. It is not some latent or passive proclivity; it is an active state, voluntarily induced. . . ."

22. *Robinson* is plain enough in declaring that it is cruel and unusual punishment to make disease-status per se a criminal offense. What is obscure, however, is the rationale for this finding. A few analogies are offered, but there is no explicit statement as to which features of the analogies are determinative. *See* Dubin, *Mens Rea Reconsidered: A Plea for a Due Process Concept of Criminal Responsibility*, 18 Stan. L. Rev. 322, 386 (1966); Note, *supra* note 11, at 649.

23. "*Robinson* stands upon a principle . . . [that] [c]riminal penalties may not be inflicted upon a person for being in a condition he is powerless to change." 392 U.S. at 567.

24. In *Easter*, for example, the court says that Congress has deemed alcoholism to be "a sickness which is accompanied with loss of power to control the use of alcoholic beverages." 361 F.2d at 52.

25. 392 U.S. at 567.

26. *Id.* at 568.

27. *Id.* at 521.

28. *Id.*

29. *Id.*

30. I shall not further consider the trial judge's third finding since it does not bear on the general issues with which I am concerned.

31. For example, Dr. Wade, the expert witness, testified that individuals such as Powell have "a compulsion, and this compulsion, while not completely overpowering, is a very strong influence. . . . " 392 U.S. at 578.

32. *Id.* at 559.

33. *Id.* at 559-60. All of the Justices seem to agree that medical knowledge of alcoholism is deficient. *Id.* at 522-23, 539, 551 n.3.

34. *Id.* at 559.

35. *Id.*

36. *Id.* at 560-61.

37. *See* pp. 800-08 *infra*.

38. 392 U.S. at 561.

39. *See, e.g.,* The Cooperative Commission on the Study of Alcoholism, Alcohol Problems 39 (prepared by T. Plaut 1967) [hereinafter cited as Plaut]; C. Rip, the Alcoholic and the Group 17 (1966); A. Ullman, To Know the Difference 8 (1960); Keller, *The Definition of Alcoholism and the Estimation of Its Prevalence*, in Society, Culture, and Drinking Patterns 310, 312-13 (D. Pittman & C. Snyder eds. 1962) [hereinafter cited as Pittman & Snyder].

40. 392 U.S. at 562.

41. Fain v. Commonwealth, 78 Ky. 183 (Ct. App. 1879). *See also* Morris, *Somnambulistic Homicide: Ghosts, Spiders, and North Koreans*, 5 Res Judicatae 29 (1951).

42. Jerome Hall states that so far as case law is concerned, "*involuntary intoxication is simply and completely nonexistent.*" Hall, *Intoxication and Criminal Responsibility*, 57 Harv. L. Rev. 1045, 1056 (1944) (emphasis in original). Although there are a few cases involving involuntary intoxication from drugs other than alcohol, *see, e.g.,* People v. Koch, 250 App. Div. 623, 294 N.Y.S. 987 (Sup. Ct. 1937), I know of only one which involves alcohol, and in this case there was no finding of involuntary intoxication. A conviction was reversed on appeal and a retrial ordered because of the trial judge's refusal to allow presentation of evidence aimed at establishing ignorance as to the effects of drinking on the part of the defendant. State v. Brown, 38 Kan. 390, 16 P. 259 (1888).

See generally, Beck, *Voluntary Conduct: Automatism, Insanity and Drunkenness*, 9 Crim. L.Q. 315 (1967); Fox, *Physical Disorder, Consciousness, and Criminal Liability*, 63 Colum. L. Rev. 645 (1963); Prevezer, *Automatism and Involuntary Conduct*, 1958 Crim. L. Rev. 361, 440.

43. Compare Plaut at 41:

> [T]he term "alcoholism" should be used with the awareness that this condition is not always easy to diagnose or to be distinguished from other types of problem drinking. In addition, even those to whom the

diagnosis is correctly given still differ greatly from one another and are likely to require different types of treatment and assistance.

44. E. Jellinek, The Disease Concept of Alcoholism 55-59, 83-86, 113-15 (1960).

45. M. Block, Alcoholism 23 (1965).

46. Chafetz, *Comment*, in *Who Is Qualified to Treat the Alcoholic?: Comment on the Krystal-Moore Discussion*, 25 Q.J. Studies on Alcohol, 347, 358 (1964).

47. See the discussion in E. Jellinek, *supra* note 44, at 13-32. In France and other beer and wine drinking countries a predominant pattern of alcoholism is the constant, daily drinking of wine, with "inability to abstain," but with control over the amount drunk at any one time so that drunkenness or incapacity to carry on with the day's activities is rare. Cessation of drinking does produce withdrawal symptoms, however. *Id.* at 25-32.

48. Keller, *supra* note 39, at 313 (emphasis in original).

49. Plaut at 39-40.

50. *Id.*

51. Glatt, *Normal Drinking in Recovered Alcoholic Addicts*, 26 Q.J. Studies on Alcohol 116 (1965).

52. *See* Easter v. District of Columbia, 361 F.2d 50, 53 (D.C. Cir. 1966); Driver v. Hinnant, 356 F.2d 761, 764 (4th Cir. 1966).

53. E. Jellinek, *supra* note 44, at 70, says that 35% of the papers he has worked with which deal generally with the etiology of alcoholism use the term "addiction" or its foreign language equivalents.

54. World Health Organization Expert Committee on Addiction-Producing Drugs, Thirteenth Report 9-10 (Tech. Rep. Ser. No. 273, 1964) [hereinafter cited as Thirteenth Report]. *See generally* Bowman, *Narcotic Addiction and Criminal Responsibility Under Durham*, 53 Geo. L.J. 1017 (1965) (discussion of the literature and development of the reasons for case-by-case analysis of the substantial variations in degree and kind of legally relevant dependence in narcotics "addiction"). Bowman's conclusions agree with those of The President's Advisory Commission on Narcotic and Drug Abuse, Final Report 3 (1963) [hereinafter cited as Final Report], to the effect that no general rule, but only case-by-case analysis, can suffice to establish whether or not a "confirmed drug abuser is so impelled by his habit that he is not accountable for his acts under criminal law."

55. Final Report at 13-16. The fourteenth report of the WHO Expert Committee on Mental Health states that dependence on alcohol and dependence on barbiturates are so similar that they "may be considered under the same heading." World Health Organization Expert Committee on Mental Health, Fourteenth Report, Services for the Prevention and Treatment of Dependence on Alcohol and Other Drugs 9 (Tech. Rep. Ser. No. 363, 1967). Furthermore, dependence of the barbiturate type is classified as producing the intermediate degree of desire, *i.e.*, "a strong desire" (but not an "overpowering" one) in the scale of degrees of dependency announced officially in Thirteenth Report at 13.

56. "After one drink, [the alcoholic] feels a physical demand for the drug so strong that he cannot stop short of intoxication." U.S. Dep't of Health, Educa-

tion, & Welfare, Alcoholism 7 (Public Health Service Publ. No. 730, rev. ed. 1965) [hereinafter cited as Alcoholism]. But note the experimental evidence to the contrary developed by Merry, *The "Loss of Control" Myth*, 1966 The Lancet, vol. I, at 1257 (summarized note 59 *infra*), and the statement by Dr. Jack Mendelson, note 57 *infra*.

. . . An interesting and concise summary of the more "physically" oriented hypotheses can be found in Siegler, Osmond & Newell, *Models of Alcoholism*, 29 Q.J. Studies on Alcohol 571, 581 (1968). The reader can find examples of most of the hypotheses I discuss here in almost any of the texts cited in this article.

57. *See* World Health Organization Expert Committee on Alcohol, First Report 5-7, 9-11 (Tech. Rep. Ser. No. 84, 1954). Aside from the controversial issue of the "compulsiveness" of the desire, it takes years as against weeks for any physical dependence to develop in the case of alcohol as compared to morphine derivatives, and tolerance levels remain comparatively very low with alcohol. Dr. Jack Mendelson, Chief of the National Center for the Prevention and Control of Alcoholism of the National Institute of Mental Health, refers to the notion of the purported "triggering" effect: "[o]nce an individual has one drink . . . he can't control his alcohol ingestion. . . . We do not believe this is the case." U.S. Dep't of Health, Education, & Welfare, Social Welfare and Alcoholism 21 (1967).

58. "All addictive alcoholics do not always drink in an uncontrolled fashion." Pattison, Headley, Gleser & Gottschalk, *Abstinence and Normal Drinking*, 29 Q.J. Studies on Alcohol 610, 624 (1968) [hereinafter cited as Pattison].

59. There is no generally agreed upon or accepted etiological pattern in connection with alcoholism. There are, however, many theories but broadly speaking they can be divided into three schools. These three are the *Physiological, the Psychological*, and the *Sociological*.

C. Rip, *supra* note 39, at 18 (emphasis in original). Rip lists four main types of hypotheses within the first category. E. Jellinek, *supra* note 44, at 82-155, lists over 50 formulations which focus on physical factors to describe alcoholism. With respect to physically oriented hypotheses and the often claimed "triggering" effect of the first drink, Merry reports his experiment in which a group of alcoholics were given a daily dose of vodka, unknown to them, and who throughout the experiment were asked to report their "craving," if any, for alcohol. No deep craving for alcohol was reported, thus tending to confirm the view that "loss of control" or "craving" after the first drink is not an automatic, physically induced phenomenon. Merry, *supra* note 56.

60. Diethelm, cited in C. Rip, *supra* note 39, at 16, argues that it can be confusing to speak of "compulsion" here because it may erroneously suggest that every chronic alcoholic has a compulsion neurosis. Other authorities imply that the vagueness of the term itself calls for caution in its use, as E. Jellinek, *supra* note 44, at 43.

61. Pittman, *Public Intoxication and the Alcoholic Offender in American Society*, in Task Force Report 13.

62. Pattison 625.

63. Forizs, *Comment*, in *Who Is Qualified to Treat the Alcoholic?: Comment on the Krystal-Moore Discussion*, 26 Q.J. Studies on Alcohol 510, 511 (1965).

64. Alcoholics Anonymous maintains that alcoholism is a "disease," but not that drinking is involuntary. On the contrary, the entire approach in Alcoholics Anonymous is to enlist the voluntary cooperation of the alcoholic, to appeal to him on moral-religious-pragmatic grounds to voluntarily abstain from drinking, and to engage in reciprocal self-help along these lines with his brother AA members. According to the U.S. Public Health Service, "[r]emarkable success . . . has been achieved" in this way. Alcoholism 10. Moreover, there is widespread recognition in the health professions that the AA approach has done at least as much, probably far more, than any other single approach to therapy for alcoholics.

> There is no longer any question that Alcoholics Anonymous has been responsible for the sobriety of more alcoholics than any other method, social, religious, or medical. Psychiatrists are now 'believers.' Our 1956 Survey shows that 99% of them approve of Alcoholics Anonymous, and 77% have referred patients to them. . . . Medical practitioners other than psychiatrists are not nearly so partial to Alcoholics Anonymous. . . . In contrast . . . Alcoholics Anonymous is now considered highly respectable and is accepted among most groups working with the alcoholic. . . . For example, 74% of State Hospitals have an Alcoholics Anonymous counselor in their alcoholism treatment program, and 82% rely on Alcoholics Anonymous for follow-up care.

M. Hayman, Alcoholism—Mechanism & Management 174-75 (1966).

65. Motivation by coercion is an important technique in inducing the alcoholic to accept help. We can include in this category any reward or punishment which is important enough to the alcoholic to cause him to forego the pleasure and needs of drinking. This could be court probation which, if broken, might lead to jail. It could be the threat of loss of financial support or the loss of a job. . . . [I]n the survey mentioned previously [*see* note 68 *supra*] 60% of psychiatrists felt that coercion in the form of legal commitment of alcoholics to state hospitals was beneficial to their treatment. Recovery and improvement rates in industrial clinics where there is considerable coercion are much higher than elsewhere. . . .

M. Hayman, *supra* note 64, at 65-66. See also the data on the favorable effect of coercion or duress in deciding to accept treatment in Lemere, O'Hollaren & Maxwell, *Motivation in the Treatment of Alcoholism*, 19 Q.J. Studies on Alcohol 428 (1958).

66. *See* M. Block, *supra* note 45, at 23-24; Eddy, Halbach, Isbell & Seevers, *Drug Dependence: Its Significance and Characteristics*, 32 Bull. W.H.O. 721 (1965); Keller, *Alcoholism: Nature and Extent of the Problem*, 315 Annals 2 (1958); *cf. Chafetz, supra* note 46, at 358 (1964) (alcoholism as symptom of chronic behavioral disorder). The definitions compiled in Alcoholism I emphasize primarily the excessiveness of an alcoholic's drinking and his consequent social and personal disabilities, rather than "loss of control."

During this discussion I have primarily mentioned only those views oriented toward "loss of control." However, many authorities flatly oppose this orientation, and, while recognizing that there may be physical factors at work, consider it essential that "there is a whole series of voluntary actions in the act of drinking; and there has to be a choice involved. . . . " Myerson, *Comments on "Institute on Modern Trends in Handling the Chronic Alcoholic Offender,"* 19 S. Car. L. Rev. 305, 348 (1967). *See also* the citations in E. Jellinek, *supra* note 44, at 58-59, and the remarks of Dr. J. Mendelson, U.S. Dep't of Health, Education, & Welfare, Social Welfare and Alcoholism 21-22, 26 (1967).

67. 392 U.S. at 560 (1968).

68. The new medical model treats alcoholism as a bona fide disease, without reservations. It is a hopeful model, and one which encourages new scientific research. It enables those using it to draw strength from the successful campaigns against other major illnesses.

Siegler, Osmond & Newell, *supra* note 56, at 584.

69. *See, e.g.*, E. Jellinek, *supra* note 44, at 161.

70. [P]hilosophically speaking, alcoholism is not a disease . . .

. . . You want to get hospitals to take in alcoholic problems, but to do so you have to hammer them on the head, to get them to accept it as a disease. So I would agree we should call it a disease. . . . It is a pragmatic definition. It has useful consequences.

Myerson, *supra* note 66, at 348. E. Jellinek, *supra* note 44, at 161, makes a similar point, and says that although there have been great strides in getting hospitals to accept alcoholics in the past few decades, this was more the exception than the rule as of 1944. Hayman, however, reports that his surveys show, as of 1966, that "there are still relatively few hospitals who will admit alcoholic patients on the basis of their alcoholism." This is in spite of the 1956 statement of the American Medical Association, and a subsequent statement in 1957 by the American Hospital Association urging general hospitals to accept alcoholic patients. For example, in 1962, there were only three hospitals in New York City which accepted chronic alcoholics on an in-patient basis. M. Hayman, *supra* note 64, at 81, 130.

71. Acknowledgment of the reluctance of both psychiatric and non-psychiatric medical men to accept chronic alcoholics as patients is a commonplace in the literature. *See* M. Hayman, *supra* note 64, at 81. Consult also, E. Jellinek, *supra* note 44, ch. IV, and Blane, Overton & Chafetz, *supra* note 19, at 658, for reviews of this situation.

72. *See* A. Ullman, *supra* note 39, at 4.

73. *See* E. Jellinek, *supra* note 44, ch. IV.6. On this and other of the "pragmatic" rather than "medical" reasons for calling alcoholism a disease, see the revealing discussion by T. F. A. Plaut, M.D., Assistant Chief of the National Center for Prevention and Control of Alcoholism, in Plaut 42-45.

74. The word "disease" has been used here as if all the modern experts were agreed that alcoholism is a disease. This is not so. However, the important

> point for us is that alcoholism is now treated by those who are responsible for the health of the community rather than by those who are responsible for the community's morals.

A. Ullman, *supra* note 39, at 5. Seeley presents a careful analysis of the concept "disease" in the context of alcoholism, and he makes plain the ineradicable element of moral judgment, the importance of the shift from one set of institutions to another, as a reason for using the concept, and, finally, the "essential" fact about applying the disease label: "that a step in public policy is being *recommended*, not a scientific discovery announced" (emphasis in original). Seeley, *Alcoholism Is a Disease: Implications for Social Policy*, in Pittman & Snyder 586, 593.

75. *See, e.g.*, Fingarette, *The Concept of Mental Disease*, in *Criminal Law Insanity Tests*, 33 U. Chi, L. Rev. 229 (1966), and a forthcoming study, Fingarette, *The Insanity Plea in the Criminal Law. See also* Swartz, *"Mental Disease": The Groundwork for Legal Analysis and Legislative Action*, III U. Pa. L. Rev. 389 (1963). Though these studies focus on the concept of "mental disease" rather than "disease" in general, they systematically relate the disease concept to issues bearing on the idea of criminal responsibility, and more particularly on the factor of volition, which is so critical in the problem of alcoholism. These studies also refer to the concept of disease more generally. *See generally* Seeley, *supra* note 74.

76. E. Jellinek, *supra* note 44, at 11-12.

77. Jellinek, *id.* at 58-59, cites seven authorities who explicitly reject the disease concept of alcoholism. He goes on to cite approvingly Leopold Wexberg's remarks based on the latter's studies of the physiology of alcoholism.

> In no other area of research and social or medical endeavor have slogans so extensively replaced theoretical insight, as a basis for therapeutic action, as in alcoholism. The emotional impact of the statement, 'Alcoholism is a sickness', is such that very few people care to stop to think what it actually means.

Jellinek's list is by no means complete as an inventory of authorities who reject the disease concept of alcoholism. Since his book, for example, Chafetz, *supra* note 46, at 358, has said, "I do not believe that there exists a disease, alcoholism, nor a particular set of personality traits we can label 'alcoholic.'" Clancy, *Comment*, in *Who is Qualified To Treat the Alcoholic?: Comment on the Krystal-Moore Discussion*, 26 Q.J. Studies on Alcohol 314, at 314 (1965), remarks that "many regard [the American Medical Association statement of 1956] as an opinion and therefore open to challenge. Differences of opinion about alcoholism as a disease still exist in the medical profession." *See also* Myerson, *supra* note 66, at 348. Swartz, a legal scholar who has done extensive work in the area of mental disease and alcoholism, says: "[T]here is considerable divergence of views even among medical men as to whether alcoholism is a disease. . . . I see alcoholism as a violation of conduct norms. . . . Violation of conduct norms . . . would in my view not, of itself, constitute disease." Swartz, *Compulsory Legal Measures and the Concept of Illness*, 19 S. Car. L. Rev. 372, 374 (1967). In addition to views such as the above, there are views which are ambiguous, vague, or borderline with respect to the question whether alcoholism is or is not a disease. For example:

> At the present time, the consensus of opinion is that the basic problem underlying the addiction to alcohol or other drugs is an emotional one. The nature of it, however, is not a simple matter. Alcoholics do not share the same emotional problems.

Krystal, *Comment*, in *Who Is Qualified To Treat the Alcoholic?: Comment on the Krystal-Moore Discussion*, 24 Q.J. Studies on Alcohol 705, 707 (1963). In the same symposium, at 712, Moore, who in many ways takes a view contrary to Krystal's, gives his view of current, sound medical doctrine:

> We are not in agreement as to etiology and there is still considerable controversy as to the best treatment techniques. Still, we feel confident that we are dealing with a tangible illness *or pathological life reaction even if we may be reluctant to call alcoholism a specific disease*.

(emphasis added). There are interesting comments and data on the "ambivalent medical attitudes about alcoholism as a disease entity," based on careful study of medical practice, as distinguished from theory, in Blane, Overton & Chafetz, *supra* note 19, at 659-60. The authors themselves do refer to alcoholism in the course of their study as a "disease" or "illness"; but when one of them in a later paper addresses himself specifically to this question, he rejects the disease concept. Chafetz, *supra* note 46, at 346.

78. With respect both to more rational and humane procedures which have already been or may be put into effect without invoking constitutional doctrine, and with respect to the inhumane aspects of procedures which have been common in recent times, the Task Force Report provides an ample review and bibliography.

POSTSCRIPT BY THE AUTHOR
September 12, 1988

As I look back at the preceding *Harvard Law Review* article one thing strikes me forcefully. The data and the theses have stood the test of time. More than that, they have been consistently, and one might even say massively confirmed by the evidence that has accumulated since then.

It is symbolic of this that in 1988 the U.S. Supreme Court could rely on that article as authority for a key element in its landmark ruling in *Traynor v. Turnage*. As in the earlier *Powell v. Texas* decision, the *Traynor* Court declined to take its own judicial stand on scientific questions such as whether alcoholism is a disease or whether all alcoholics drink voluntarily. But in *Traynor* it did make a key decision: It sustained the VA rule being challenged. That VA rule held that where alcoholism is without psychiatric disorder—i.e., in the great majority of cases—there is no need to examine the individual case, for *all* such alcoholics drink wilfully (voluntarily). Citing the lower Court's prior holding and the *Harvard Law Review* article, the Court said that such a general rule is not arbitrary but is based on substantial medical evidence. Of course it follows that if such a rule is medically reasonable for one agency it is medically reasonable no matter who makes it.

In my book *Heavy Drinking* I have brought the evidence relating to this conclusion up-to-date. A large experimental and clinical literature now attests repeatedly to the following theses: Alcoholics have a good deal of control over their drinking. Many alcoholics effectively choose to turn back from their gross abuse of alcohol, and they do so in about the same proportions regardless of whether it is in the context of "treatment" programs, organizations like A.A., or on their own initiative without any formal help. There are many patterns of drinking, and no single sharply differentiated "alcoholism" pattern. While biological and genetic factors can play a significant role in some alcoholism, they do not destine a person to become an alcoholic. It is the individual's mind, character, and motivation, the family and cultural background, and the social status and relationships that most powerfully explain the variance between those who do and those who do not move into an alcoholic way of life. And, regardless of the talk about alcoholics being diseased and without self-control over their drinking, when it comes to actual practice almost all those who seek to help the alcoholic take it as the immediate and absolutely essential postulate that the drinker can and must take responsibility and use self-control. Whatever the doctrine or organizational format, the objective is always to influence the drinker's motivation—to inform, to reason with, in one way or another to persuade the alcoholic to cease abusive drinking, and to re-shape his or her life so as to minimize or eliminate the mental and social incentives to drink. While there are many theories about how best to motivate the alcoholic to cease abuse of alcohol, the key remains not physical change but motivational change.

If I were to modify anything I said in the *Powell* article, it would be to make more specific the final statement of why the alcoholic's choice to stop is so very difficult. In 1970 I had to leave this phrased in terms of a miscellany of factors in just about every dimension of human life. Now one sees that while this is true, it is the *pattern* – the shape of the person's way of life – that is of the essence. Gradually, usually unwittingly over the course of years, the alcoholic has come to favor drinking as a "solution" to life-difficulties, and quite understandably has come to find congenial acquaintances, situations, and social strategies that sustain the drinking ethos and that wall off criticism. In time, this route leads to perceiving the world in terms of drinking, and reacting to it in terms of drinking. When drinking has become a central thread around which a whole way of life is woven, it is by then extremely difficult to change. Simplistic notions like "disease," "sin," "bad character," or "bad habit" distract us from the complex truth. *Everything* about such a life conspires to incite drinking. As a result, mere rational reflection, or even emotional shock, while they may at last lead to a vivid awareness of how destructive that life is, can easily be no match for the innumerable incentives and evasive strategies by now built into daily life. All these, when the chips are down, can lead the alcoholic to choose to drink in spite of prior good resolutions in the abstract.

This momentum that the way of life takes on is in no way unique to the alcoholic. After all, if people were always prudent and rational, changing the way they live whenever Reason so dictated, no one would ever come to lead a destructive or even imprudent pattern of living. The tragic truth is otherwise, of course. So we have to look at alcohol abuse not as a unique and alien disease that makes one a helpless victim, but instead as an unhappy manifestation of human fallibility. "Alcoholism" is a vague label for a heterogeneous population of individuals who for all sorts of different reasons have increasingly centered their life around drinking, first as a response to life's challenges, but then eventually as a way of life with its own autonomy and inner dynamic.

REFERENCES

Fingarette, H. 1970. "The Perils of Powell: In Search of a Factual Foundation for the 'Disease Concept of Alcoholism'." *Harvard Law Review* 83:793-812.
Fingarette, H. *Heavy Drinking – The Myth of Alcoholism as a Disease*. Berkeley: University of California Press, 1988.
Powell v. Texas 392 US 514 (1968)
Traynor v. Turnage 99 LEd 2d 618 (1988)

The Heritability of Alcoholism: Science and Social Policy

David Lester

SUMMARY. During a brief period, from perhaps 1943 to 1970, there appeared to be a consensus that social and cultural influences played a decisive role in the development of alcoholism. Increasingly thereafter, a belief in "clear" and "stunning" evidence for the heritability of alcoholism has taken hold in the scientific professions and research supporting agencies, and among alcoholism professionals and (not least) in the lay publics. This review attempts to make plain that the factual support for the present consensus is, at best, weak—and that the consensus in the main reflects a victory for ideology over rigorous scientific methodology and solid data, a triumph of fancy over fact, subversive of sound public policy.

ELEMENTS OF GENETIC THEORY

Genetics deals with characters transmitted from parents to offspring; such traits are "inborn" and hereditary, not acquired, and are related to specific facets of the organism's biological structure and function. "Inborn errors of metabolism" account for a wide variety of human maladies. The goal of studies on the possible hereditary nature of alcoholism is an attempt to elucidate the biologi-

---

David Lester is Professor (II) Biochemistry, Emeritus, Center of Alcohol Studies, Rutgers University, New Brunswick, NJ 08903.

Mailing address: David Lester, 29 Forester Drive, Princeton, NJ 08540.

This paper appeared in slightly different form as Chapter 1 (Genetic Theory: An Assessment of the Heritability of Alcoholism) in the book Theories on Alcoholism, Eds.: C.D. Chaudron and D.A. Wilkinson, Addiction Research Foundation, Toronto, 1988. The author is grateful to those editors for permission to rework the material. This paper has been expanded with new material, including references as recent as December, 1988.

cal mechanisms responsible for the development of alcohol abuse and alcoholism, and thus, as with phenylketonuria, to be in a position to provide rational counseling, prevention or treatment methodology. My aim here is to examine, critically, the reports of those investigations which deal with this issue, focusing especially on those reports of the last several decades which have led most people to accept as proven the heritability of alcohol abuse and alcoholism.

Molecular biology has established the structural reality of the units of heredity, the genes. Because offspring share 50% of the genes of each parent, their own assemblage of genes, their genotype, is unique and not the same as that of either parent; the parent genotypes are disassembled and reconstituted in the progeny from the transmitted genes in ovum and sperm. As the organism develops prenatally and postnatally, under a variety of changing environmental circumstances, the interaction of genotype and environment produces the multitudinous characters and traits which we recognize as the individual's phenotype(s). The science of genetics deals with the transmission and combinations of genes, first elucidated by Gregor Mendel. The expression of the genotypes as observable wrinkling of peas, blood groups, eye color, stature, butterfat yield, abdominal bristle number in Drosophila, and like traits has long been a staple of biology. The development of a specific genotype in varying environments (the environment being both the genetic and the nongenetic environment) can result in the production of a range of such phenotypes: the functional relation between phenotype and varying environment for a specific genotype is the norm of reaction (Lewontin, 1982).

For plants and for some species of animals, whose genotype can be isolated, propagated and controlled, the norm of reaction is determinable: the genotype can be replicated, the environment altered, and a variety of outcomes measured. Although human genotypes in all probability exhibit such norms of reaction, no such experiment appears likely. Such an experimental program is restricted to a narrow range of genotypes and their phenotypes, to relatively simple traits in which a straightforward cause and effect relation can be established. For concepts like intelligence, or schizophrenia, or alcoholism, there is no evidence that simple relationships exist; indeed, there is every reason to believe that the highest levels of organismic function are involved, embracing the most complex developing and evolving relationships of humans as social beings. It will be argued that to assign values to the contributions of "nature" and "nurture" appears a not particularly scientific exercise for the elucidation of such specifically human problems as alcoholism.

Falconer (1964) points out that the study of variation of metric characters, e.g., height, and the partition of this variance into components attributable to different causes, is the way genetic questions are formulated. The relative magnitude of these components, the variance of genotype (V_g) and of environment (V_e), determines the degree of resemblance between relatives; the genotypic variance is composed of the breeding value [the additive variance: (V_a)], and the dominance (where the effect of the gene is recognized in the heterozygote), interaction and environmental variances. The relationship is the heredity [$V_a/(V_g + V_e)$], and it assesses the relative importance of the breeding value as a portion of the total variance of the phenotype. For nonmetric, qualitative traits, genetic involvement is assessed (e.g., in twin pairs) by concordance rates; a twin pair is usually considered concordant if either both or neither possess a particular trait and discordant if one of the pair possesses the trait and the other does not (Stern, 1960; p. 554). In some cases (e.g., Kaij, 1960a), concordance has been defined as only the possession of the trait by both co-twins, excluding the case where neither possesses it.

The heritability value is of undoubted importance to the animal breeder who seeks increased milk production in cattle whose life cycle is under almost total control. Its importance for humans, subject to a variety of biological and social influences is, at best, substantially less. There is, today, no evidence of a correspondence between human alcoholism and one gene or constellation of genes, and unless it can be shown that a significant hereditary component is present, research investigations in this area would appear to be pursuing a scientific will-o'-the-wisp. In any case, the demonstration of a hereditary component does not, of course, indicate the specific genetic involvement: further investigation is required to elucidate the mechanism of action.

HISTORICAL DEVELOPMENT

An appropriate starting point for any discussion of heredity and alcoholism is the position taken by Goodwin (1982) vis-à-vis Elvin M. Jellinek's (1945) 1944 review of the "Heredity of the Alcoholic." Goodwin contends that Jellinek was dogmatic in stating that alcoholism was transmitted socially. The dogma of the day, however, was that alcoholism was hereditary, and it was indeed challenged by Jellinek's assessment of the contemporary evidence. That the "notion that alcoholism is hereditary is old" has, in fact, been asserted by Goodwin himself (1976). It is thus not amiss to emphasize that for many decades prior to 1944 (and thereafter) the laws of the various states allowed the compulsory sterilization of those considered genetically degenerate, including (in addition to the insane, feebleminded, moral and sexual perverts, habitual criminals, and rapists) drunkards, epileptics and syphilitics, and that such laws carried (in an 8 to 1 decision) the 1927 legal imprimatur of the Supreme Court of the United States (Buck v. Bell, Superintendent; Paul, 1973). For Jellinek to conclude that ". . . no evidence has ever been adduced to show that this heredity, by *necessity* [my emphasis], had to express itself in inebriety" was to judge the evidence fairly, and he continued by stating that "The only permissible conclusion is that not a disposition toward alcoholism is inherited but rather a constitution involving such instability as does not offer sufficient resistance to the social risks of inebriety. The inherited constitution is merely a suitable breeding ground for inebriety" (p. 109).

Careful study of Jellinek's 1944 lecture should convince readers that the admittedly undogmatic Jellinek believed firmly that no matter what weight was assigned to hereditary factors, the mental hygienist was, in fact, "not faced by implacable fate" (p. 110). Having worked for many years as a statistician concerned with plant breeding, Jellinek was well aware that even a perfectly heritable trait could be substantially changed by environment. How tangled the web that, on the one hand, the creator of the "disease concept" of alcoholism (Jellinek, 1960) is criticized as a dogged opponent of the hereditary nature of alcoholism (Goodwin, 1982), while, on the other hand, Peele (1984), who favors a social explanation, notes,

> The disease theory of alcoholism has the merit of bringing troubled people into the care of hospitals and doctors, an advantage appreciated particularly by physicians themselves, who tend to see human problems in terms of the medical model: disease, treatment, cure. Yet it posits an inborn organic cause, a bodily deficiency, where there may be none, and for this reason the theory is troubling. Alcoholism may at its roots be a social and cultural problem, not a medical one. (p. 15-16)

It is sadly ironic how Jellinek's views on alcoholism and heredity have been misinterpreted, otherwise how to explain the serious suggestion by an adherent of all-encompassing hereditary doctrine that alcoholism be renamed Jellinek's Disease (Fitzgerald, 1983)?

CHARACTERISTIC METHODS

The methodology used in research on the heritability of alcoholism is characteristic of most investigations dealing with complex traits. None of the methods employed are original in the sense that they have been developed for the study of alcoholism, nor are they applied in a manner fundamentally different from that in which they have been applied to the study of other human aberrations, e.g., schizophrenia. Because the definitions of complex traits such as alcoholism can be narrow or broad, the definition to be employed is of cardinal importance: how else recognize the appearance of the trait?

Breeding as a possible methodology is excluded on ethical grounds, as it is not for infra-human animals; but even if an animal model of alcoholism were possible (Lester, 1982), its inadequacies make it of doubtful relevance. Other methodologies are discussed in later sections of this paper, and deal with the specific manner in which the actions of the genes are purportedly separated from the actions of their environments: comparison of identical and nonidentical twins, the use of half siblings raised with and without their biological parents, adoptees separated from their biological parents shortly after birth, the association of "alcoholism" with characters known to be genetically transmitted (markers), and the presumed correlation of heredity and elimination (metabolism) of alcohol.

Many proponents of the view that alcoholism is heritable are aware that alcohol use, and most especially alcohol abuse, introduces the special methodological problem of assessing the consequences of its antecedent chronic use upon preceding measurable attributes; there seems to be no manipulation, other than a prospective study, that avoids this pitfall. To employ an acceptable definition of alcoholism, to mount an adequately sized prospective study in which the data are generated by the study itself (rather than by uncontrolled outside agencies), and to evaluate the weight to be given to the genes (by methodology akin to that of Cloninger et al., 1981), is a formidable task. The risk in such prospective studies is that there is never a guarantee that all the right questions (Regier et al., 1984; Robins et al., 1984) will have been asked, let alone that significant answers will be found, but if alcoholism is to any extent heritable in any context, then such a study should be the next one pursued.

BOUNDARIES OF GENETIC THEORY

Given a demonstration of the weight to be given to the "heritability" of alcoholism, some important limitations of such a finding would still have to be borne in mind. As Lewontin et al. (1984) state (anent IQ):

> The heritability of a trait only gives information about how much genetic and environmental variation exists in the population *in the current set of environments* [emphasis in the original]. It has absolutely no predictive power for the result of changing the set of environments.

And further,

> The confusion of "heritable" with "unchangeable" is part of a general misconception about genes and development. The phenotype of an organism is changing and developing at all times. Some changes are irreversible and some reversible, but these categories cross those of heritable and nonheritable. The

> loss of an eye, an arm, or a leg is irreversible but not heritable. The appearance of Wilson's disease [a defect of copper metabolism inherited as a single gene and curable by the administration of penicillamine] is heritable but not irreversible. The morphological defect that causes blue babies is congenital, nonheritable, irreversible under normal developmental conditions, but reversible surgically. The extent to which morphological, physiological and mental characteristics do or do not change in the course of individual lifetimes and the history of the species is a matter of historical contingency only. The variation from person to person in the ability to do arithmetic, whatever its source, is trivial compared to the immense increase in calculating power that has been put into the hands of even the poorest student of mathematics by the pocket electronic calculator. The best studies in the world of the heritability of arithmetic skill could not have predicted that historical change. (pp. 116-117)

Lewontin (1981) previously addressed the notion that biological constraints necessarily limit culture, pointing out that "culture is precisely a *negation* of individual limitations."

Placing a value on the heritability of alcoholism, which is assuredly far less than 1.0, tells us nothing about the biochemical, morphological, physiological or other biological substrata which may be necessary if alcohol abuse or alcoholism is to be manifest, let alone the variety of social, cultural, economic, historical and other environmental factors which may be, and in all probability are, involved.

The determination of the heritability of alcoholism has, of course, been attempted on many occasions, and it is of obvious interest to examine the results. My present assessment of the studies of the last 40 years leads me to conclude that little change is required in the 1944 judgement of Jellinek. Previous reviews of the heredity of alcoholism have in large part been uncritical, but several excellent reviews on different aspects of this topic have been recently published (Cabaniss, 1979; Murray et al., 1983).

RESEARCH RESULTS

I hope here to extend the critiques of Cabaniss (1979) and Murray et al. (1983); these authors, in lengthy reviews, have examined the available twin, adoption and half sibling studies, indicating their many methodological and other deficiencies, and reaching essentially the same conclusions. Cabaniss concludes (p. 61) that "the evidence for a genetic factor in alcoholism which acts selectively on some individuals and not on others is less than adequate," while Murray et al. conclude that there may be a "modest genetic effect on both normal drinking and alcoholism in men, though similar evidence for women is so far lacking." Many of the deficiencies noted by these critics overlap, and many do not; despite this, many other serious deficiencies have been overlooked by them and will be examined in what follows. I restrict my critique to those well known reports which allowed evaluation of the study's conclusions because they employed adequate numbers of subjects, applied appropriate definitions of alcohol abuse and alcoholism, and provided a sufficiency of data for analysis.

TWIN STUDIES

Twin studies compare monozygotic (MZ: arising from a single ovum and sperm) and dizygotic (DZ: arising from two separate ova and sperm) twins, the MZ twins with identical genotypes and the DZ twins (same-age siblings) sharing only half their genes; DZ twins may thus be fraternal, sororal or of unlike sex. Except as specifically noted, most of the studies have employed male twin pairs. For any qualitative character or trait, greater concordance (similarity) between MZ pairs as compared to DZ pairs is taken to result from the MZ's genetic identity and the ratio of their concordances reflects the degree of genetic input; any discordance in an MZ pair is assumed to be the result of environmental differences acting on an identical genotype.

Twin studies depend on various assumptions, some of questionable validity. They assume that mating of the parents has been random (there is no conscious preference for marriage partners with similar obvious traits), that no dominance or other genetic effects are involved in the particular trait (the trait may arise from asymmetry of alleles at a locus or loci), and that within-pair environmental variance is the same in DZ as in MZ twins. The degree of assortative (nonrandom) mating among alcoholics is not known, but it is known to be high for traits such as height and body size. It is almost certainly the case that DZ twins are exposed to more dissimilar environments than MZ twins; indeed, this is obviously true from conception onward: DZ twins generally develop in separate placentas and postnatally the environments diverge even more, MZ twins being confused with one another and being treated as the same person. Because they share fewer traits, DZ twins are more likely to differ in their talents, interests, friends, and occupations, and share far fewer common experiences; their greater genetic dissimilarity ensures that the sets of environments that they experience will be more dissimilar than the sets encountered by MZ pairs. The fact that intra-pair environmental variances are unequal means that the ostensible heritability calculated perforce includes these unequal variances.

In addition to this basic conceptual deficiency, there is the possibility of misclassification of MZ and DZ pairs. Other limitations are discussed by Stern (1960).

In the first study using twins, Kaij (1960a, 1960b) drew his sample of 48 MZ and 126 DZ (27.6% MZ) twin pairs from all male sets of twins born between 1890 and 1939 in Skane (southern Sweden) in whom at least one of each pair (an index twin, or proband) had at some time been registered with either of the region's two County Temperance Boards. [The 27.6% of MZ twins appears to be representative of all twins born: in the period 1941-1960, for example, the percentage of MZ pairs born in Sweden was 24.6% (National Center for Health Statistics).] Each of the twins was categorized as to drinking on the basis of official register information on a scale from *a* to *e*, and also categorized with information obtained at their interview with Kaij on a scale from *0* (abstainer) to *4* (chronic alcoholic); the latter classification was not made on about 10% of the pairs, so that only official register data was used. To the best of my knowledge, if the co-twin did not appear in the Temperance Boards' registers, there could be no "official register" information; but Kaij does not enlighten the reader how he obtained information about drinking habits in the absence of registration of the co-twin; I assume that, on the basis of the interview with the proband (or with another informant), Kaij himself decided how to categorize the co-twin, thus introducing risk of further bias.

Those abusers of alcohol who came to the attention of the Temperance Boards are those who made a public display of their abuse, while other, more private, abusers were excluded. Cabaniss thus finds herself in agreement with Kaij that the sample of abusers, although representative of those registered with the Boards, are not representative of alcohol abusers, and may be, admittedly, psychopaths and not primary alcoholics. Cabaniss points out that of 74 MZ individuals, only 17 were adjudged "normal and healthy." Interviewing was not blind: Kaij might well have assigned twins looking more alike to the same class than he would those looking more unlike.

Murray et al. (1983) indicate that the element of uncertainty with regard to the zygosity of the twin pairs employed may be higher than expected, pointing (probably inaccurately) to the low proportion of MZ twins in the sample: Kaij, unable to obtain blood groups on all pairs, states that ". . . a few MZ pairs may be concealed in the DZ group," which Murray et al. believe " . . . raises the question of whether MZ twins discordant for drinking, who often look very different, may have been wrongly considered DZ"—which would increase the concordance rate for MZ. Obtaining information from relatives and nonaffected MZ co-twins may lead to a denial of monozygosity, inflating concordance for MZ and discordance for DZ pairs. With regard to the representativeness of the sample, Murray et al. make the further criticism that there was a much higher rate of alcohol-related criminal acts in the Kaij sample than in most samples of alcoholics. These authors then consider the problem posed by the fact that DZ twins were interviewed only once, for no longer than 60 minutes, while most of the MZ pairs received a far lengthier and detailed psychometric examination in a University setting: more information was thus elicited about the drinking habits of MZ than DZ pairs.

While the classification based on official records indicated that 25.4% (15 of 59) of the MZ pairs and 15.8% (23 of 146) of the DZ pairs fell into the same drinking class (with a chi square of 2.0012, p = .157), Kaij's own additional "compound" classification yielded a concordance of 53.5% (31 of 58) for MZ and 28.3% (39 of 138) for DZ pairs (p < .0014). But as Murray et al. point out ". . . co-twins less adequately investigated might have appeared wrongly discordant, thus lowering the DZ concordance rates," and inflating the calculated contribution of heredity.

A major point made by Cabaniss relates to the definition of concordance employed by Kaij. She points out that the differences in concordance obtained by Kaij from his Table 12 (and shown in Kaij's Table 13) are calculated from pairs where both possessed the trait (from any of the classes), with a chi square of 10.21 (p < .0015). Cabaniss recalculated the differences for each of Kaij's classes 1 to 4 (using the data for *all* twin pairs), defining concordance as 100% minus the percent discordant for that class, and for none of the 4 classes are the concordances of MZ pairs significantly higher than for DZ pairs (Cabaniss: Table 2, p. 22), there being, under this traditional definition, a concordance of 77.6, 65.5, 79.3 and 89.7% (N = 58) for MZ twins in Classes 1 to 4, respectively, versus 58.7, 60.9, 73.2 and 81.9% among DZ twins. The legitimacy of this argument may be questioned because of the large number of pairs in which neither member of a pair possessed the trait denominating one of the four categories. But it is unarguable that if any one of the four classes is analyzed separately, using Kaij's definition of concordance, only class 2 shows a significant difference in concordance between MZ and DZ pairs.

Neither Cabaniss nor Murray et al. noticed other defects in Kaij's study. For example, MZ pair #47 adjudged concordant (both officially *a*), is described in this manner:

> The information about this pair is derived from a 13-year younger brother, who saw the author [Kaij] on account of heavy alcohol abuse. He said his parents had died when he was young, and he did not know much about them. The twins were said to have been very much alike and often mistaken for each other. Both went to sea in early years, and the informant had not seen much of them. One of them was killed in a shipwreck at age 20. The other is still at sea. He was convicted at age 23

(then proband) and at ages 24, 30 and 33. (Kaij, 1960a, p. 118)

So much for monozygosity! At least one of the tables (Table 12) contains information at variance with Table 26, showing 4 pairs of MZ twins at a concordant Class 1 while Table 26 has a count of six—and so on! There are many other inconsistencies within and between tables which do not enhance confidence in Kaij's conclusions.

Cabaniss and Murray et al. accept Kaij's count of 59 MZ and 146 DZ pairs, yet Kaij chose only 48 and 126 such pairs. Actually Kaij found 64 probands among MZ twins and 150 probands among DZ twins; but the 64 MZ probands ". . . were members of 48 twin pairs" and 150 DZ probands were members of 126 DZ pairs. Nine pairs (5 MZ and 4 DZ) were eliminated, leaving 59 MZ and 146 DZ. Kaij justifies this increase (48 to 59 and 126 to 146) by stating: "When comparisons of *intrapair* correlations of drinking habits between DZ and MZ pairs are made, Weinberg's so-called 'proband method' was used, which means that when both members of a pair are probands the pair is counted twice" (p. 30). No reference is given for Weinberg, but it is undoubtedly to the method proposed by Weinberg (1912, 1928) and misapplied by Kaij. [Weinberg, later others, proposed a method for rectifying incomplete sibling data when calculating the frequencies of a recessive trait; see, for example, the discussion by Bailey (p. 216, 1951).] The event, therefore, of appearance on the register of the Temperance Boards allows some pairs to be counted more than once: Kaij's Table 26 indicates that 16 of the 48 MZ pairs were counted twice; similar data on DZ pairs are not supplied. The major effect may be inflation of the concordance rate for MZ pairs.

I can only conclude that Kaij's study is so flawed that no conclusion, least of all about the hereditary nature of alcoholism, can be drawn. This examination has served the purpose, I hope, of demanding the closest scrutiny to such studies, made possible, of course, by the indefatigability of Lennart Kaij.

In one of the largest studies reported, Partanen et al. (1966) examined 902 male twin pairs chosen from all twins born in Finland between 1920 and 1929 and registered with the Finnish Central Statistical Office; a total of 641 DZ, 198 MZ and 63 twin pairs of undetermined zygosity were studied. The zygosity of each pair was determined by the similarity of a variety of measures, including stature, eye and hair color, and blood typing. DZ twins comprised pairs discordant for blood type(s) or with physical attributes incompatible with MZ status. Where blood samples were unobtainable, close physical similarities alone decided the choice for MZ placement.

For six measures connected with the drinking of alcoholic beverages—density (frequency of alcohol consumption), amount (consumption per drinking session), loss of control (ability to abstain from drinking), drunkenness arrests, addictive symptoms, and social complications—only the heritability values for density and amount (0.39 and 0.36) suggested an influence of heredity (as did the values for drinking coffee or smoking tobacco). The other measures, which would also appear to reflect alcohol abuse and to be correlated with density and amount, had nonsignificant values for heritability. The tenuous nature of the apparently significant heritability values is seen in the loss-of-control measure: younger twins gave a value of 0.54, but the value for older twins was −0.07, interpretable as the cumulative effect of the environment, and paradoxical too because in the age range used older twins might have been expected to exhibit more fully developed signs of alcohol abuse. The disparity between the values for density and amount versus those for the other measures suggests that we lack some understanding of the meaning of these measures or that sampling error has produced some significant result. Because the sample contained few heavy drinkers or alcoholics, indicants such as hospitalization or liver cirrhosis were not used.

Various other twin studies reviewed by Cabaniss and Murray et al. add little to the present discussion. However, Murray et al. report in a preliminary manner on their own study, which had (at the time of their review) examined 56 pairs of twins, in which zygosity was established, for their concordance rates for "dependence on alcohol." They found 21% of the MZ and 25% of the DZ twins concordant for this trait, an obviously nonsignificant difference, albeit weighted towards a negative heritability.

The differences in intra-pair environmental variances would be reduced if twins raised apart from an early age were to be studied, but few such pairs exist, and the few in which drinking habits are known (Newman et al., 1937; Shields, 1962; Kaij, 1960) were not actually raised completely apart: in every instance the co-twins had knowledge of each other.

HALF SIBLING STUDIES

In three papers, Schuckit et al. (1972a, 1972b, 1972c) reported upon various stages of their investigation of a group of alcoholic probands and their half siblings. These individuals have differing genetic and environmental relatedness depending on their parentage, and thus offer a means of evaluating the contribution of heredity. The 69 probands were chosen from patients admitted to the alcohol unit of the Malcolm Bliss Mental Health Center and from the Renard Hospital (both in St. Louis, Mo.) on the basis of ". . . severe life problems as a consequence of alcohol abuse," defined as alcoholism: the consequence of alcohol abuse was the presence of (1) a divorce or legal separation, or (2) a job loss, or (3) two or more nontraffic arrests, or (4) a hospitalization for a physical or psychiatric consequence of excessive drinking other than the index admission. Persons with any preexisting psychiatric disorder were excluded. In addition to meeting one of the mentioned criteria, the probands also had to have half siblings: 164 were found. From the probands, and 90 of their relatives, was obtained a ". . . history of psychiatric illness in their biologic parents, in all parent figures, and in full siblings and half siblings, as well as in biologic parents and parent figures of the half siblings."

The half siblings can be divided into 4 groups (Table 3; Schuckit et al., 1972c) on the basis of whether there was an alcoholic biologic parent or not and whether the half sibling was raised with or without such a figure: of the 46 with an alcoholic biologic parent, 24 were raised with that parent and of these 11 were alcoholics, while of the 22 raised without an alcoholic parent figure, 11 were also alcoholics; of the 118 without an alcoholic biologic parent, 14 (of whom 2 were alcoholics) were raised with an alcoholic parent figure and 104 (of whom 8 were alcoholics) were raised without such a figure. There were thus 32 alcoholics among the 164 half siblings, 22 of whom had an alcoholic biologic parent, and of the 132 nonalcoholic half siblings, 24 had such a parent: thus, 69% of the alcoholic half siblings had an alcoholic biologic parent compared to only 18% of the nonalcoholic half siblings, a ratio of almost 4 ($p < .0005$). Either this table or the preceding Table 2 (or both) are in error, Table 2 showing 20 (62%) of the 32 alcoholic half siblings and 26 (20%) of the 132 nonalcoholic half siblings to have an alcoholic parent, while Table 3 gives these numbers as 22 and 24. At an earlier stage of the study (Schuckit et al., 1972a), a similar Table 2 seems to contain a similar type of error: according to the table, 61% of 23 (N = 14) alcoholic half siblings and 19% of 75 (N = 14) nonalcoholic half siblings had an alcoholic biologic parent, from which a chi square of 16.141 is calculated for the comparison; yet such numbers (14 and 9 versus 14 and 61) would yield a chi square of 13.3635; if the percentage of alcoholic biologic parents were 65% (15 rather than 14 parents), not 61%, then the chi square is indeed 16.141. These errors raise doubts about the care which the authors gave to other, more critical, parts of the study. Further, even if the values favoring a greater hereditary involvement (from Table 3) are used, and a comparison made between the numbers of alcoholic and nonalcoholic half siblings with and without an alcoholic biologic parent, but raised with such a parent figure, the comparison is between 11 and 13 of the former and 2 and 12 of the latter: this gives a chi square of 2.6339 ($p = .105$). This particular comparison highlights the thinness of the results and indicates the importance to be given the authors' own rather curiously obscure caveats, as when they state:

> The limitations of this type of study must be kept in mind. It is possible that a nonalcoholic biologic parent determines in some subtle way the development of alcoholism in children raised by neither biologic parent. (1972c, p. 1135)

Cabaniss deplores the incomplete, and arbitrary, decision of the authors to place half siblings in either the group "raised with" an alcoholic parent figure or "raised without": in the former group were half siblings who resided a minimum of 6 years (before the age of 17) while the latter group contained those residing for less than 6 years. She suggests that living with an alcoholic parent figure for a substantial period of time (i.e., just short of 6 years) could have affected the development of alcoholism, and that a more decisive division between those half siblings who never lived and those who lived throughout the childhood years would have provided a more suitable comparison. Schuckit et al. note that the time interval was chosen not only to provide a substantial time of exposure to the parent but also to yield groups of sufficient size; they also indicate that an attempt to consider this effect yielded such small numbers in any category that ". . . a larger sample would be needed to provide a definitive answer" (Schuckit et al., 1972c, p. 1134).

Murray et al. (1983), while praising the methodological strategy, believe that the results might have been related to the 81% of the alcoholic half siblings who lived in a broken home. They also consider it "strange" that there was a lesser likelihood to become an alcoholic in those half siblings raised with the alcoholic proband. And finally, they believe the definition of alcoholism used was so broad as to mischaracterize the study as one concerned with the genetics of alcoholism, and would rather speak of it as dealing with alcohol abuse and problem drinking.

The answer to the deficiencies noted by Cabaniss, Murray et al., and not least by Schuckit et al., in addition to those already given, appears also to lie in carefully selecting a large group of probands each matched (at random) with a single same-sex half sibling. Such an approach, though it makes for the exclusion of many possible probands, and thus makes the achievement of a subject pool more difficult, has the decided advantage of providing a justifiably better answer.

ADOPTION STUDIES

Following the lecture of E. M. Jellinek (1945) on "Heredity of the Alcoholic" (Lecture 9) came the lecture of Anne Roe (1945) on "Children of Alcoholic Parents Raised in Foster Homes," a report of a study of adopted children of alcoholics. It not only preceded by more than 20 years the wider recognition of this particular strategy for genetic research in behavior, but it is also obvious that Jellinek was well aware of Roe's work before its presentation and that it influenced his own critique of prior work (both Jellinek and Roe were associates in what was to become the Center of Alcohol Studies at Yale University). In contrast to the work criticized by Jellinek, Roe concluded "... that the reported high incidence of alcoholism and psychosis in the offspring of alcoholics is not explicable on the basis of any hereditary factor." However, Roe's work has been faulted on several grounds, including the use of adoption records for the classification of the parents, the imprecision of the definition of alcoholism, and the differences between the probands and the controls as to sex, age at placement in a foster home, and so on.

Current interest in the possible hereditary nature of alcoholism began with the study by Goodwin et al. (1973) of male adoptees with a biological parent who had been hospitalized primarily for alcoholism. These "index" adoptees were chosen from among all those adopted outside their own families (N = 5,483) in Copenhagen and its immediate environs from 1924-1947, a pool established for the study of schizophrenia by Kety and others. The criteria for an index case included: alcoholic parentage (85% were the biologic father), adoption by nonrelatives before the seventh week of life, maleness, and no known contact with biological relatives. Sixty-seven adoptees were selected. Two control groups were chosen, the first consisting of 70 adoptees meeting the index criteria (matched for age, sex and time of adoption), except that neither biologic parent had a hospital record of alcohol abuse or alcoholism, and the second group of 37 adoptees "... had a biological parent hospitalized for a psychiatric condition *other* than alcoholism" (p. 238). The number of adoptees thus totaled 174, 67 index cases, and 70 and 37 control adoptees.

Of the sample of 174, 41 (14 probands) could not be found or refused their participation. Another adoptee was eliminated because it was not known which of two possible biologic fathers was the real one: whether this adoptee originally belonged to the index or the control groups is not stated. The subjects were interviewed (in Danish, later translated into English) by a psychiatrist (without knowledge of their proband or control status). Information about demographic matters, parents, drinking practices, life style, psychopathology, et cetera, was secured in a structured 2 to 4 hour interview. Since there were no differences between the control groups, they were combined. This would seem to leave a total of 132 adoptees (174 minus 41 minus 1), but the authors' arithmetic gives 133. Similarly, one would expect to have 53 (or possibly 52) probands (67 minus 14, or 67 minus 14 minus 1), but the authors calculate this as 55 probands; where one might expect 80 (or possibly 79) controls (70 plus 37 minus 27, or 70 plus 37 minus 27 minus 1), the authors give the total as 78. These unexplained arithmetical inconsistencies, as well as others to be discussed, raise questions about the care with which the study was conducted.

The adoptees were placed in one of 4 drinking categories (there were no teetotalers among the adoptees): moderate, heavy, problem drinker, and alcoholic. Problem drinkers and alcoholics met the criteria for a heavy drinker, with the former having insufficient problems from drinking to be classed alcoholic, the latter having problems from 3 of 4 areas: social disapproval of immediate family, including marital problems; job or police troubles from drinking; frequent blackouts and other consequences of intoxication and withdrawal from alcohol; and loss of control or morning drinking. In addition to being placed in one of these 4 groups, alcohol's effects and consequences (e.g., hallucinations, morning drinking, drunken driving arrests, hospitalization for drinking, etc.) and the extent of psychopathology (e.g., anxiety neurosis, depression, psychiatric treatment, etc.) were noted and comparisons made between probands and controls.

The statistical tests employed were chi square (two-tailed, with Yates' correction), and appropriate Student's t test. In the evaluation of the chi square statistic, the use of the two-tailed probability implies no a priori knowledge that, for example, probands (or controls) are more (or less) likely to manifest a particular symptom or to be categorized as a moderate, heavy or problem drinker, or as an alcoholic. The one-tailed probability is one-half of the two-tailed probability, but it demands, for the validity of its use, that any discrepancy in a direction opposite to that noted be unrelated to factors relevant to the study (Bliss, 1967; Fisher, 1954). Thus the assumption of the authors is clear: the direction of expected frequencies of the enumerations employed was not known for the two groups of adoptees. Although the authors' calculations of chi square

are mostly correct, it is not always possible to gauge how they arrived at their inconsistent estimates of the probability. In some instances, Yates' correction is not used; in other instances, the one-tailed probability is used. Such usages obviously either increase the calculated chi square, thereby lowering the probability, or lower the calculated p directly: the result is to enhance, falsely, the plausibility of the authors' arguments for the heritability of alcoholism.

Where the data are available, I have recalculated the values of chi square and the probability associated with it. For example, Table 3 (Goodwin et al., 1973, p. 240) shows that 22 (40%) probands and 19 (24%) controls required some psychiatric treatment, and a footnote indicates that $p < .01$: to emphasize the significance of this difference, the authors state: "Nearly half of the probands had received psychiatric treatment as compared to one quarter of the controls" (pp. 239-240); but for this item, chi square actually equals 3.0034 with $p = .083$. The next line of the table offers an opposite example: 8 probands and 2 controls received psychiatric hospitalization for which a $p < .05$ is shown; but the chi square is 5.0475 and $p = .025$. In Table 4, for the items hallucinations, lost control and morning drinking, 3, 19 and 16 probands, and 0, 13 and 9 controls exhibited the respective symptoms with p values of $< .05$, $< .02$ and $< .02$; but the chi squares are 2.2303, 4.7069 and 5.4114 with p values actually equal to .135, .030 and .020. Further, in the text itself, the authors note that 16 of the proband parents and 10 of the control parents had been arrested at some time for drunkenness, with a chi square of 4.441 and $p < .02$; but the value of p equals .035, somewhat weaker support for "the validity of the hospital diagnosis of alcoholism in the parents of the probands" (p. 241).

Table 4 also shows that, at some time in their lives, 10 of the probands and 4 of the controls could be designated as alcoholics ($p < .02$); with a chi square of 4.5320, $p = .033$. If the definitions of problem drinker and alcoholic are considered to overlap and these categories are combined, then there are 15 probands and 15 controls who manifested the appropriate symptomatology, yielding a chi square of 0.7782 ($p = .378$). At a minimum, one must conclude that a lesser significance should be attached to the previous p value of .033. This criticism has been made most cogently by Murray et al. (1983). They state:

> If the cut-off point for abnormality is widened to include not just alcoholism but also problem drinking, then evidence for any genetic predisposition vanishes. Indeed, the control adoptees were more frequently categorized as heavy or problem drinkers than the index adoptees (Table V). This finding contradicts the evidence of Kaij's twin study and Cloninger's adoption study (*vide infra*) that not only alcoholism but also milder alcoholic abuse is under some degree of genetic influence. Furthermore, this finding runs counter to all the evidence that heavy drinking and alcoholism are closely related. Could it be that Goodwin's findings are simply an artifact produced by the threshold for alcoholism accidentally dividing heavy drinkers in the index and control groups unevenly? (p. 42)

In light of the present examination of this study, this interpretation seems likely to be more than the mere possibility suggested by Murray et al. (1983).

Goodwin et al. determined the current status of the adoptees with regard to the designation alcoholic; whereas in Table 4 the listing depended on whether the adoptee had met the criteria for at least a year at some time, they also assessed his current status and found that 8 of the probands and 3 of the controls exhibited the appropriate alcoholic symptoms at the time of interview. For this comparison they calculated a chi square of 4.8671 (with $p < .05$), but the correct chi square is 3.5589, with $p = .059$. How did they obtain the value of 4.8671? In this instance, the authors did not use the Yates correction, though their methods section asserts that they did.

Although it may be churlish to contest their arithmetic, the errors are not few in number and establish the likelihood that other errors, not visible in the data presented, also occurred. It must be concluded that genetic disposition was indeed unproven.

The more general criticisms of this investigation, made by Cabaniss (1979) and by Murray et al. (1983), are concerned with the composition of the control group and with the diagnosis. Since 70 of the originally identified adoptees had no biological parents with a recorded psychiatric hospitalization, it would appear that this would have been sufficient in number as a control; as it turned out, there would have been 50 in this control group, close to the 53 probands (67 minus 14). Yet this group was combined with 28 (from 37) adoptees whose biological parents had been hospitalized for nonalcohol-related psychiatric illness. Murray et al. state

> One would have thought that the first group would have provided a "pure" control, but for some unspecified reason, the two control groups were combined. . . . Could this have been to increase the likelihood of finding significant differences? Since certain psychiatric conditions associated with diminished alcohol consumption are also partly heritable, e.g., obsessional neurosis, this combined control group cannot be regarded as satisfactory. (p. 41)

In a major study by Cloninger et al. (1981) employing a pool of 862 Swedish males adopted by nonrelatives before the age of 3, 151 of whom had some record of alcohol abuse (characterized as mild, moderate and severe), the authors

> . . . distinguish two forms of alcoholism that have distinct genetic and environmental causes and differ in their association with criminality, severity of alcohol abuse, and the frequency of expression in biological mothers. Postnatal milieu determines the frequency and severity of expression of the common types of susceptibility in both men and women. In contrast, the less common type is highly heritable in men but is seldom expressed in mothers of affected men. (p. 861)

The adoptees comprised an unselected population, one in which no specific types of parents or children were sought, and included all illegitimate children born in Stockholm between 1930-1949 and adopted. Because of the range of this population, the investigators studied ". . . how adoptees with particular types of congenital background react to different types of adoptive placement. This is called a cross-fostering analysis because each possible combination (cross) of genotype and environment is studied." (p. 862)

Extensive data about the adoptees were obtained from child welfare, Temperance Board, criminal, and National Health Insurance registers, and from the records of psychiatric hospitals. A discriminant function analysis yielded background variables which set apart the alcohol abusers from all others. Various other statistical procedures were also used in a complex and sophisticated analytical scheme. The manner of data presentation makes it difficult to assess the extent to which errors in arithmetic or in statistical assessment occur, but in their initial paper (Cloninger et al., 1981), and in their following paper (Bohman et al., 1981), there are errors in the calculation of chi square (see especially p. 966, e.g., significance of the four-fold increase in alcohol abusers among 29 daughters of mothers who abused alcohol compared to the daughters with neither biological parent an alcoholic). Although the authors conclude that their results "reconcile" earlier adoption studies (Roe, Goodwin et al.), this reconciliation fails to take into account the unacceptability of these studies. Moreover, since Roe found no genetic influence, Goodwin et al. found genetic influence for alcoholism but not for problem drinking, and Cloninger et al. found genetic influence for problem drinking but not for alcoholism, these contradictory results challenge the possibility of "reconciliation."

Cloninger et al. discerned no continuum of genetic influence. Given the categories of mild, moderate and severe abuse, they concluded that ". . . environmental factors largely determine severity of abuse given a genetic predisposition to either mild or severe abuse"; and that ". . . most moderate alcohol abusers had another distinct kind of predisposition that was highly heritable in men regardless of their postnatal environment" (p. 865). Their analysis also indicated ". . . that unidentified factors or unspecified interactions were determining the development of severe abuse" (p. 865).

The alleged implacability of alcoholism is highlighted by the extraordinary logic of the authors' discourse on the high prevalence of nonfamilial (sporadic) alcoholism: they hypothesize that if children's alcoholism is not reflected in any signs of vulnerability to alcoholism on the part of their biological parents, this is because the latter ". . . are not themselves exposed by virtue of their drinking customs. Thus, *alcohol abuse itself is not a sensitive criterion of genetic susceptibility*" (p. 867, emphasis mine). The authors thus posit a widespread genetic susceptibility to alcohol abuse which is not manifested because social custom inhibits contact with alcohol. In this manner, it is implicitly asserted that no weight should be given to the estimated 47 to 82 percent of alcoholics who had no alcoholic parents (Cotton, 1979). For an inherited trait *not* to occur in one's relatives seems most peculiar. What then is the weight to be given heredity? Here the authors cavil, saying:

> . . . the demonstration of the critical importance of sociocultural influences in most alcoholics suggest that major changes in social attitudes about drinking styles can change dramatically the prevalence of alcohol abuse regardless of genetic predisposition. (p. 867)

Unlike that of Goodwin et al. or that of Kaij, the Cloninger et al. study involved interviews with none of the adoptees, and relied exclusively upon official registers. As Kaij points out, reliance for the diagnosis of alcoholism on the data of the Temperance Board register is likely to introduce sample bias by identifying as alcoholics those individuals who are also psychopaths. Thus, Murray et al. are led to conclude, as one must, that despite the sophisticated statistical analyses of the data, ". . . one has doubts about the validity of the original distinctions" (p. 43).

GENETIC MARKERS AND ALCOHOLISM

About 20 years ago I suggested (Lester, 1966) that "an association of alcoholism with other characteristics known to be inherited would appear to offer some support for a biological factor in the etiology of alcoholism" (p. 420). Among these inherited characteristics are the blood groups and other serum proteins, phenylthiocarbamide taste sensitivity, defects of color vision, and (non)secretion of ABH blood group substances into the saliva. The "association" essentially says that since the genetic marker is inherited, so too, in some fashion, is the disease. Although individuals afflicted with cancer of the breast, the colon, or the rectum, or with substantial hypertension, do not appear to possess differing blood group frequencies than persons without these diseases, people with duodenal ulcers have a higher (55% vs. 47%) frequency of blood group O; since the relative incidence of this disease is not different among those in A, B, and AB blood groups, it may be estimated that the likelihood of getting duodenal ulcers is some 40% higher for blood group O than non-O individuals. Similarly, it is surmised that individuals who taste phenylthiocarbamide (PTC) as bitter are less likely to develop nodular goiters than nontasters of PTC.

Swinson (1983) has reviewed published reports beginning in 1959, which examined the association between genetically determined characteristics and alcoholism. These genetic markers include the ones named above. Swinson concludes that there is no association between alcoholism and blood groups, and that any significant association between alcoholism and the three other polymorphisms may well result from prior alcohol intake: an effect, not an antecedent, of alcohol use; Swinson is guarded on this issue, suggesting that further investigation in this area might fruitfully lead to greater clarity, especially if family studies and prospective assessments were to be made. I have no reason to disagree with this assessment.

These three reviews (Cabaniss, Murray et al., and Swinson) represent excellent, even-handed, cautious and careful probing of the evidence, and they suggest that genetic involvement in the etiology of alcoholism, however structured, is weak at best. My present examination of part of the evidence extends, and I believe, strengthens, these previous judgments.

PHARMACOGENETICS AND ALCOHOL METABOLISM

Much attention has been paid to apparent pharmacogenetic support for the weight to be assigned heredity in the etiology of alcoholism. Many authors (e.g., Shields, 1977; Rutstein and Veech, 1978; Erwin and McClearn, 1981; Goodwin, 1982; Schuckit, 1984) have accepted the work of Vesell et al. (1971) which reported virtually absolute genetic control of alcohol metabolism. In two subsequent papers by Vesell (1972a, 1972b), the original 1971 data on 7 MZ and 7 DZ pairs of twins were repeated, although for reasons not made known to the reader, the Federation Proceedings paper (1972b) roughly doubled the rates of ethanol metabolism (mg/ml/

hr) shown in the tables of the other papers! Other values (ID, age and body weight) were unchanged. The conclusions reached in these papers remain unchanged (Vesell and Penno, 1983).

While the original paper and that in the Annals of the New York Academy of Sciences (1972a) reported a heritability of 0.98, the Federation Proceedings paper reported the heritability to be 0.99, albeit based on different rates (in most cases doubling those previously reported) of ethanol metabolism. My own calculations of the heritability yield values of 0.98 and 0.973, respectively (employing the authors' definitions of variance and heritability). Unfortunately, the values for DZ twins are unacceptable in at least 2 cases. For example, as judged by the slope of the lines representing the disappearance of alcohol from the plasma (mg/ml/hr), twin F.D. metabolizes ethanol at more than twice the rate of twin P.D. (0.24 vs. 0.11), and twin H.H. metabolizes ethanol some 43% more rapidly than P.M. (0.20 vs 0.14). Yet if the alcohol concentrations are extrapolated to zero concentration, twin P.D. manages to eliminate the same ethanol dose in less time than twin F.D. (4.5 vs. 5.0 hours), and twin P.M. eliminates the ethanol dose in 5.2 vs. 6.2 hours (for twin H.H.). The seeming paradox apparently arises from differences in absorption and distribution of alcohol, factors not taken into account by these investigators: although these particular sets of twins had identical body weights, their heights may have differed, thus resulting in differences of body water space. Whatever the reason, these values cannot be used. If they are excluded, the heritability decreases to 0.934, based on the original data (for the data in Federation Proceedings, the value falls to 0.895). It would also appear reasonable to include only same-sex twins in the dizygotic group; using same-sex twins, however, leaves only 3 pairs of fraternal twins, and it would be ridiculous to perform further calculations with such data.

Using appropriate data from these reports, heritability values for body weight can also be calculated: it turns out that the variance of body weight is greater in identical than in fraternal twins! I have indicated elsewhere (Lester, 1988) other difficulties with the reports of Vesell et al. (e.g., Wagner and Patel, 1972; Wagner, 1973).

The first problem with the cited experiment, which affects other similar investigations, is the confounding effect of differences in body water and in absorption of alcohol from the stomach. To obtain reliable results for the rate of disappearance of alcohol, the solution is to administer alcohol intravenously. The second problem is that only same-sex fraternal twins should be used and that the number of twins should exceed 7 by at least a magnitude (Martin et al., 1981).

These problems are also evident in the work of Luth (1939), though to a lesser degree. [Vesell et al. (1971) were apparently unaware of their predecessor of 32 years, a situation not yet rectified (Vesell and Penno, 1983).] Luth studied the rate of ethanol elimination in 10 pairs of identical and 10 pairs of same-sex fraternal twins. Although he concludes that there is a genetic component (by comparing the mean intrapair differences between the groups), he did not calculate the heritability. Such a calculation yields values of 0.63 for ethanol elimination and 0.67 for body weight. With larger numbers of twins for the calculation of the heritability of body weight, a value of about 0.8 is ordinarily obtained (never 1.00).

In 1977, Kopun and Propping carefully studied 19 identical and 21 fraternal twin pairs, also assessing intrasubject variation in ethanol metabolism. Their heritability value for ethanol elimination (mg/ml/hr) was 0.46, for absorption (mg/m1/30 min) was 0.57, and for ethanol degradation (mg/kg/hr) was 0.41. They concluded that these parameters "although to some extent under genetic control, is [sic] appreciably influenced by environmental factors" (p. 344). They attribute the high values of Vesell et al. (1971) to the relatively small number of twin pairs and to their inhomogeneity with respect to sex and age. Kopun and Propping are sufficiently self-critical to realize the problems of their own study: thus they find greater concordance for the absorption of alcohol in their identical twin pairs than for the intrasubject measure in single subjects: "We can only speculate and cannot explain these findings" (p. 343). When other time intervals (between 30 and 60 minutes) were used for estimation of absorption, "no influence of genetic factors could be established" (p. 343). It seems essential in such studies to remove the confound of absorption by giving alcohol intravenously, and as Kopun and Propping imply they understand, to give the dose of ethanol based upon the volume of body water, that is, to take account of age and height differences in addition to those of weight (Watson et al., 1981; Lester, 1988). The necessity for such experimental rigor is underlined by the fact that, in a later paper, reporting the greater concordance of the EEG in MZ versus DZ twins after alcohol ingestion, Propping (1978) remarks that ". . . during the period of the main effect of alcohol, i.e., between 60 and 180 min after alcohol intake, blood alcohol curves of MZ twins are not more similar to one another than those of DZ twins" (p. 94). It is unfortunate that the results on alcohol elimination find their way so readily and uncritically into a textbook (Vogel and Motulsky, 1982), and especially that the papers by Vesell et al. are now enshrined as Holy Writ.

Martin and his co-workers (1981; see also Gibson and Oakeshott, 1981) have embarked on a broad ranging study of a similar, though more encompassing, nature. By 1981, they had already tested 79 pairs of 18- to 35-year-old twins and aimed "to collect data on at least 200 pairs of twins . . . " (p. 90). These pairs, fraternal and identical, attend an 8-hour test session during which they receive 0.75 g ethanol/kg about one hour after a light, nonfatty breakfast. A variety of measures are made, including the absorption and elimination of ethanol, psychomotor and cognitive tasks, and hematological and biochemical assays some of which have been suggested to be indicators of previous experience with alcoholic beverages. The authors make clear their view that previous studies in this area (Luth, 1939; Vesell et al., 1971, etc.) ". . . involving fewer than 100 pairs have a very low probability of providing a critical test of relevant hypotheses when used for traits that are incompletely inherited" (p. 90). Unfortunately, at least for the rate of alcohol elimination, their use of oral administration of alcohol may also confound the results they will obtain. In their 1981 paper, they offer a preliminary analysis of the effects of alcohol on an arithmetic computation task, concluding

> It is clear that if there are genetic differences affecting performance deterioration under alcohol on this task, then they are of small effect compared with individual environmental experiences and with the genetic differences that affect performance

> on all occasions, regardless of whether alcohol is present or absent. (p. 95)

I can only join these authors in the hope that their analysis of data on the projected 200 twin pairs will provide valid and acceptable values on genetic involvement in some of alcohol's effects. For the present, however, the conclusion offered by Gibson and Oakeshott (1981), co-investigators of Martin, seems appropriate: "*In toto* the published studies on the inheritance of alcohol metabolism in man emphasize more the inadequacies of available data than provide insight into the causes of the variation" (p. 131).

This conclusion was drawn despite the seeming acceptance by Gibson and Oakeshott of reports of higher levels of blood acetaldehyde after alcohol ingestion in siblings or sons of alcoholics compared to controls with no familial alcoholism (Schuckit and Rayses, 1979). Such higher levels of acetaldehyde have also been considered the basis of the "flushing" reaction, an inborn reaction to alcohol with presumably aversive consequences. The evidence that an aldehyde dehydrogenase deficiency is responsible for elevated levels of acetaldehyde and flushing in certain Orientals (Okada and Mizoi, 1982; Tsukamoto et al., 1982) and other ethnic groups is also on not particularly firm ground until methodological problems associated with the analysis for acetaldehyde are rectified. But that the conclusion of Gibson and Oakeshott remains warranted is made plain by the recent review of blood acetaldehyde levels by Eriksson (1983). Eliminating the sources of artefactual production of acetaldehyde has produced a situation wherein "acetaldehyde is not, at least with current analytical procedures, detectable in human venous blood during ethanol intoxication in subjects having neither a deficiency in, nor inhibition of, aldehyde dehydrogenase activity" (pp. 147-148), a conclusion buttressed recently by Nuutinen et al. (1984). Even in subjects who might have such a deficiency, Eriksson's Table 1 makes clear that the 10-fold higher blood acetaldehyde levels in Japanese flushers compared to Japanese nonflushers and the 5-fold higher levels in Japanese flushers compared to Japanese alcoholics is still subject to analytical caveats. The negative association between flushing and frequency of drinking has, however, been reported to be significant only for Japanese men, not for

Japanese women (Schwitters et al., 1982); these investigators conclude that ". . . once persons drink at all, whether flushing occurs following the use of alcohol has only a trivial effect on drinking behavior" (p. 1262).

Much the same situation prevails with regard to ethnic differences (Caucasians versus Eskimos versus Native Americans, et cetera) in rates of ethanol disappearance. Small numbers of subjects, inattention to state of alimentation, and the confound introduced by the oral administration of alcohol raise serious doubts about the import of these studies for the involvement of heredity and alcoholism. More than a little weight must be given to the excessive use of alcohol by individuals "intolerant" (flushers) to alcohol and to the overwhelming numbers of "tolerant" (nonflushers) individuals who do not become alcoholics.

PRACTICAL IMPLICATIONS

The factors that enhance risk, or offer protection from risk, from nature and nurture, are the meaningful objectives of inquiry. For the greatest part, the search for a genetic influence in alcoholism has cast no more light on factors identifying the individual at risk for alcoholism than did an earlier, different and abortive attempt by Williams et al. (Williams, 1947; Williams et al., 1949; 1949a); the fault, to some degree, with Williams's approach was to disregard, in the alcoholic, alcohol-induced perturbations.

The possible causes and mechanisms whereby alcoholism develops have been set out by Clare (1979), Goodwin (1979, 1979a, 1979b, 1979c), and Grove and Cadoret (1983), among numerous others. The list is long, encompassing many possibilities and some improbabilities (e.g., Sudduth, 1977), derived from biology, psychology and sociology. From proposers entranced with heredity (Goodwin; Grove and Cadoret), the list is hardly short and its length implies that not one but a panoply of genes are necessary, especially if genetic theory is to embrace aspects of personality like shyness and social insecurity, à la sociobiology. I cannot but agree with the views of Richardson (1984), in an analogous context, ". . . that the credence accorded the views is disproportionate with their theoretical and empirical warrant. It is, furthermore, suggested that the proper explanation for the attraction and persistence of such views lies in their conformity with ideological norms'' (p. 396). Richardson might well have added ''propagation'' to ''attraction and persistence.''

A revealing, important, and recent example is the publication by the U.S. National Institute on Alcohol Abuse and Alcoholism (1985) of a 39-page pamphlet titled *Alcoholism: An Inherited Disease*. One of the authors of the preface to the pamphlet is C. Robert Cloninger; the preface is an unabashed paean to the importance, value and social impact that knowledge of the genetic factors in alcohol abuse and alcoholism will have for prevention and treatment. The preface assumes, and the remainder of the pamphlet assures the reader in most uncritical fashion, that the evidence is ''impressive'' for the genetic transmission of alcoholism. The pamphlet stresses the importance of genetic factors in the ''majority'' of alcoholics, and follows the logic previously alluded to: the high prevalence of nonfamilial alcoholism (hardly ''sporadic'' at a frequency of between 47 to 82 percent) is because the social customs of parents disallowed contact with alcohol. This is a most curious inhibitor in societies in which the drinking of alcoholic beverages is engaged in not simply by a majority, but by an overwhelming majority of the population. One example must suffice to illustrate the bias: to show how impressive is the evidence for a genetic factor, the pamphlet informs the reader that, ''(Goodwin's) study was based on a large sample population of 5,483 individuals who had been adopted in early childhood'' (p. 4), in contrast to the 133 (maximum) adoptees who were actually studied. Needless to say, the review by Murray et al. is not mentioned, nor is the admonition given by Cloninger et al. (1981) that ''. . . the demonstration of the critical importance of sociocultural influences in most alcoholics suggest that major changes in social attitudes about drinking styles can change dramatically the prevalence of alcohol abuse regardless of genetic predisposition'' (p. 867). The differences in event-related potentials (ERP) between children of alcoholics and children with no alcoholic biological relatives, one of the assessed ''Markers of inherited susceptibility to alcoholism'' discussed in the pamphlet, is given a less than critical appraisal. Independent investigators, using the same subjects and procedures as described in one of the two papers (discussed in the pamphlet) upon which the presumed success of this marker is based, were unable to replicate the results; in a subsequent investigation of ERP, Polich et al. (1988) conclude, delicately, that "The results suggest that the relationship between the P300 ERP and the inheritability of alcoholism is not yet clear and may be subject to modulation by task requirements, population differences, and subject sex." In other words, another "marker" has failed to exhibit any predictive strength.

The pamphlet provides a rationale for genetic theory and alcoholism: as stated in the preface, it is not only that, "Knowing that alcoholism is heritable should make it easier for us to rethink our cultural attitudes toward alcoholism and to accept it for what it is— " but that alcoholism is "a disease with a molecular basis, . . . " (Preface). Reducing alcohol abuse and alcoholism to a molecular level means that one need no longer tinker with social and cultural attitudes; rather our efforts will be rewarded by designing "specific pharmacological interventions to prevent it and treat it" (p. 36).

Although the NIAAA pamphlet was hardly required to set the tone for these views, it does appear to have fostered an outpouring of similar tracts and expressions. On 2-3 April 1987, the New York State Division of Alcoholism and Alcohol Abuse held a national conference (in cooperation with 12 other organizations, including Children of Alcoholics Foundation, Inc.); the title "A Family Legacy. The Genetics of Alcoholism" gives the essence of the affair. Thus, the Director of the Division (Robert V. Shear) characterized the status of the field by stating that the ". . . developments in genetic research in this area have been stunning . . . " and averred that he was "electrified" when he encountered the 1973 paper of Goodwin et al. More recently, Fitzgerald (1988) has embodied her no nonsense hereditarian views in a book, which, in all kindness, must be said to be not only a hodgepodge of misunderstandings and misinterpretations, but also wrong. Goodwin's suggestion (Goodwin, 1987) that "the illness *may* [my emphasis] have a genetic component" and that nature vs. nurture is a debate are rejected: for her, there is neither a guarantee nor a debate because nature is the clear and acknowledged winner. The magazine *Newsweek* (Monmaney et al., 1988) generally echoes this picture, but does allow that there is some dissent. However, in a book

(Light, 1988) presumably directed to a professional audience, the author's presentation seems calculated *not* to exercise any criticism and no dissenting or different views receive mention. The hereditary nature of alcoholism receives its latest, though subdued, imprimatur from U.S. Patent 4,770,996 (Tabakoff, 1988) wherein it is asserted that "The development of a diagnostic criterion to identify individuals at risk for becoming alcoholic is currently based upon the *clear demonstration* [my emphasis] that genetic factors are important to the development of alcohol-related problems in a significant portion of the alcoholic population."

These expressions find a ready acceptance by most alcoholics, and such notions at least dilute the responsibilities of the individual and the experienced guilt.

Unrelated human beings, differing in many genes but holding untold numbers of genes in common, display similar onsets, courses and outcomes in relation to alcohol; it is not unreasonable to believe that alcoholism is the result of man's biology *and* the personal and social circumstances of his existence, external to but yet created by him. How then can the fate be fate, let alone implacable, if only a small portion of identical twin pairs share an alcoholic destiny? Despite the identity of 100% of the genes in each member of a such a pair, and a far higher common nurture than fraternal twins, the fact of the existence of a nonalcoholic co-twin argues for more than the effect of one or more heritable traits. Nurture, in the larger sense of its intertwining with the genotype, must play a far greater and more decisive role than the proponents of heredity appear willing to concede. Furthermore, even if it were possible to partition such contributions without error in particular populations, we would still not know how to act absent an etiological mechanism.

Scientific inquiry would be the victim if any simplistic ideology of genetic theory and alcohol abuse and alcoholism were not questioned. And the spirit of the scientific enterprise would be diminished if this, or any other alternative perspective, were not criticized.

I believe that no elucidation of the etiology of alcoholism is possible without a prospective longitudinal study embracing the assessment of probable mechanisms from the biological to the sociocultural. Such a holistic approach rejects the simplistic and reductionist search for a single cause, the "Thomas switch" which Goodwin (1982) admires and apparently expects will one day appear, ready to turn alcoholism, like syphilis, "on and off" (Thomas, 1979). To believe this is truly to believe in the implacable fate. It is noteworthy that the examples given by Thomas are tertiary syphilis, chronic tuberculosis and pernicious anemia, the switches being the spirochete, the tubercle bacillus, and a vitamin deficiency, all causes *external* to the organism. Unless we are asked to believe that alcoholism arises from an analogous external cause, the comparison may be inapplicable. Or is the availability of alcoholic beverages the cause, and prohibition the switch? If something external to the organism can be modulated in some manner, say by decreasing the effect of alcohol, will this eliminate alcoholism?

It does not appear that Goodwin would accept such an external mechanism. For genetics to have a place in such a schema, something internal to the organism must be switched. Since Thomas also believes ". . . that schizophrenia will turn out to be a neurochemical disorder, with some central, single chemical event gone wrong," I assume that Goodwin too expects the rectification of a neurochemical event to transform the alcoholic; both would appear to accept the heritability of schizophrenia despite the steady decrease in the estimate of its value over the years. In 1980, Cassou et al., after an impressively lengthy and exhaustive reevaluation, concluded that there was a total absence of proof of a genetic effect in the schizophrenic process. Then, in 1981 and again in 1983, Lidz and his co-workers came to the same conclusion, that ". . . the investigators' more direct study of the adopted-away offspring of schizophrenic parents failed to provide statistically significant evidence of a genetic influence . . . " Given the interactions and interrelationships of the increasing numbers of presumed neurotransmitters, Thomas' exuberance appears overdone; the nature of the genetically related neurochemical has, so far, been sought in vain.

RELATIONS TO OTHER THEORIES

It is my belief that a theory involving the interaction of genetics and environmental influences is compatible with many theories from many disciplines. I thus assert that no single factor or event "causes" alcoholism, that it is, to use what is to some an overworked phrase, a disease, syndrome or process of a multifactorial nature. And its etiology will be found, variously, in the results of investigations from neurobiology and neuropsychology to politics and economics. I also believe that only the kind of longitudinal prospective study previously described, asking the right questions, will provide the answers.

The work to be done demands not only exemplary rigor but also the closest scrutiny by others because its effects on public policy are, and would be, hardly trivial. Kitcher (1985) has put the issue explicitly: discussing the English scientific scoundrel Sir Cyril Burt and his pernicious effects on British education, he states:

> My aim is not to vex Sir Cyril's ghost but to draw a moral. Those who frame social policies often look to the findings of the sciences for guidance. If the studies they consult are incorrect, then the mistakes may reverberate through the lives of millions. Dogmatic faith, wedded to deliberate fraud, is only the most glaring (and surely the least common) source of socially costly scientific error. From the point of view of those who ultimately suffer, however, the source does not greatly matter. For those of my friends whose talents were left to moulder because of a benighted educational policy, it would hardly be a consolation to know the error arose from carelessness rather than deliberate deception. The moral is transparent. When scientific claims bear on matters of social policy, the standards of evidence and of self-criticism must be extremely high. (p. 3)

Feldstein (1988) provides additional evidence from the area of epidemiology for the vital necessity of "High-quality data" and ample criticism of published investigations.

CONCLUSION

Scientists in this area commonly focus on the relatively small number of genes which confer biological individuality (Williams,

1956) on those genes that divide us, for example, into the races of man. But our common genetic endowment, the result of a long biological history, would seem to be the great base upon which our culture and social history acts. There will then be many "switches," turned on and off, in the complex network of interactions between the individual's biology and culture that produce the alcoholic process.

The alcoholic is not doomed by any biological constraints or immutable laws of nature. The social organization in which the individual at risk for alcoholism has developed also has available many compassionate helping hands. However described, whether disease, process or syndrome, whether physical and/or mental, the individual also can agree with Henley (1875) and say:

> I am the master of my fate;
> I am the captain of my soul,

understanding that few captains or masters ever operated without a helping crew to keep the ship from foundering.

REFERENCES

Bailey, N.T.J. The estimation of the frequencies of recessives with incomplete multiple selection. *Annals of Eugenics*, 1951, *16*, 215-222.

Bliss, C.I. *Statistics in Biology*. New York: McGraw-Hill Book Company, 1967.

Bohman, M., Sigvardsson, S., & Cloninger, C.R. Maternal inheritance of alcohol abuse. *Archives of General Psychiatry*, 1981, *38*, 965-969.

Buck v. Bell, Superintendent. United States Reports (Cases adjudged in the Supreme Court at October Term, 1926). Decided 2 May 1927. Vol. 274, pp. 200-208. Washington: United States Government Printing Office, 1928.

Cabaniss, N. *Is alcoholism an inherited disorder? An evaluation of twin, half-sibling and adoption studies of drinking behavior*. Unpublished senior honors thesis, Princeton University, 1979.

Camps, F.E. Genetics and alcoholism. *Annals of the New York Academy of Sciences*, 1972, *97*, 134-137.

Cassou, B., Schiff, M., & Stewart, J. Genetique et schizophrenie: reevaluation d'un consensus. *Psychiatrie de l'Enfant*, 1980, *23*, 87-201.

Clare, A.W. The causes of alcoholism. In G. Edwards & M. Grant (Eds.), *Alcoholism. New Knowledge and New Responses*. Baltimore: University Park Press, 1977.

Cloninger, C.R., Bohman, M., & Sigvardsson, S. Inheritance of alcohol abuse.

Archives of General Psychiatry, 1981, *38*, 861-868.

Cotton, N.S. The familial incidence of alcoholism. *Journal of Studies on Alcohol*, 1979, *40*, 89-116.

Eriksson, C.J.P. Human blood acetaldehyde concentration during ethanol oxidation (Update 1982). *Pharmacology Biochemistry & Behavior*, 1983, *18*, 141-150.

Erwin, V.G. & McClearn, G.E. Genetic influences on alcohol consumption and actions of alcohol. *Currents in Alcoholism*, 1981, *8*, 405-420.

Falconer, D.S. *Introduction to Quantitative Genetics*. New York: The Ronald Press Company, 1964.

Feinstein, A.R. Scientific standards in epidemiologic studies of the menace of daily life. *Science*, 1988, *242*, 1257-1263.

Fisher, R.A. *Statistical Methods for Research Workers*. New York: Hafner Publishing Co., Inc., 1954.

Fitzgerald, K.W. Living with Jellinek's Disease. *Newsweek*, 17 October 1983, p. 22.

Fitzgerald, K.W. *Alcoholism: The Genetic Inheritance*. New York: Doubleday, 1988.

Gibson, J.B. & Oakeshott, J.G. Genetics of biochemical and behavioural aspects of alcohol metabolism. *Australian & New Zealand Journal of Medicine*, 1981, *11*, 128-131.

Gleibermann, L., Gershowitz, H., Harburg, E., & Kuusinen, S. Blood groups and alcohol use. *Journal of Studies on Alcohol*, 1981, *42*, 557-563.

Goodwin, D.W. *Is Alcoholism Hereditary*? New York: Oxford University Press, 1976.

Goodwin, D.W. Alcoholism and heredity, a review and hypothesis. *Archives of General Psychiatry*, 1979a, *36*, 57-61.

Goodwin, D.W. The cause of alcoholism and why it runs in families. *British Journal of Addiction*, 1979b, *74*, 161-164.

Goodwin, D.W. Genetic determinants of alcoholism. In J.H. Mendelson & N.K. Mello (Eds.), *The Diagnosis and Treatment of Alcoholism*. New York: McGraw-Hill, 1979c.

Goodwin, D.W. Genetics of alcoholism. In R.W. Pickens & L.L. Heston (Eds.), *Psychiatric Factors in Drug Abuse*. New York: Grune and Stratton, 1979d.

Goodwin, D.W. Alcoholism and heredity: update on the implacable fate. In E.L. Gomberg, H.R. White & J.A. Carpenter (Eds.), *Alcohol, Science and Society Revisited*. Ann Arbor, MI and New Brunswick, NJ: University of Michigan Press, Rutgers Center of Alcohol Studies, 1982.

Goodwin, D.W. *Children of Alcoholics*. Luncheon address at a conference on "A Family Legacy. The Genetics of Alcoholism." N.Y. State Division of Alcoholism and Alcohol Abuse, 2-3 April 1987, Penta Hotel, New York City.

Goodwin, D.W., Schulsinger, F., Hermansen, L., Guze, S.B., & Winokur, G. Alcohol problems in adoptees raised apart from alcoholic biological parents. *Archives of General Psychiatry*, 1973, *28*, 238-243.

Goodwin, D.W., Schulsinger, F., Moller, N., Hermansen, L., Winokur, G., &

Guze, S.B. Drinking problems in adopted and nonadopted sons of alcoholics. *Archives of General Psychiatry*, 1974, *31*, 164-169.

Grove, W.M. & Cadoret, R.J. Genetic factors in alcoholism. In B. Kissin & H. Begleiter (Eds.), *The Pathogenesis of Alcoholism; Biological Factors*. New York: Plenum, 1983.

Henley, W.E. Invictus. In W.R. Benet & C. Aiken (Eds.), *Anthology of Famous English and American Poetry*. New York: Modern Library, 1944.

Jellinek, E.M. Heredity of the Alcoholic. In *Alcohol, Science and Society* (pp. 105-114). New Haven: Quarterly Journal of Studies on Alcohol, 1945.

Jellinek, E.M. *The Disease Concept of Alcoholism*. New Haven, CT: Hillhouse Press, 1960.

Kaij, L. *Alcoholism in Twins. Studies on the Etiology and Sequels of Abuse of Alcohol*. Stockholm: Almquist and Wiksell, 1960a.

Kaij, L. *Alcoholism in Twins. Studies on the Etiology and Sequels of Abuse of Alcohol. Case Reports*. Stockholm: Almquist and Wiksell, 1960b.

Kevles, D.J. *In the Name of Eugenics. Genetics and the Uses of Human Heredity*. New York: Adolf A. Knopf, 1985.

Kitcher, P. *Vaulting Ambition. Sociobiology and the Quest for Human Nature*. Cambridge: The MIT Press, 1985.

Kopun, M. & Propping, P. The kinetics of ethanol absorption and elimination in twins and supplementary repetitive experiments in singleton subjects. *European Journal of Clinical Pharmacology*, 1977, *11*, 337-344.

Lester, D. Self-selection of alcohol by animals, human variation, and the etiology of alcoholism. A critical review. *Quarterly Journal of Studies on Alcohol*, 1966, *27*, 395-438.

Lester, D. An animal model of alcoholism. In E.L. Gomberg, H.R. White, & J.A. Carpenter (Eds.), *Alcohol, Science and Society Revisited*. Ann Arbor, MI and New Brunswick, NJ: University of Michigan Press, Rutgers Center of Alcohol Studies, 1982.

Lester, D. Genetic theory. An assessment of the heritability of alcoholism. In C.D. Chaudron & D.A. Wilkinson (Eds.), *Theories on Alcoholism*. Toronto: Addiction Research Foundation, 1988.

Lewontin, R.C. Sleight of hand. (A review of Genes, Mind, and Culture by Lumsden, C.J. & Wilson, E.O.) *The Sciences*, 1981, *21*, 23-26.

Lewontin, R.C. *Human Diversity*. New York; Scientific American Library, W.H. Freeman and Company, 1982.

Lewontin, R.C., Rose, S., & Kamin, L.J. *Not in Our Genes*. New York: Pantheon Books, 1984.

Lidz, T., Blatt, S., & Cook, B. A critique of the Danish-American studies of the adopted-away offspring of schizophrenic parents. *American Journal of Psychiatry*, 1981, *138*, 1063-1068.

Lidz, T. & Blatt, S. Critique of the Danish-American studies of the biological and adoptive relatives of adoptees who became schizophrenic. *American Journal of Psychiatry*, 1983, *140*, 426-435.

Light, W.J.H. *Alcoholism and Women, Genetics, and Fetal Development*. Springfield: C.C Thomas, 1988.

Luth, K.-F. Untersuchungen uber die Alkoholconzentration nach Alkoholgaben bei 10 eineiigen und 10 zweieiigen Twillungspaaren. [Investigations of the alcohol blood level in 10 monozygotic and 10 dizygotic pairs of twins.] *Deutsche Zeitschrift fur die gesamte gerichtliche Medizin*, 1939, *32*, 145-164.

Martin, N.G., Gibson, J.B., Oakeshott, J.G., Wilks, A.V., Starmer, G.A., Craig, J., & Perl, J. A twin study of psychomotor performance during alcohol intoxication: early results. In *Twin Research 3: Epidemiological and Clinical Studies*. New York: Alan R. Liss, Inc, 1981.

Monmaney, T., Springen, K., & Hager, M. Heredity and drinking: how strong is the link? *Newsweek*, 18 January 1988, pp. 66-67.

Murray, R.M., Clifford, C.A., & Gurling, H.M.D. Twin and adoption studies: how good is the evidence for a genetic role? In M. Galanter (Ed.), *Recent Developments in Alcoholism* (Vol. 1). New York: Plenum, 1983.

Newman, H.H., Freeman, F.N., & Holzinger, K.J. *Twins: A Study of Heredity and Environment*. Chicago: University of Chicago Press, 1937.

National Center for Health Statistics. These data were obtained from the Office of International Statistics through the courtesy of Dr. Robert B. Hartford, Assistant Director.

National Institute on Alcohol Abuse and Alcoholism. *Alcoholism: An Inherited Disease*. DHHS Publication No. ADM 85-1426, 1985.

Nuutinen, H.U., Salaspuro, M.P., Valle, M., & Lindross, K.O. Blood acetaldehyde concentration gradient between hepatic and antecubital venous blood in ethanol-intoxicated alcoholics and controls. *European Journal of Clinical Investigation*, 1984, *14*, 306-311.

Okada, T. & Mizoi, Y. Studies on the problem of blood acetaldehyde determination in man and level after alcohol intake. *Japanese Journal of Alcohol and Drug Dependence*, 1982, *17*, 141-159.

Partanen, J., Bruun, K., & Markkanen, T. *Inheritance of drinking behavior; a study on intelligence, personality and use of alcohol in adult twins*. Helsinki: Finnish Foundation for Alcohol Studies, 1966.

Paul, J. State eugenic sterilization history: a brief overview. In J. Robitscher (Ed.), *Eugenic Sterilization*. Springfield: Charles C Thomas, 1973.

Peele, S. The new prohibitionists. *The Sciences*, 1984, *24*, 14-19.

Polich, J., Burns, T., & Bloom, F.E. P300 and the risk for alcoholism: family history, task difficulty, and gender. *Alcoholism: Clinical and Experimental Research*, 1988, *12*, 248-254.

Propping, P. Alcohol and alcoholism. *Human Genetics*, 1978, Suppl. 1, 91-99.

Regier, D.A., Myers, J.K., Kramer, M., Robins, L.N., Blazer, D.G., Hough, R.L., Eaton, W.W., & Locke, B.Z. The NIMH epidemiological catchment area program. *Archives of General Psychiatry*, 1984, *41*, 934-941.

Richardson, R.C. Biology and ideology: the interpenetration of science and values. *Philosophy of Science*, 1984, *51*, 396-420.

Robins, L.N., Helzer, J.E., Weissman, M.M., Orvaschel, H., Gruenberg, E.,

Burke, J.D., Jr., & Regier, D.A. Lifetime prevalence of specific psychiatric disorders in three sites. *Archives of General Psychiatry*, 1984, *41*, 949-958.

Roe, A. Children of alcoholic parents raised in foster homes. In *Alcohol, Science and Society* (pp. 115-127). New Haven: Quarterly Journal of Studies on Alcohol, 1945.

Rutstein, D.D. & Veech, R.L. Genetics and addiction to alcohol. (Editorial.) *New England Journal of Medicine*, 1978, *298*, 1140-1141.

Schuckit, M., Goodwin, D.W., & Winokur, G. The half-sibling approach in a genetic study of alcoholism. In M. Roff, L.N. Robin, & M. Pollack (Eds.), *Life History Research in Psychopathology* (Vol. 2). Minneapolis: University of Minneapolis Press, 1972a.

Schuckit, M.A., Goodwin, D.W., & Winokur, G. Genetic investigation in alcoholism—the half-sibling approach. *International Symposium Biological Aspects of Alcohol Consumption*, 27-29 September 1971b. Helsinki: Finnish Foundation for Alcohol Studies, 1972b, *20*, 163-167.

Schuckit, M.A., Goodwin, D.W., & Winokur, G. A study of alcoholism in half-siblings. *American Journal of Psychiatry*, 1972c, *128*, 1132-1136.

Schuckit, M.A. & Rayses, V. Ethanol ingestion: differences in blood acetaldehyde concentrations in relatives of alcoholics and controls. *Science*, 1979, *203*, 54-55.

Schuckit, M.A. Prospective markers for alcoholism. In *D.W. Goodwin, K.T. Van Dusen & S.A. Mednick (Eds.), Longitudinal Research in Alcoholism*. Boston: Kluwer-Nijhoff Publishing, 1984.

Schwitters, S.Y., Johnson, R.C., McClearn, G.E., & Wilson, J.R. Alcohol use and the flushing response in different racial-ethnic groups. *Journal of Studies on Alcohol*, 1982, *43*, 1259-1262.

Shields, J. *Monozygotic Twins: Brought Up Apart and Together*. London: Oxford University Press, 1962.

Shields, J. Genetics and Alcoholism. In G. Edwards & M. Grant (Eds.), *Alcoholism. New Knowledge and New Responses*. Baltimore: University Park Press, 1977.

Stern, C. *Principles of Human Genetics*. San Francisco: W.H. Freeman and Company, 1960.

Sudduth, W.H. The role of bacteria and enterotoxemia in physical addiction to alcohol. *Journal of the International Academy of Preventative Medicine*, 1977, *4* (No. 2), 23-46.

Swinson, R.P. Genetic markers and alcoholism. In M. Galanter (Ed.), *Recent Developments in Alcoholism* (Vol 1). New York: Plenum, 1983.

Tabakoff, B. *Identification of Individuals Predisposed to Alcohol Abuse*. U.S. Patent 4,770,996. Washington, DC, 13 September 1988.

Thomas, L. The medusa and the snail. In *Medical Lessons from History*. New York: Viking Press, 1979.

Tsukamoto, S., Sudo, T., Karasawa, S., Kajiwara, M., & Endo, T. Quantitative recovery of acetaldehyde in biological samples. *Nihon University Journal of Medicine*, 1982, *24*, 313-331.

Vesell, E.S. Ethanol metabolism: regulation by genetic factors in normal volunteers under a controlled environment and the effect of chronic ethanol administration. *Annals of the New York Academy of Sciences*, 1972a, *197*, 79-88.

Vesell, E.S. Introduction: genetic and environmental factors affecting drug response in man. *Federation Proceedings*, 1972b, *31*, 1253-1269.

Vesell, E.S., Page, J.G., & Passananti, G.T. Genetic and environmental factors affecting ethanol metabolism in man. *Clinical Pharmacology & Therapeutics*, 1971, *12*, 192-201.

Vesell, E.S. & Penno, M.B. Intraindividual and interindividual variations. In J. Caldwell & W.B. Jakoby (Eds.), *Biological Basis of Detoxication*. New York: Academic Press, 1983.

Vogel, F. & Motulsky, A.G. *Human Genetics*. Berlin: Springer-Verlag; 1982.

Wagner, J.G. Intrasubject variation in elimination half-lives of drugs which are appreciably metabolized. *Journal of Pharmacokinetics and Biopharmaceutics*, 1973, *1*, 165-173.

Wagner, J.G. & Patel, J.A. Variations in absorption and elimination rates of ethyl alcohol in a single subject. *Research Communication in Chemical Pathology & Pharmacology*, 1972, *4*, 61-76.

Watson, P.E., Watson, I.D., & Batt, R.D. Prediction of blood alcohol concentrations in human subjects. *Journal of Studies on Alcohol*, 1981, *42*, 547-556.

Weinberg, W. Weitere Beitrage zur Theorie der Vererbung. 4. Uber Methode und Fehlerquellen der Untersuchung auf Mendelesche Zahlen beim Menschen. *Archiv fur Rassen – und Gesellschaftsbiologie*, 1912, *9*, 165-174.

Weinberg, W. Mathematische Grundlagen der Probandenmethode. *Zeitschrift fur Induktive Abstammungs-und Vererbungslehre*, 1928, *48*, 179-228.

Williams, R.J. The etiology of alcoholism: a working hypothesis involving the interplay of hereditary and environmental factors. *Quarterly Journal of Studies on Alcohol*, 1947, *7*, 567-587.

Williams, R.J. *Biochemical Individuality*. New York: John Wiley, 1956.

Williams, R.J., Berry, L.J., & Beerstecher, E., Jr. Individual metabolic patterns, alcoholism, genetotrophic diseases. *Proceedings of the National Academy of Sciences*, 1949, *35*, 265-271.

Williams, R.J., Berry, L.J., & Beerstecher, E., Jr. Individual metabolic patterns, alcoholism, genetotrophic diseases. *Science*, 1949, *109*, 441.

Is Risk for Alcoholism Predictable? A Probabilistic Approach to a Developmental Problem

Robert A. Zucker

A man I know is a cook in the State Prison of Southern Michigan, one of the largest walled prisons in the world. When one compares his work to that of most others, it is clear that he is in substantially greater danger of assault, and possibly even death, than is true of others of his occupation. And yet he reports, I believe accurately, that should an uprising come down, his life would be protected although he is unarmed, because he has befriended a "natural lifer" who is a man both of large physical stature and of considerable political power in the prison social structure. He notes as well that his life would probably be in less jeopardy than that of one of the armed but disliked guards in the prison.

The relevance of this little vignette to the topic under consideration is that both my story and the problem I address have to do with the anticipation of problematic outcomes in risky circumstances. The story makes the point that even living in risky environments does not automatically preclude successful outcomes, and that the possession of protective factors does not insure successful ones; contextual factors, that are themselves the outgrowth of an interaction, and a set of processes that unfolds over some time sequence, may make the difference between a safe and a damaged ending. The present review deals with these issues in detail, elaborating on the

---

Robert A. Zucker is Professor of Psychology, Department of Psychology, Michigan State University, East Lansing, MI 48824.

Preparation of this article was supported in part by National Institute on Alcohol Abuse and Alcoholism Grant AA07065.

nature of risk itself, examining the theoretical structure which has guided much of the research relevant to risk for alcohol problems and alcoholism, briefly summarizing the evidence upon which current predictive statements are made, and addressing the question of the extent to which certainty about outcome can be anticipated on the basis of a knowledge of risk factors alone.

THE CONCEPT OF RISK

Webster's New International Dictionary (1956) lists the following as alternative definitions of *risk*:

1. The chance of loss or peril;
2. The degree of probability of such loss;
3. Abbreviation for "amount at risk"; that is, the amount which the (insurance) company may lose;
4. The character of hazard involved (syn.:danger).

These definitions deal with three aspects of the phenomenon; risk implies an *anticipated outcome* (i.e., the occurrence of a negative event, called a loss). It also implies a *likelihood estimate*; or to put the matter another way, the concept of risk is a probabilistic statement. It implies the attachment of some kind of weight to the possibility of occurrence of a future event. And last, the concept implies that there are some attributes of the ongoing event structure, prior to outcome, that are best characterized as *hazard or danger*. This attribute of risk implies an actuality of the moment as well as the possibility of a later troublesome consequence. As in my story, that which is dangerous at the moment may still be negotiated without jeopardy, but it is usually considered to require greater attentiveness to the process, and to the details of the negotiation than would be the case were one not in a dangerous situation.[1] Such is the nature of risk.

To pursue this definition a bit further, risk is an attribute of populations rather than individuals, and is typically inferred on the basis of an observation that some proportion of a group with specified characteristics eventually displays some sign or symptom. It is the manifest display, the actuality of risk transformed into bona fide trouble, which then becomes the basis for prospective statements about risk characteristics for a new, but similar population.

Elements of risk or danger are inferential in a different sense at the individual level; they are best regarded as signs of covert processes that only some of the time are detectable by their overt display. This is precisely the dilemma in anticipating individual outcome for such a disorder as alcoholism.[2] One needs to infer and understand the interplay of factors that may never come to fruition, but that nonetheless must be regarded as still present and operational. The remainder of the paper deals with the evidence relating to the presence of such factors, and the processes which undergird them. First along the way, we consider the theory structure that guides much of this research, as it has in some instances helped and in others hindered a comprehensive understanding of these phenomena.

FACTORS NECESSARY FOR THE ANTICIPATION OF RISK: THE PROBLEM OF THEORY IN ETIOLOGIC RESEARCH

Despite the weights assigned to different factors in a predictive equation, one can never hope to be successful in accounting for individual variation if the variables included are trivially to nonexistently related to the criterion. Similarly, if the measures used to assess a factor are crude or heavily laden with error, the estimates of variance accounted for will only be imprecise and low-order bounds for the amount of variation attributable to that factor. When these principles are stated in the abstract form just used, they are truisms that one would expect a first year graduate student to understand after having completed a course in experimental design or multivariate statistics. Yet when these same principles are applied as judgement criteria, in a practical sense, for some of the most significant research programs attempting to map and understand alcoholic etiology, they are too often violated. The result is that our knowledge of etiologic connections—the basis for both prediction of risk and outcome—continues to be more flawed than it needs to be.

From the perspective of theory, there are five types of conceptual or design problems that have repeatedly invaded major research studies of the past decade, in ways that make it difficult to come to a more definitive understanding of causes and outcomes:

1. *Failures to adequately sample the domain of known and significant influences*: for example, within the realm of psychosocial influences upon behavior, it has repeatedly been demonstrated in research on the development of drinking and problem drinking, that the role of peers in introducing, stabilizing and reinforcing these drug use patterns is one of the most powerful sources of variation of any in the variable domain (Kandel, 1980; Jessor & Jessor, 1977; Zucker & Noll, 1987). A like pattern of salience of the peer influencing structure—at the level of the family group—is also more recently being demonstrated for older, alcoholic drinkers (Jacob & Seilhamer, 1987). Despite the major power of this level of influencing structure, it is more often noticeable by its absence than by its presence in all but the studies which explicitly are concerned with charting its power as a main effect.

This problem is not one found only among the more biologically based research community; given the strong evidence for a genetic component operating in the regulation of differences in pattern of alcoholism (Cloninger, Bohman, & Sigvardsson, 1981) it becomes increasingly important for primarily psychosocially focused research to attempt to mark and evaluate this source of contributory variation. At the moment such efforts most often are confined to high-risk research paradigms (cf. Begleiter, 1988; Goodwin, Van Dusen, & Mednick, 1984) than to the mainstream of etiologically focused studies.

2. At a more general level, what is perhaps most unfortunate about this state of affairs is that the discussion of domain issues in understanding this complex set of phenomena is still quite rare, with some exceptions (e.g., Tarter, Alterman, & Edwards, 1985; Cloninger, 1987; Zucker & Gomberg, 1986). It is noteworthy that the Institute of Medicine, in its most recent review of the state of research in the alcohol field (1988), acknowledges this as a major research issue for the '80s, and points up the need for multi-disciplinary research to explicitly address the across domain inter-relationships that are so much a part of alcoholic phenomena (cf. Institute of Medicine, 1987, p. 12). The IOM recommendation points up the

second set of design flaws, namely: *Failure to adequately represent the interactional nature of this disorder*.

Alcoholism is, after all, a biobehavioral disorder. At the biological level it is most appropriately classified as a pharmacogenetic disorder, that involves the interaction between a self-administered pharmacologic agent and a neurophysiologic system that – to some degree – has been hard wired by way of the genetic structure. At the same time, it is a distinctly different disorder than schizophrenia, whose primary manifestations are best understood as involving central nervous system deficits. In contrast, the self-administered nature of the agent of damage means that, for an adequate model of alcoholic etiology, there must be adequate representation of an ecology of contexts of availability and social structures, within which patterns of use are shaped, reinforced and punished. Along with the biological sequelae of sustained alcohol involvement (those factors that lead to tolerance and dependence), there are a massive set of social sequelae of use that play a role in the cumulation process, a process that eventuates, for some individuals, in the development of an alcoholic career.

This issue of neglected interactional influences, as well as of failures to adequately assess the domains of causal structure is nowhere better illustrated than in the Cloninger et al. (1981) Stockholm Adoption Study. These investigators conclude that, among men, there are two kinds of genetic predisposition to alcoholism, one substantially limited by the postnatal environment (called Type I, or milieu-limited), the other, apparently unaffected by environmental variations (called Type II, or male-limited). In an incisive re-analysis of these data, Searles (1988) calls attention to the exceptionally sparse and inadequate set of environmental variables included (age at final adoptive placement, extent of postnatal hospital care, occupational status level of adoptive father, rearing by biological parent for more than six months, adoptive parents' alcohol abuse record and criminality record). He notes that the manner in which the data are presented obscures the heavy contribution of unspecified (and unmeasured) environmental variation to the outcome of alcohol abuse, and demonstrates that the effect size for these influences is "substantially more important in determining alcohol abuse than are genetic factors" (p. 161).

One last point about the mapping of causal domains as this contributes to the evaluation of risk; the Stockholm study is but one example of an inadequate set of measures with which to chart environmental variation. Given the field's current ability to begin to assess genetic load by way of family history measurement, the lack of studies which adequately assay both sets of domains ends up restricting our ability to capture interactional variations that might contribute to a more precise anticipation of differences in alcohol abuse outcome.

3. *Failure to understand the importance of "nonspecific factors" in etiology*: Despite the articulate and carefully reasoned assaults on the disease model over this last generation (Cahalan, 1970; Peele, 1986), it is still with us in ways that erode the research models we construct and the studies we carry out to understand alcoholic etiology. The disease model carries within it the promise that a set of factors can be identified which will be the *sine qua non* of the disorder (cf. Meehl, 1989). Such factors, particularly when they may involve a heritable element, are most often construed to be alcohol-specific in their mechanism (cf. National Institute on Alcohol Abuse and Alcoholism, 1985). In one instance, nonspecific factors have been rejected outright as inappropriate elements to even include in the etiologic equation (Nathan, 1988).

Such a perspective is limiting in two ways: first, it avoids dealing with the empirical criterion of amount of predictive variance apportionable to particular factors; yet from both predictive and public health vantage points, this is undoubtedly a central issue in any theory and any research program. Ultimately, the isolation of a "that without which" is of little practical use if it does not contain the key to modification of the disorder. Yet this solution is not always in the "specific factor" realm (e.g., draining swamps to cure malaria).

Second, it currently leads investigators into a research paradigm that ends up avoiding some of the most substantial sources of variation in patterns of alcohol (and other drug) involvement of any now known (see point 1 above; also, Kandel, 1978; Peele, 1988). Severe drug involvement is a human act, involving a biopsychosocial process over long spans of developmental time. As such, it is probably not adequately capturable by an etiologic paradigm which ignores nonalcohol-specific, but powerful ecological factors along the way (Jessor & Jessor, 1973; Moos, 1979).

4. *Failure to take account of the developmental nature of alcoholic processes, which involve several alcoholisms as well as the more moderate forms of abuse*: If there is one characteristic that is both troublesome and ubiquitous about alcohol involvement at different levels of severity, it is that the phenomenon is a fluid one, shifting over developmental epochs, remaining steady for some drinkers and shifting for others, changing from problem to nonproblem status or vice versa, etc. (Zucker, 1979; Kandel & Logan, 1984; Cahalan, 1970; Fillmore, Bacon, & Hyman, 1977). Current evidence indicates that this statement is as true for the severe and chronic end of the alcohol abuse continuum—what gets called alcoholism—as it is for more moderate and more acute manifestations of drinking difficulty (Goodwin et al., 1971; Polich, Armor, & Braiker, 1980; Roisen, Cahalan, & Shanks, 1978; Skog & Duckert, in press).

The field is increasingly aware of the evidence for epiphenomenality. However, what is still missing is an awareness that the move into and out of severe drinking difficulties occurs in a developmental, life trajectory context, and that the difficulties are likely to have different long term ramifications *depending upon the developmental context in which they appear* (Zucker, 1987; 1988). Thus, onset of drinking problems is a different issue when it occurs at age 11 than when it occurs at age 16, and different than either of these two when it occurs at age 65 (Robins, 1984; Gomberg, 1982). The recalcitrance of the problem and its susceptibility to outside modification may be very different at these different developmental epochs, *because of the meaning structure that surrounds the abuse at the time it takes place, and because the processes that work to create the problematic outcome may, in fact be different in these different periods* (e.g., Kandel & Andrews, 1987; Robins & Przybeck, 1985).

A related developmental issue that is only beginning to receive attention is the need to distinguish between a variety of different "alcoholisms," which are marked by different etiologies and different developmental pathways (Zucker, 1987; Cloninger, Sigvardsson, & Bohman, 1988; McCord, 1988). Thus, the appearance of a symptomatic display that is part of several different alcoholic trajectories will tell us nothing about risk if we cannot simultaneously identify which pathway it maps onto. Accurate assessment of risk needs to take account of these different developmental trajectory and contextual issues in weighting relative impact.

5. *Failure to distinguish between maintenance processes and onset processes in the formulation of etiologic paradigms*: Related to points 3 and 4 above, if one conceives of alcoholism (alcohol dependence) in its full blown form to be closely tied to, if not synonymous with the *alcohol dependence syndrome* (Edwards & Gross, 1976), then it is not surprising that one would heavily emphasize the role of alcohol-specific factors in its etiology, and one would heavily direct research to those neurobiological factors that control the syndrome. Conversely, if one understands that the onset and early movement into heavy alcohol involvement is largely controlled by contextual, attitudinal and social influence structures (Kandel, Kessler, & Margulies, 1978; Jessor & Jessor, 1977) then it is not surprising that one would heavily direct research to understand the interplay and timing of these variables. The current evidence implicates both sets of factors, but the timing, and the role that each plays has not been well enough emphasized (Zucker & Gomberg, 1986). The former appear to be elements concerned more with maintenance of the processes, the latter appear to be concerned more with onset. This distinction rarely is made; more importantly, studies tracking the relative importance of one vs. the other, that simultaneously allow for evaluation of the time-linked nature of the relative contributions, have not yet been carried out.

ANTICIPATING RISK FOR ALCOHOLISM: EVIDENCE FOR CONTINUITY AND CUMULATION OF PROCESS

The above points need to be taken as a series of lenses through which to scrutinize existing studies. Despite the relative lack of awareness of these issues, some sets of influences have systematically been replicated in longitudinal data sets with fairly large variable domains. Thus, as when assembling two identical jigsaw puzzles, both of which have lost pieces (but not the same ones), it is possible to reconstruct more of the shape of the lost original than would be true were only one of the puzzle copies available. We turn now to the replicated evidence which identifies some common factors indicating continuity of outcome of alcoholic process.

The first work we examine involves six studies, all of which originated in childhood and adolescence, followed respondents on into adulthood rather than terminating in adolescence, and all of which established a diagnosis of either alcoholism or problem drinker (what would be called alcohol abuse in this era of DSM IIIR terminology) when respondents reached adulthood. Thus all of these studies began at a time where it is reasonable to infer that none of the subjects were yet alcoholic, although it is equally reasonable to expect that drinking had already been in place among a substantial subset of those who were adolescent at the T_1 data collection. The studies referred to are the Oakland Growth Study, the St. Louis Child Guidance Clinic Study, the Columbia Follow-up Study, The Cambridge-Somerville Youth Study, and the Physique and Delinquency Study. A series of papers over the last decade carefully describes these studies in detail, reviews their commonalities, and also points up correspondences between the longitudinal work and other studies of high-risk but not yet alcoholic samples (Zucker, 1979; Zucker & Noll, 1982; Zucker & Gomberg, 1986). Drawing primarily from the Zucker and Gomberg review, the following points summarize the across study commonalities:

1. childhood antisocial behavior is consistently related to later alcoholic outcome (5 studies);
2. more childhood difficulty in achievement related activity is consistently found in those who later become alcoholic (4 studies);
3. males who later become alcoholic are more loosely tied to others interpersonally (4 studies);
4. heightened marital conflict is reported with consistently greater frequency in the prealcoholic[3] homes (4 studies);
5. parent-child interaction in prealcoholic homes is characterized by inadequate parenting and by the child's lack of contact with the parent(s) (all 6 studies);
6. parents of prealcoholics are also more often inadequate role

models for later normality; they are more likely to be alcoholic, antisocial, or sexually deviant (4 studies);

7. greater activity level in childhood is identified as a precursor in two studies;
8. ethnic differences are systematically linked to alcoholic outcomes; within the range of ethnic heritages sampled, alcoholics are more likely to come from Irish than Italian backgrounds (3 studies).

These across study correspondences are significant, but from a developmental perspective they still leave several issues untouched. Given that the bulk of this work begins at the end of middle childhood, it does not inform us about what might be taking place earlier on, that is itself precursive to the events of later childhood. However, there is another set of studies that is useful in filling in some of the gaps; I refer to those several longitudinal projects that have begun to examine what early childhood characteristics might be antecedent to an alcohol (or in some cases drug) involved outcome during the teen years. The special utility of these studies—even though coming from quite diverse populations—is that they examine some of the same attributes that were identified as important in the later stage longitudinal studies. Thus they allow us to fill in the developmental flow chart running from childhood to adulthood. Table 1 lists the relevant studies, and Table 2 charts the extent to which they provide evidence for correspondence with the findings of the later stage, high-risk longitudinal studies just summarized.

Given the diversity of populations examined here, and the substantial lack of risk loading in two of the four of the studies (Brook et al.; Block et al.), the evidence for continuity of behavior from the preschool years onward is significant if not impressive. In every area where an association could be tested, the relationships either parallel or do not contradict what has been observed in the studies of older populations. Further, the evidence for a precursive relationship between early childhood antisocial involvement and alcohol related problem outcomes in later years seems at this juncture to have been sufficiently replicated among boys so as to be regarded as an established sequence. Evidence from the Michigan State University Longitudinal study is consistent with all elements of this picture

TABLE 1. Prospective Studies of Influences During Early Childhood Related to Alcohol and Drug Involvement in Adolescence: Study Characteristics

Study	Subject Characteristics and Source	Age at first contact	Age at follow-up
1. Rydelius (1981;1984) Nylander (1960)	229 Stockholm children with severely alcoholic, clinic treated fathers (50%M) and 163 matched "social twins" without paternal alcoholism	4-12	24-32
2. Kellam et al (1980;1983) Ensminger et al (1982)	Complete population sample; N = 1242 black 1st graders; approx. 50% M; from South side Chicago	6	6-7; 9; 16-17
3. Brook et al (1986)	N = 356; 94% white; 49% M@ T1; random selection from 2 NY counties	5-10	13-18
4. Block et al (1988); Block & Block (1980)	N = 105; 67% white; 49% M; recruited through nursery schools, over represents middle class	3	4; 5; 7; 11; 14

TABLE 2. Correspondences Between Earlier Stage Developmental Studies and Later Stage, High-Risk-for-Alcoholism Longitudinal Studies

	STUDY			
	Rydelius/ Nylander	Kellam et al	Brook et al	Block et al
CHARACTERISTICS IDENTIFIED IN LONGITUDINAL STUDIES WITH OLDER Ss[a]				
1. CHILDHOOD ANTISOCIAL BEHAVIOR/AGGRESSION	+	+ (Boys) 0 (Girls)	+[a]	+[b]
2. CHILDHOOD ACHIEVEMENT PROBLEMS	+	0	0[c]	--
3. POORER CHILDHOOD INTERPERSONAL CONNECTIONS	--	+(Boys)[d]	0[c]	+
4. HEIGHTENED ACTIVITY LEVEL IN CHILDHOOD	+	--	0	+ (Boys) 0 (Girls)
5. LESS PARENT-CHILD CONTACT & MORE INADEQUATE PARENTING IN CHILDHOOD	+	--	--	+ (Girls) 0 (Boys)
6. MORE MARITAL CONFLICT IN CHILDHOOD HOMES	--	--	--	--
7. PARENTS MORE OFTEN INADEQUATE ROLE MODELS/ WITH MORE PSYCHOPATHOLOGY AND NO ALCOHOLISM AND OTHER PSYCHOPATHOLOGY	+[e]	--	--	--

TABLE 2 (continued)

Note: A (+) in the columns indicates a correspondence between the later age longitudinal studies and the earlier developmental stage studies; a (0) indicates no relationship; a (-) indicates an obverse correspondence, and a (--) indicates no data available on this issue.

In all of the above tallies, a correspondence is judged to be present if in the younger sample, the identified characteristics is precursive of later, greater alcohol involvement, more alcohol related problems, or a later stage of alcohol/drug use (cf. Kandel, 1975)

Table 3 (continued)

[a]Predelinquency measure was related; aggression against peers and siblings was not

[b]Marginally significant in girls

[c]Earlier childhood factors only influenced by way of their impact upon later (adolescent) factors

[d]Trend for shyness together with aggressiveness

[e]True of both parents

(Zucker, 1987). Over an anticipated 20 year time span, this project is following families, initially with children between 3 and 6 years of age, who are at high risk for alcoholism in later life by way of their being male and also the children of alcoholic fathers. The work is especially relevant to the evolution of risk because it utilizes a population based sample of families, and is able to identify alcoholism in the parent before any formal diagnosis or treatment of the problem has taken place.

In this data set, as hypothesized, cross-sectional evidence is already accumulating that the familiarity with alcoholic beverages, and the development of cognitive structures about them (relating to being able to identify alcohol and have a clearer sense of the appropriate contexts of its use) differentiates the high-risk children from matched controls as early as three years of age (Noll & Zucker, 1983). Other analyses (Reider, Zucker, Noll, Fitzgerald, & Maguin, 1988) of the marital patterns in these very young families, are consistent with the longitudinal evidence just reviewed concerning parental behavior and risk in adolescence and thereafter (i.e., the later stage studies). Quite strong relationships also are noted between extent and severity of parents' alcohol problems and the levels of current violence displayed in these families. In addition, severity of parents' alcohol problems is positively and strongly related to their own antisocial histories. These are two sets of characteristics not well covered by the studies summarized in Table 2; the evidence here, albeit cross-sectional, is thus consistent with what one would again expect on the basis of a continuity-of-process hypothesis going back at least as early as age 3.

SPECIFIC VS. NONSPECIFIC ETIOLOGY: A CAUTIONARY NOTE

On all of these grounds the evidence for a steady progression is incomplete but very strong. Both longitudinal data sets and a subset of high-risk but not yet alcoholic cross-sectional studies are in accord on these points. In addition, the individual difference findings among the children suggest that the *problem behavior syndrome* – identified by Donovan and Jessor (1985; Donovan, Jessor, & Costa, 1988) in adolescent and young adult populations as the core of a variety of delinquent, substance abusing, and precociously unconventional activities – may be found in place as early as the preschool years in these very high-risk families; this aggressive/antisocial component appears to provide the core around which other elements of the syndrome may accrete.[4] The evidence is consistent with such a hypothesis, but the longitudinal work following it from early on, and tracking it into adulthood needs elaboration in several different directions.

1. The above review implies that the pathway into problematic alcohol involvement is by way of influences that are nonspecific to alcoholism. The fact that parallel findings concerning this syndrome are also noted in studies that have tracked alcoholic outcome

from homes where there was no alcoholic parent (McCord, 1988) lends additional support to this position. But given the likelihood that some aspects of the ultimate disorder are under genetic control, what these studies do not clarify is the extent to which these manifestations are simple prolegomena to the later alcoholic syndrome, rather than being core *mediational* structures which form an intrinsic part of the etiologic chain. Current evidence is more consistent with the second alternative (Hesselbrock et al., 1984; Cadoret, Troughton, O'Gorman, & Heywood, 1986), but without factoring some measure of genetic loading, however crude, into the data set, these alternate etiologic pathways cannot be differentiated. This was in fact done in McCord's very elegant data set, but since the focus of her report was upon parent contributions to child's alcoholism, the regression analysis she reports does not allow us to evaluate comparative effects.

2. Alcohol-specific factors[5] (as opposed to alcoholism-specific ones) operate both in and outside of alcoholic homes, and can be expected to be a significant dimension of exposure around which the learning of drinking takes place (Cahalan, Cisin, & Crossley, 1969). Earlier formulations in this arena have focused almost exclusively on the adolescent years as the developmental time frame within which such exposure takes place and needs to be understood (Kandel, 1978). However, recent studies with children as young as three years of age indicate that learning about alcohol takes place far earlier than had previously been suspected. Eight investigations have been carried out with younger groups. These studies, summarized in a recent review paper (Zucker & Noll, 1987), indicate that young children already are well on their way to developing internalized schemas about alcohol, as a drug, its effects, and its appropriate contexts of use. Some evidence also exists for the presence of individual differences in the development of this knowledge base as a function of parent use patterns (Noll et al., 1986).

Given these findings, and the strong correlation commonly noted between exposure to these experiences (i.e., exposure to drinking peers) in later childhood and exposure to other aspects of the problem behavior syndrome, the contribution of each of these separate sources of variation to the problem outcome of alcohol abuse is not clear. And insofar as the biological aspects of alcoholism are linked intimately to the antecedents, sequelae and consequences of consuming alcohol in varying amounts and schedules, it is critical at the behavioral level to distinguish among these different sources of risk variation.

ANTICIPATING RISK FOR ALCOHOLISM AND ALCOHOL ABUSE: EVIDENCE FOR DISCONTINUITY AND FOR THE OPERATION OF MEDIATIONAL AND AMELIORATIVE PROCESSES

The current clinical myth, based upon research with alcoholic individuals drawn from treatment settings, is that the disorder is an irreversible one which may remit, but not reverse itself (American Psychiatric Association, 1987). The controversy about controlled drinking (Marlatt, 1983) is precisely about this issue, although it rarely is formulated in this way. Disagreements about whether or not alcoholism is a disease also are, in part, concerned with this question.

From a risk perspective, those who adhere to an irreversibility position are implicitly making the case that a set of factors have coalesced (or have always been present, but have evolved to an advanced enough stage) such that a process is in place which is no longer capable of being disaggregated. In fact, the evidence reviewed above points in just such a direction, although the data suggest that what is operating is more an accretion process than an irreversible syndrome. However, to make this issue a bit more interesting (and challenging), it is also important to note that the figures on continuity of such processes in risky environments (such as having an alcoholic parent) show that it is *the minority* of children who move on to develop the problematic, alcohol abusive outcome (Cotton, 1979).[6]

What makes the difference? Two projects currently have data sets that are far enough along in a developmental sense, encompass measures of alcohol and drug involvement (i.e., the end criterion of risky processes), and also address the question of relative risk in early childhood. One is the already cited Brook, Whiteman, Gordon and Cohen (1986) longitudinal study (see Tables 1 and 2), which explicitly examines the issue of risk dilution as well as risk enhancement, albeit at an early stage of the drug involvement career. In a creative set of interactive analyses, these investigators demonstrated that the presence, in adolescence, of greater tolerance for deviance, impulsivity, aggression toward peers, and a variety of other measures that may be subsumed under the Donovan and Jessor problem behavior syndrome rubric (also the Block & Block [1980] Ego Undercontrol rubric), all operated to vitiate earlier childhood (T_1) factors that, on their own, would have moderated level of drug involvement (and most probably level of alcohol problems). Conversely, a variety of high-risk characteristics of earlier childhood (ages 5 to 10), involving both the problem behavior syndrome and other characteristics (depressive mood, eating problems), were ameliorated by factors in adolescence that indicated a low level of the problem behavior cluster.

It is important, in this context to stress that this is an interaction effect, which occurs in addition to a main effect. The main effect is for continuity of behavior, by way of a *mediational sequence*. This process operates by way of chaining: childhood personality characteristics shape adolescent personality traits (i.e., a process of continuity in development), which in turn impacts level of adolescent drug involvement. The interaction effect, to either enhance or dilute adolescent drug involvement, overlays and runs counter to the mediational main effect sequence.

There is another critical question which needs to be posed: given that the more straightforward, main effect sequence involves continuity, the interaction-effect-shifts in problem behavior from childhood to the adolescent years thus involve an invasion upon such continuity of process. How can this be accounted for? The Brook et al. study does not speak to this question, but other of these investigators' work (Brook, Whiteman, & Gordon, 1983) demonstrates that more than personality factors are in operation here: level of drug involvement in that study was related to the influence of peer and family factors, and to their interaction with personality variables.

The other study is McCord's Cambridge-Somerville project. Her 1988 paper does not explicitly focus on issues of risk amelioration, but the study's findings concerning pathways leading into alcoholism, are interpretable in the obverse direction as protective factors. Shyness in childhood (circa age 10) is a protective factor; so also is coming from a home without an alcoholic father. But most importantly, this study shows that pathways into (and out of risk) are different for children who have an alcoholic father as compared to those who do not. For the former, mother's *low* esteem for her alcoholic husband is a protection; for the latter, a different set of issues appears central, namely, mother's *high control* over her son during adolescence appears to be more salient as a protection against the son's later becoming alcoholic.

Such studies, that are able to evaluate interactional processes in the earlier childhood years, that deal with the possibility of multiple pathways into and out of risk, and that are able to spread a net across a sufficient array of the salient predictive domains, are critical if the field is to become better able to specify level of risk. Equally central in this process is the willingness of investigators to formulate models of developmental interplay that take account of mediational effects, chaining sequences, and the vulnerability and opportunity to change that seems to be present at key turning points in people's lives (Elder & Caspi, 1989). This work is already taking place in other areas of developmental child psychopathology (e.g., Ensminger, Kellam, & Rubin, 1983; Rutter, 1987) but it has not yet heavily penetrated the alcohol field.

A PROBABILISTIC FRAMEWORK FOR RISK AND OUTCOME

The studies reviewed above provide evidence for both continuity and discontinuity in risk progression over time. Were one not to have a developmental lens through which to view such findings, one would be forced to conclude that the data are conflicting, but that is not at all the case. To understand this apparent contradiction it is necessary to move away from the notion of course as an unvarying coherency of process over developmental time, and to view it instead as the outcome of a probabilistic process, the result of multiple factors that independently come into play, sometimes simultaneously and sometimes at different developmental periods (Zucker, 1987). This perspective requires a life course framework, or risk grid, that maps both multiple domains of influence and the succession of developmental periods, within which extent of risk for alcohol use, and/or problems may build up, remain steady or subside. Such a model has been presented in detail elsewhere (Zucker, 1987; Zucker, 1988).

Within the context of such a model, the rudimentary element of risk becomes the *event*, the display of an individual or contextual attribute (separately or in interaction), which—if repeated often enough—will eventuate in a troublesome (i.e., symptomatic) outcome. The probability of such a display is lessened when the high-risk attribute driving it is diluted by an insulating attribute; it is also lessened if the contextual attribute necessary for an environmental trigger is not present. Conversely, the probability of repeated display, and damaged outcome, is heightened when contextual risk or trigger factors are densely packed around the individual, or when repetition itself allows for the evolution of a hierarchized display structure (Zucker, 1988) wherein the elicitation of one component is more likely to trigger the appearance of a variety of related components. Such a framework is better able to handle the complex nature of the evidence for both stability and reversibility of risk than is true of schemas like the disease model, which postulate irreversibility of course.

Thus developmental stage changes in alcohol abuse, noted in the longitudinal studies that have tracked this process from adolescence into adulthood (Fillmore et al., 1977; Yamaguchi & Kandel, 1984) are accounted for by differences in the salience of contextual triggers for alcohol involvement across the stages. Similarly, the substantial evidence for migration into and out of alcohol abuse in adulthood, noted in both alcoholic (Skog & Duckert, in press) and nonalcoholic (Cahalan, 1970) populations is understandable by way of the occurrence of an event structure that has neither been repeatedly internally driven nor externally triggered sufficiently to cumulate. The obverse is also true: in studies of the manifestations of risk from birth to adolescence (Werner, 1986), within adolescence itself (Labouvie & McGee, 1986), and from middle childhood into middle adulthood (McCord, 1988), when risk is cumulated by way of the presence of multiple risky components, the probability of a hazardous outcome is increased to substantially over the 50 percent mark. The currently available data suggest that this cumulation process is strictly additive, but this issue has not been explored in any systematic way.

Within the context of such a probabilistic model it becomes reasonable to look early on in the life span for precursors of later, especially abusive alcohol involvement. One would be particularly interested in individuals and environments where there is (1) early appearance of the problem behavior syndrome, and the endogenous factors (e.g., temperament, activity level) which may drive it; (2) inheritance of positive alcohol-specific endogenous factors; (3) early exposure to alcohol use, and to environments that are favorable in their attitudes about heavy alcohol use, and (4) contextual support for the practice and stimulation of the behaviors which emerge as a result of (1) to (3); one would anticipate such support and stimulation would be most forthcoming from family and peer social structure. These circumstances, operating in concert, can be expected to enhance hazard and cumulate risk. Conversely, cumulation into abuse should be less likely to occur if exposure and involvement is in ameliorative environments. As a corollary to this, if one's interest is in the prevention of abusive alcohol involvement at the individual level, it is most reasonable to intervene in those environments where a greater number of factors suggest the likelihood of cumulative process.

NOTES

1. In fact, from the perspective of prevention, it is essential that these precursive, inferred processes be attended to, if one is concerned that the hazard *not* manifest itself.

2. "Alcoholism" is the generic term being used in this discussion to refer to the propensity for individuals to have chronic, alcohol related troubles which operate as a syndrome, and which have been shown to have elements of a common etiology and course. The terms "alcohol dependence" or "chronic problem drinking" could just as easily be substituted instead.

3. This term refers to the child's status; in fact, parents frequently are already alcoholic, and this itself is a common contributor to risk (see point 6).

4. Recent work by Cloninger and his colleagues (Cloninger, Sigvardsson, & Bohman, 1988) is also consistent with this conclusion. Although the Washington University group set their categories within the framework of a much more strictly clinical vocabulary, they appear to be replicating and rediscovering a set of phe-

nomena that have repeatedly been implicated in the etiology of youthful problem alcohol involvement, and that have been reported in the literature at least since 1968 (Jessor, Graves, Hanson, & Jessor, 1968; Zucker & Fillmore, 1968).

5. Also termed "drinking specific factors" (Zucker, 1979) and "proximal influences" (Jessor & Jessor, 1977).

6. This statement needs to be tempered by awareness that the damaged alternative is the less probable outcome when this factor is the only one present. As will be discussed below, when several risk factors are present, the probabilities become greater.

REFERENCES

American Psychiatric Association. (1987). *The Diagnostic and Statistical Manual of Mental Disorders–Third Edition–Revised*. Washington, DC: American Psychiatric Association.

Begleiter, H. (1988). Symposium: The Genetics of Alcoholism: Introduction to the Symposium. *Alcoholism: Clinical and Experimental Research*, *12*, 457.

Block, J.H., & Block, J. (1980). The role of ego-control and ego-resiliency in the organization of behavior. In W.A. Collins (Ed.), *Development of Cognition, Affect, and Social Relations* (pp. 39-101). Hillsdale, NJ: Lawrence Erlbaum Assoc.

Block, J., Block, J.H., & Keyes, S. (1988). Longitudinally foretelling drug usage in adolescence: Early childhood personality and environmental precursors. *Child Development*, *59*, 336-355.

Brook, J.S., Whiteman, M., & Gordon, A.S. (1983). Stages of drug use in adolescence: Personality, peer, and family correlates. *Developmental Psychology*, *19*, 269-277.

Brook, J.S., Gordon, A.S., Whiteman, M., & Cohen, P. (1986). Dynamics of childhood and adolescent personality traits and adolescent drug use. *Developmental Psychology*, *22* (3), 403-414.

Cadoret, R.J., Troughton, E., O'Gorman, T.W., & Heywood, E. (1986). An adoption study of genetic and environmental factors in drug abuse. *Archives of General Psychiatry*, *43*, 1131-1136.

Cahalan, D., Cisin, I., & Crossley, H. (1969). *American drinking practices: A national study of drinking behavior and attitudes*. New Brunswick, NJ: Publications Division, Rutgers Center for Alcohol Studies.

Cahalan, D. (1970). *Problem Drinkers*. San Francisco, CA: Jossey-Bass.

Cloninger, R., Bohman, M., & Sigvardsson, S. (1981). Inheritance of alcohol abuse: Cross-fostering analysis of adopted men. *Archives of General Psychiatry*, *38*, 861-867.

Cloninger, C.R., Sigvardsson, S., & Bohman, M. (1988). Childhood personality predicts alcohol abuse in young adults. *Research Society of Alcoholism*, *12*, 494-505.

Cotton, N. (1979). The familial incidence of alcoholism. A review. *Journal of Studies on Alcohol*, *49*, 89-116.

Donovan, J.E., & Jessor, R. (1985). Structure of problem behavior in adolescence and young adulthood. *Journal of Consulting and Clinical Psychology*, *53*, 890-904.

Donovan, J.E., Jessor, R., & Costa, F.M. (1988). Syndrome of problem behavior in adolescence: A replication. *Journal of Consulting and Clinical Psychology*, *56* (5), 762-765.

Edwards, G., & Gross, M. (1976). Alcohol dependence: Provisional description of a clinical syndrome. *British Medical Journal*, *1*, 1058-1061.

Elder, G.H., & Caspi, A. (In press). Studying lives in a changing society: Sociological and personological explorations. In A.I. Rabin, R.A. Zucker, R.E. Emmons, & S.J. Frank (Eds.), *Studying persons and lives*. New York: Springer.

Ensminger, M.E., Brown, C.H., & Kellam, S.G. (1982). Sex differences in antecedents of substance use among adolescents. *Journal of Social Issues*, *38* (2), 25-42.

Ensminger, M.E., Kellam, S.G., & Rubin, B.R. (1983). School and family origins of delinquency: Comparison by sex. In S.A. Mednick (Ed.), *Prospective Studies of Crime and Delinquency*. Boston: Kluwer-Nijhoff Publishing Co.

Gomberg, E.S.L. (1982). Alcohol use and alcohol problems among the elderly. *Alcohol and Health Monograph*, *4*, 263-290.

Goodwin, D.W., Crane, J.B., & Guze, S.B. (1971). Felons who drink: An 8-year followup. *Quarterly Journal of Studies on Alcohol*, *32*, 137-147.

Hesselbrock, M.N., Hesselbrock, V.M., Babor, T.F., Stabenau, J.R., Meyer, R.E., & Weidenman, M. (1984). Antisocial behavior, psychopathology and problem drinking in the natural history of alcoholism. In D.W. Goodwin, K.T. Van Dusen, & S.A. Mednick (Eds.), *Longitudinal research in alcoholism*. Boston: Kluwer-Nijhoff Publishing.

Institute of Medicine. (1980). *Alcoholism, Alcohol Abuse, and Related Problems: Opportunities for Research*. Washington, DC: National Academy Press.

Institute of Medicine. (1987). *Causes and Consequences of Alcohol Problems: An Agenda for Research*. Washington, DC: National Academy Press.

Jacob, T., & Seilhamer, R.A. (1987). Alcoholism and Family Interaction. In T. Jacob (Ed.), *Family interaction and psychopathology: Theories, methods and findings*. New York: Plenum.

Jessor, R., Graves, T.D., Hanson, R.C., & Jessor, S.L. (1968). *Society, personality, and deviant behavior: A study of a tri-ethnic community*. New York: Holt, Rinehart, & Winston.

Jessor, R., & Jessor, S.L. (1973). The perceived environment in behavioral science: Some conceptual issues and some illustrative data. *American Behavioral Scientist*, *16*, 801-828.

Jessor, R., & Jessor, S.L. (1975). Adolescent development and the onset of drinking: A longitudinal study. *Journal of Studies on Alcohol*, *36*, 27-51.

Kandel, D.B. (1978). Convergences in prospective longitudinal surveys of drug use in normal populations. In D.B. Kandel (Ed.), *Longitudinal research on drug use: Empirical findings and methodological issues*. Washington, DC: Hemisphere.

Kandel, D.B., Kessler, R.C., & Margulies, R.Z. (1978). Antecedents of adolescent initiation into stages of drug use: A developmental analysis. In D.B. Kandel (Ed.), *Longitudinal research on drug use: Empirical findings and methodological issues* (pp. 73-99). Washington, DC: Hemisphere.

Kandel, D.B. (1980). Drug and drinking behavior among youth. In J. Coleman, A. Inkeles, & N. Smelser (Eds.), *Annual Review of Sociology Vol. 6* (pp. 235-285). Palo Alto, CA: Annual Reviews, Inc.

Kandel, D.B., & Logan, J.A. (1984). Patterns of drug use from adolescence to young adulthood: I. Periods of risk for initiation, continued use, and discontinuation. *American Journal of Public Health, 74* (7), 660-666.

Kandel, D.B., & Andrew, K. (1987). Processes of adolescent socialization by parents and peers. *International Journal of the Addictions, 22* (4), 319-342.

Kellam, S.G., Ensminger, M.E., & Simon, M.B. (1980). Mental health in first grade and teenage drug, alcohol, and cigarette use. *Drug and Alcohol Dependency, 5*, 273-304.

Kellam, S.G., Brown, C.H., Rubin, B.R., & Ensminger, M.E. (1983). Paths leading to teenage psychiatric symptoms and substance use: Developmental epidemiological studies in Woodlawn. In S.B. Guze, F.J. Earls, & J.E. Barrett (Eds.), *Childhood Psychopathology and Development* (pp. 17-47). New York: Plenum Press.

LaBouvie, E.W., & McGee, C.R. (1986). Relation of personality to alcohol and drug use in adolescence. *Journal of Consulting and Clinical Psychology, 54*, 289-293.

McCord, Joan. (1988). Identifying developmental paradigms leading to alcoholism. *Journal of Studies on Alcohol, 49*, (4), 357-362.

Meehl, P.E. (In press). Schizotaxia as an open concept. In A.I. Rabin, R.A. Zucker, R.E. Emmons, & S.J. Frank, (Eds.), *Studying persons and lives*. New York: Springer.

Moos, R. (1973). Conceptualization of human environments. *American Psychologist, 28*, 652-665.

Nathan, P.E. (1988). The addictive personality is the behavior of the addict. *Journal of Consulting and Clinical Psychology, 56* (2), 183-188.

National Institute on Alcohol Abuse and Alcoholism (1985). *Alcoholism: An inherited disease*. (DHHS Publication No. ADM 85-1426). Washington, DC: U.S. Government Printing Office.

Noll, R.B., & Zucker, R.A. (1983, August). *Developmental findings from an alcoholic vulnerability study*. Paper presented at the annual meeting of the American Psychological Association, Anaheim, CA.

Noll, R.B., Zucker, R.A., Gonzalez-Maurer, G., & Greenberg, G.S. (1986, August). *Development of cognitive structures about alcoholic beverages among preschoolers: II*. Paper presented at the annual meeting of the American Psychological Association, Washington, DC.

Peele, S. (1986). The implications and limitations of genetic models of alcoholism and other addictions. *Journal of Studies on Alcohol*, *47*, 63-73.

Peele, S. (1988). A moral vision of addiction: How people's values determine whether they become and remain addicts. In S. Peele (Ed.), *Visions of Addiction* (pp. 210-233). Lexington, MA: Lexington Books.

Reider, E.E., Zucker, R.A., Noll, R.B., Maguin, G., & Fitzgerald, H.E. (August 1988). Alcohol involvement and family violence in a high-risk sample: I. Spousal violence. Paper presented at the American Psychological Association Meetings, Atlanta, GA.

Robins, L.N. (1984). The natural history of adolescent drug use. *American Journal of Public Health*, *74*, 656-657.

Robins, L.N., & Przybeck, T.R. (1985). Age of onset of drug use as a factor in drug and other disorders. In C.L. Jones, & R.J. Battjes (Eds.), *Etiology of Drug Use: Implications for Prevention* (pp. 178-192). (DHHS Publication No. ADM 87-1335.) NIDA Research Monograph 56, A RAUS Review Report. Washington, DC: U.S. Government Printing Office.

Roizen, R., Cahalan, D., & Shanks, P. (1978). "Spontaneous remission" among untreated problem drinkers. In D.B. Kandel (Ed.), *Longitudinal Research on Drug Use* (pp. 197-221). Washington, DC: John Wiley & Sons.

Rutter, M. (1987). Psychological resilience and protective mechanisms. *American Journal of Orthopsychiatry*, *57*, 316-331.

Rydelius, P. (1981). Children of alcoholic fathers: Their social adjustment and their health status over 20 years. *Acta Paediatrica Scandinavica*, *286*, 1-83.

Rydelius, P.A. (1984). Children of alcoholic fathers—a longitudinal prospective study. In D.W. Goodwin, K.T. Van Dusen, & S.A. Mednick (Eds.), *Longitudinal Research in Alcoholism*. Boston: Kluwer-Nijhoff Publishing.

Searles, J.S. (1988). The role of genetics in the pathogenesis of alcoholism. *Journal of Abnormal Psychology*, *97*, 153-167.

Skog, O., & Duckert, F. (In press). The stability of alcoholics' and heavy drinkers' consumption: A longitudinal study. *Journal of Studies on Alcohol*.

Tartar, R.E., Alterman, A.I., & Edwards, K.L. (1985). The vulnerability to alcoholism in men: A behavior-genetic perspective. *Journal of Studies on Alcohol*.

Webster's New International Dictionary, second edition. (1956). Edited by W.A. Neilson, & D.W. Carhart. Springfield: Merriman.

Werner, E.E., (1986). Resilient offspring of alcoholics: A longitudinal study from birth to age 18. *Journal of Studies on Alcohol*, *47*, 34-40.

Yamaguchi, K., & Kandel, D.B. (1984). Patterns of drug use from adolescence to young adulthood: III. Predictors of progression. *American Journal of Public Health*, *74*, 673-681.

Zucker, R.A. (1979). Developmental aspects of drinking through the young adult years. In H.T. Blane, & M.E. Chafetz (Eds.), *Youth, alcohol, and social policy* (pp. 91-146). New York: Plenum Press.

Zucker, R.A., & Noll, R.B. (1982). Precursors and developmental influences on drinking and alcoholism: Etiology from a longitudinal perspective. In National Institute on Alcohol Abuse and Alcoholism (Ed.) *Alcohol and Health Mono-*

graph No. 1: Alcohol consumption and related problems. (DHHS Publication No. (ADM) 82-1190, pp. 289-330). Rockville, MD: National Institute on Alcohol Abuse and Alcoholism.

Zucker, R.A., & Gomberg, E.S.L. (1986). Etiology of alcoholism reconsidered: The case for a biopsychosocial process. *American Psychologist*, *41*, 783-793.

Zucker, R.A. & Noll, R.B. (1987). The interaction of child and environment in the early development of drug involvement: A far ranging review and a planned very early intervention. *Drugs & Society*, *2*, 57-97.

Zucker, R.A. (October 1988). Alcohol involvement over the lifespan: A developmental perspective on theory, course and method. Paper presented at the First Vanderbilt Conference on Lifespan Developmental Alcohol Research, Vanderbilt University School of Medicine and Institute of Public Policy Studies, Nashville, TN.

The Problems of Nosology in Alcoholism Treatment and Research

Thomas P. Beresford, MD
Frederic C. Blow, PhD
Kirk J. Brower, MD
Jack G. Modell, MD
Cindy Kracht, MSW

SUMMARY. The authors review the purpose of establishing nosologies for alcoholism and identify two: description of natural history and identification of discrete treatment populations. Reviewing the various nosologic schemes thus far presented for alcoholism, they conclude that nosologic research thus far has yielded a useful clinical discrimination between primary alcoholics and primary polysubstance abusers. They point to further work-in-progress separating groups of alcoholics with and without concurrent major mental illness. They suggest that further nosological advances will rest upon a new understanding of biogenetic markers, further measures of affinity between alcoholics and ethyl alcohol (measures of craving) and, finally, on understanding patients' conceptions of nosological models.

Despite the ubiquity of alcoholism as a clinical problem, no consistent nosology has emerged with sufficient clarity of definition to command widespread acceptance and use by either treatment or research centers over long periods of time. The purposes of the present discussion are to review some of the efforts at nosology that

---

Thomas P. Beresford, Frederic C. Blow, Kirk J. Brower, Jack G. Modell, and Cindy Kracht are affiliated with University of Michigan Alcohol Research Center, Ann Arbor, MI 48104.

This work was supported in part by NIAAA grants R0-1-AA-07325-02 and 1-P50-AA07378-01.

have taken place over the last 40 years and to attempt to assess the likely use of nosologies in the future.

PURPOSES OF NOSOLOGY IN ALCOHOLISM

To begin, it is important to review the purpose of any nosology applied to a clinical problem. In most cases, this purpose is two-fold. First, the nosology should, in naming a type or sub-type of a general clinical syndrome, describe or define a natural history associated with that type or nosology alone. By so doing, the nosological description, based on empirical data, offers a baseline of the natural course of an illness or a condition against which efforts to treat may be measured. It follows that any useful nosology should be based on empirical observation of an illness course. Such observations are best done using prospectively applied measures of a clinical population studied over the usual course of the illness. This is true whether one is studying diabetes, cancer, or alcoholism. Prospective studies in the latter condition are especially difficult owing to the extreme length of the natural course of the illness, varying from a few years to as many as twenty or more. This approach to nosology assumes a "disease model," one facet of which is the natural decline as the disease progresses.

The second purpose in establishing a nosology is simply to be able to select study subjects appropriately in order to select treatments and to assess their outcome properly. It is obvious to most investigators in the field of therapeutics that without a proper understanding of the natural history as a baseline, without proper definition of outcome measures, and finally without proper selection of appropriate treatment/no treatment subjects, little sense can be made of the value of any attempt at intervention. This has certainly been true of medical conditions, such as angina pectoris, in which the efficacies of various treatments have been promulgated, only to be discarded when investigators applied proper therapeutic assessment methods. This difficulty is worse in considering treatment for alcoholism since, up to this time, no effective biological treatments for alcoholism have emerged and none appear likely in the immediate future. This circumstance restricts treatment of alcoholism to the realm of psycho-social interventions. To the researcher in therapeutics this means that most of the available treatments for alcoholism depend upon the patients themselves as the primary agent for recovery: the degree to which any given patient believes over time that he or she will get better relates directly to remission. Because of this, non-blinded studies of treatment efficacy must generally reach success rates of 60 to 70% in order to establish a credible rate of efficacy. Indeed, most treatments for alcoholism, over the short term of six months to two years do achieve such success rates (Emrick, 1975). The difficulty is that in alcoholism, with a natural history of ten or more years, little is known about either the strengthening or the attenuation of the patients' beliefs and hopes over a course of illness as long as a decade. Because of this, nosological concerns become even more salient as treatment researchers attempt to define specific kinds of psycho-social treatments that are likely to have *long-lasting* effects and to match those treatments with specific symptom constellations that may differentiate patients who seek help.

The problems of nosology in alcoholism, then, may be summed up as (1) a nosology that includes cross-sectional validity in describing symptom complexes for discrete groups of patients, (2) very long-term, longitudinal validity that can predict the course of an illness over ten or more years, and (3) a clear set of criteria by which specific treatments matched to specific patients can be measured both in the short and in the long term course of alcoholism. This is a tall order for any nosology and far more complex than most of the nosologies currently in effect in medical or psychiatric practice. Because of this complexity, investigators used to simpler modes of nosological description, for example in surgical or medical therapeutics, may easily bypass a consideration of therapeutics in alcoholism as overly diffuse. We hope to avoid this pitfall in the present paper and would like to underscore the problem of nosology in alcoholism as being an exceedingly complex one. As a result, we offer the following discussion in the spirit of collegial inquiry in the hopes that a review and some criticism of current nosologies would be useful in edging us toward a more broadly applicable nosologic system for alcoholism.

NOSOLOGIC SYSTEMS

Symptom Comparisons

One way of understanding attempts at nosology is to consider a dichotomy between the subjective experience of alcoholism as manifested by the history of symptoms that any given patient may bring to a clinical situation, as opposed to those phenomena, such as the longitudinal course, the drug of choice, and others, that may be more readily observed by objective means. For purposes of discussion, we have presented the existing nosologic systems using this dichotomy in Tables 1 and 2. The reader may note that some nosologic systems for alcoholism, such as the St. Louis (Feighner) criteria and the Research Diagnostic Criteria are not present in this list. We have elected not to include these since, in clinical usage, the DSM-III-R (1987) system has all but supplanted these earlier attempts at a similar diagnostic approach. On the other hand, we have included the concept of juvenile delinquency as researched by the Gluecks (1950, 1968) in order to provide a historical counterbalance for a trend in the current literature: later researchers have rediscovered or verified, depending on one's point of view, the characteristic natural histories of persons who abuse alcohol and who present pre-existing character problems consistent with sociopathy or conduct disorder, depending on age of onset (Cloninger, 1987). We believe this is an unfortunate trend that serves to obscure rather than to enlighten the usefulness of nosologies in alcoholism. We beg the readers' pardon if we have omitted one or another nosological system with which the reader may be familiar. Our attempt has been to examine those that appear to have the widest use in clinical practice as well as the widest empirical basis, judging from present clinical reports.

The first and arguably one of the most detailed nosologic systems was that worked out by Jellinek (1960) in the years prior to the publication of his landmark book. His four types of alcoholism, alpha through delta (we have viewed "epsilon" as a variant of "delta" rather than as a separate type), attempted to explain the differing phenomenologies of the patients who sought assistance in the Yale Alcohol Study Center. As Jellinek noted, these ranged

Table 1

Overall Comparison of Nosologies

NOSOLOGIC SYSTEM	COURSE	DRUG OF CHOICE	ASSOCIATED DIAGNOSES	SOCIAL EFFECTS	AGE
Jellinek					
alpha	+ +			+ +	
beta	+ +		++ (medical)		
gamma	+ +				
delta	+ +				
Gluecks					
juvenile delinquent			++ (sociopathy/conduct disorder)	+ +	+ + +
Cahalan				+ + +	
Vaillant					
alcoholism	+ + +	+ +		+ +	
polydrug abuse	+ + +	+ + +	+++ (sociopathy)	+ +	+ + +
Schuckit					
primary alcoholic		+ + +			
secondary alcoholic			+++ (Axis I or II of DSM-III-R)		
Cloninger					
Type 1	+	O	O	+ +	
Type 2	+ + +	O	+++ (sociopathy/conduct disorder)	+ + +	+ + +
DSM-III-R					
abuse	+	+ +	+ + +	+ +	
dependence	+	+ + +	+ + +	+ + +	
other substance abuse	+	+ +	+ + +	+ + +	
other diagnoses	+	+ +	+ + +	+ + +	+ + +

Table 2

Comparison of Symptom Weights In Various Nosologic Schemes

NOSOLOGIC SYSTEM	SYMPTOMS						
	social problems	psychologic "dependence"	medical complications	tolerance	withdrawal	loss of control	craving
Jellinek							
alpha	foremost	foremost	no	no	no	no	no
beta	possible	possible	foremost	no	no	no	no
gamma	possible	possible	possible	foremost	foremost	foremost	possible
delta	possible	possible	possible	foremost	foremost	possible	foremost
Gluecks							
juvenile delinquent	foremost	possible	possible	possible	possible	possible	possible
Cahalan							
problem drinking	foremost	possible	possible	possible	possible	possible	possible
Vaillant							
alcoholism	foremost	possible	possible	probable	probable	foremost	possible
polydrug abuse	foremost	foremost	possible	probable	probable	probable	foremost
Schuckit							
primary alcoholic	possible	foremost	possible	foremost	foremost	foremost	possible
secondary alcoholic	possible	possible	posible	probable	probable	probable	possible
Cloninger							
Type 1	possible	possible	possible	probable	probable	probable	probable
Type 2	foremost	foremost	possible	probable	probable	probable	probable
DSM-III							
abuse	foremost	foremost	possible	possible	possible	infrequent	possible
dependence	probable	probable	probable	foremost	foremost	foremost	possible
other substance abuse	foremost	possible	possible	foremost	foremost	probable	foremost
other diagnoses	probable	probable	infrequent				

from persons with relatively mild social difficulties due to drinking, through alcoholics presenting with clear physical dependence who were locked in the cycle of tolerance and withdrawal. It is a system based heavily on the disease concept of alcoholism (the title of Jellinek's book) and, as compared in Table 2, depends very heavily on the symptoms of physical and psychological dependence as well as on the medical complications ensuing from the latter. It is interesting to note that despite the careful attention to definition that Jellinek provided, very few current treatment or research institutions use his categorizations. Despite this, however, Jellinek's clear insistence on differentiation with respect to social problems, psychological dependence, medical complications, and the symptoms and signs of physical dependence have all found their way into current, more widely used nosological systems such as the diagnoses of alcohol abuse and alcohol dependence currently promulgated by the American Psychiatric Association in its Diagnostic and Statistical Manual (3rd Edition Revised) (1987). For example, the alpha alcoholic in Jellinek's original discussion was someone who had encountered serious social difficulties because of their drinking and had most often been using alcohol as a means of "relaxation" or other "recreational" purpose that would qualify him or her as an alcohol *abuser* under the DSM-III-R criteria. At the same time, Jellinek's gamma symptoms of physical dependence, along with the key phenomenon of "loss-of-control," are considered an essential part of the DSM-III-R criteria for alcohol *dependence*.

Some might argue that the two phenomenon, noted by both Jellinek and the authors of the DSM-III-R, are merely symptoms of alcoholism viewed at two different points in the course of the disease: early and late. Jellinek himself argued this same point in his famous description of the course of alcoholism. The DSM-III-R criteria, by contrast, offer little in the way of attention to the long-term course of the disease, as is noted in Table 2. The DSM-III-R generally assesses symptoms that have been in place for a month or more but makes no mention beyond this period of time, except to say that six months of abstinence is required to diagnose a "full remission." The DSM-III-R also makes an attempt at categorizing severity as mild, moderate or severe. By contrast, in Jellinek's discussion of the downhill course of the disease, we are given a view of alcoholism as a process over many years. Nonetheless, whether stated in Jellinek's early terms or in the current DSM-III-R, it is clear that nosologic tools can be used both in attempting to differentiate alcoholics as to severity of the illness and in attempting to pinpoint their location in the natural progression of the illness. The accuracy with which this can be managed is, of course, dependent both on the specific course of the illness in any given individual and on the state of development of the clinical observer's skills at the time of observation and formulation. There is very little question, however, that any observer or clinician attempting to assess an alcohol use problem who ignores any of the major symptom categories noted at the top of Table 1, will be attempting a less than thorough assessment. Whether one uses Jellinek's symptom categories, those of the DSM-III-R or others, we owe Jellinek the debt of having outlined the symptom constellations in a clear and organized way in the early stages of clinical research in alcoholism. After his efforts, any understanding of one nosology against another may be reasonably considered as an exercise in translation rather than in discovery.

Diagnostic Comparisons

Translation is once again necessary when considering another trend in nosologic discussions of alcoholism. At a time approximately contemporaneous with Jellinek's research, the Gluecks began studying the causes of juvenile delinquency. In the course of that study they outlined a profile of sociopathic characteristics found in childhood (currently referred to as conduct disorder in the DSM-III-R) that included polydrug abuse. On most occasions, one of the drugs of abuse was alcohol and for many of the subjects of the Gluecks' study, a career in alcoholism ensued.

This latter fact was borne out by the follow-up study conducted by Vaillant (1983) of the Gluecks' original sample of inner-city youth. From their original study, it was clear that there was a high association between alcoholism in the context of multiple drug abuse and the sociopathic or deviant characteristics seen in children, especially males, at an early age.

Vaillant, both in the follow-up study of the Gluecks' sample and in earlier studies (Vaillant, 1966) of drug addicted subjects, pointed out that alcoholic and polydrug abusing groups represent two distinct clinical populations with different natural histories. The two groups can be separated with reasonable clinical clarity. Some of the differentiating factors between these two groups of patients, in addition to the presence of sociopathic symptoms among the polydrug group, included the use of a series of abused drugs as opposed to alcohol alone or as a first choice of abuse, an age of onset that varied among the alcoholic group but was largely restricted to adolescents in the polydrug group, the presence of pre-existing personality traits demonstrated on psychometric personality inventories in the polydrug group but not in the alcoholic groups, and finally the much more striking rate of recovery among the alcoholic patients and the more dismal prognosis of the polydrug addicted patients (Vaillant, 1978). We have summarized these characteristics in Table 3. The distinction between the two groups fulfills our original requests of a nosologic system: that the nosology define a specific natural course of an illness and that the nosology points out a differential response to treatment. In other words, treatments designed specifically for one or the other of these two groups may not work particularly well for the opposite nosologic set.

The same nosologic differences have been confirmed lately by Cloninger (1987) in his approach from the perspective of family history and putative genetic influences. Cloninger's investigations verified the presence of pre-existing personality traits among those subjects with pre-existing histories of social deviance, along with a proclivity to abuse alcohol as one of a series of drugs.

Schuckit (1984), by contrast, moved beyond the mere association of sociopathic tendencies and alcoholism in his designation of a primary and secondary alcoholic state. In the former, alcoholism exists without any prior diagnosis of either major psychiatric illness or of character disorder. In this view, primary alcoholism is a disease unto itself resembling the gamma and delta alcoholics originally described by Jellinek. In Schuckit's approach, anyone with pre-existing evidence of a major psychiatric syndrome (axis 1 of the DSM-III-R) or of clear disorder of character (axis 2 of the DSM-III-R) is considered as having developed alcoholism secondary to the pre-existing illness. In this regard secondary alcoholism has come to be known as "dual diagnosis" in the everyday lexicon of mental

Table 3

Comparison of Nosologies For The Polydrug Dependence Syndrome

	A	B	C	D	E	F
1	VARIABLE	Gluecks (1950)	Vaillant (1978)	Schuckit (1984)	Cloninger (1987)	DSM-III-R (polydrug abuse)
2						
3	Age Of Onset	Child/Adolescent	same	same	same	no mention
4	Polydrug Use Including Alcohol	yes	yes	yes	yes	yes
5	Sociopathic/Conduct Disorder Traits	yes	yes	yes	yes	yes
6	Family History Of Alcohol Abuse	yes	possible	likely	likely	no mention
7	Course	no mention	20-40 years	no mention	no mention	no mention

health and substance abuse workers if not in the more formal nosologies.

As Schuckit rightly points out and as others have noted in establishing the DSM-III-R, evidence of a second or third or more specific psychiatric syndrome may indicate specific treatment, as for example in co-existing schizophrenia or mania. This specific treatment may sometimes improve the prognosis from alcoholism. An example might include a schizophrenic patient whose drinking occurs during decompensation of the schizophrenia but not when the schizophrenic symptoms remain under careful control with appropriate medicine. For Schuckit, the natural history of alcoholism that co-exists with other psychiatric disorders depends on which of the two is the primary illness. The natural history, by his schema, most closely resembles the natural history of the primary disorder. When using this nosology, therefore, alcoholics with co-existing disorders require a careful evaluation to determine which illness is primary. Unfortunately, in actual practice this determination is often difficult to make.

Clearly this dichotomy in nosology is a useful one to make and is one that is shared by the DSM-III-R. Indeed, this latter document takes the process one step further in that many of the symptoms of a number of the entities discussed in the DSM-III-R may be mimicked by alcoholism. As Vaillant has pointed out recently (Vaillant, 1988), the likelihood of having one DSM-III-R diagnosis is highly associated with having *three or more* concurrent diagnoses. While this may be a source of confusion for some clinicians, to clinical researchers it represents the present edge of our knowledge in being able to differentiate specific clinical syndromes in the context of alcoholism. This state of nosologic clarity leaves much to be desired and has spawned the search for biological markers and other forms of recognition that would allow for further nosological differentiation. Needless to say, for the practicing clinician, this state of affairs requires a settling into one or another of the nosologic systems listed in Table 1 and a belief in a clinical history that can assess the symptoms and signs listed in the various symptom categories in Table 1.

Already complicated nosologic difficulties are made even more complex by the work of social scientists who may write of symptoms and other phenomena based on large survey data sets rather than by smaller, more intense observation seen in the clinical setting. A good example of this, listed in Table 1, is the Cahalan Problem Drinking Scale (Cahalan, 1970). While it notes many of the symptoms of psychological and physical addiction outlined by Jellinek, Cahalan's scale gives a more equitable distribution to other phenomenon such as those involving the various social effects of the illness. In this regard, Cahalan's Problem Drinking Scale, and its subsequent assignment to problem drinking categorization, may be regarded as heavily weighted towards social effects of drinking. While this is entirely appropriate for large scale social surveys, it may or may not be of use in screening or diagnosing large numbers of patients presenting for medical care or for substance abuse or for specific alcoholism treatment. It is certainly an important approach when considering the long-term natural course of the illness. Vaillant's Problem Drinking Scale (Vaillant, 1983) in fact assesses many similar phenomenon although with a different weighting system.

Focusing upon the wider range of phenomena presented in Table 2, it is clear that many of the newer versions of nosological classification attempt to account for areas in which the older versions were somewhat deficient. For example, in Jellinek's original version, little mention was made of other drugs of abuse in addition to alcoholism, as a way of differentiating alcoholic and polydrug abusing patients. The alcoholic versus polydrug abuse dichotomy, by contrast, is clearly reflected in Vaillant's, Schuckit's and the DSM-III-R approach to understanding different kinds of alcoholism. Cloninger, despite a rather clear congruence between his Type 2 alcoholic, Vaillant's polydrug abuser, and Schuckit's secondary alcoholic with primary sociopathy, gives surprising little mention to this phenomenon. While this may have been an oversight, it is clear from his other descriptions that his Type 2 alcoholic very closely resembles the earlier dichotomizations around polydrug abuse or pre-existing sociopathy.

Age Comparisons

Consideration of the age at onset of alcoholic dependence may have nosologic applicability beyond the alcoholism-polydrug abuse dichotomy. Recent surveys of persons found to be alcohol dependent in the sixth decade of life and beyond suggest that as many as one in three began dependent drinking in the previous five years. (Gomberg, 1980; Maddox et al., 1986) This has led to the suggestion of early versus late onset alcoholics, referring to the age at onset. Others have taken issue with this description, suggesting that age is less important than the length of time dependent drinking has been going on (Gomberg, 1985). The more useful nosologic distinction therefore should be that between recent versus long term drinkers at any age. While empirical data remains to be gathered in support of either position, present knowledge of the physical and other sequelae of alcoholism are associated with the length of time spent in addictive style drinking, suggesting that the recent onset description may be a useful one clinically as well as prognostically.

In sum, nosologic considerations to this point have advanced our understanding of alcoholism in at least three ways. First, they have outlined large symptom complexes that must be assessed in order to allow for an accurate description of an alcoholic person at any given point in time. Hopefully this will result in a clearer knowledge of the course of alcoholism and the course of its treatment over long periods of time, knowledge to be gained through prospective longitudinal research. Secondly, the nosological efforts to date have succeeded in outlining the clinically useful dichotomy between persons abusing alcohol in the absence of pre-existing character or major mental illness and those abusing alcohol either concurrently with, or as a consequence of, a character disorder or a major mental illness. Although in clinical practice the primary-secondary distinction can sometimes be difficult to determine, the diagnosis of co-existing psychopathology is important both clinically and nosologically and remains open for much more study. Thirdly, the age of onset, viewed both in chronologic age and in the length of time between dependence and clinical recognition, appears to provide a useful nosologic distinction both in younger and elderly alcoholics.

A number of areas of nosology remain that, to our way of thinking, have not been adequately assessed. One is the role of genetic markers for alcoholism. This will most likely await the elucidation of specific bio-genetic markers that can be associated with predictable forms of familial alcoholism. To the best of our knowledge, those methods have not yet been developed. In the meantime, we are left with the simple typology of familial and non-familial alcoholism, one that may be clinically useful for prevention efforts among the children of alcoholics and possibly in predicting outcome in adult alcoholics.

Similarly, a useful approach might lie in some valid and reliable measurement of the affinity between a given alcoholic patient and the drug itself. This challenges us to develop new and more effective ways of measuring the "craving" for alcohol that Jellinek described long ago in his delta alcoholic. Along the same lines, ways of describing and measuring the loss-of-control (gamma alcoholic) phenomenon may prove useful in determining further nosologic characteristics that might elucidate the natural histories of subgroups of persons suffering from alcoholism. Much remains to be learned.

Nosology and Treatment Modeling

A further area that may open new useful nosologic distinctions may lie in both the patient's ability to accept treatment and the ability to respond to treatment. The former brings to mind the work recently done on ego-defense mechanisms as ways of understanding a given patient's ability to perceive and cope with naturally occurring forms of anxiety. Interesting data from the Toronto research group suggests that ego strengths, measured by others through the use of ego-defense measurement systems, appear correlated with the patient's ability to derive benefit from specific forms of psychotherapeutic treatment (Annis). In their study, measures of ego strength strongly predicted the long-term outcome of patients subjected to extremely vigorous therapy for alcoholism and drug abuse. This remains an untapped area of nosologic inquiry and one that appears to offer much gain.

A second area of further nosological research may well include patient beliefs with respect to the various models of alcohol addiction. We (Brower et al., 1989) have previously summarized these models and present them in Table 4. Against six models of alcohol-

Table 4

Comparison of Nosologic Schemes With Brower's Description of Treatment Models

	A	B	C	D	E	F	G
1				MODELS			
2		Moral	Social	Learning	Self Medication	Disease	Pluralistic
3	NOSOLOGY						
4	Jellinek					+ + +	
5	Glueck		+ + +		+ +		
6	Vaillant				+ +	+ + +	
7	Schuckit					+ + +	
8	Cahalan		+ + +				
9	Cloninger				+ +	+ + +	
10	DSM-III-R					+ + +	+ +
11	Alcoholics Anonymous	+ +				+ + +	

ism, we have diagrammed the nosologic approaches noted above. It is interesting to note that a preponderance of the present nosologies fit best with the disease model of alcoholism. This is despite the fact that many other models such as the social model or the moral model (recently reflected in a famous Supreme Court decision) are very often commonly held models among patients seeking assistance. Little to this date has been done in understanding the nosological implications of the various models that *patients* bring to treatment. This approach may offer a significant nosological gain in amplifying our ability both to identify measures of outcome and to provide the means of matching patients to treatment. In a field as diverse as alcoholism treatment, in which both patients and therapists may approach the clinical encounter from widely separate and often poorly articulated models of the illness, attention to the patient's and therapist's beliefs alike may serve to open windows for treatment matching that have heretofore remained closed. This appears to us to be a very vibrant and very useful area for future research.

CONCLUSION

As we noted above, the complexity of nosological considerations in alcoholism may serve for a time to put off the interest and efforts of those among us who seek to find the simple in the complex. This is true in the case of nosologic considerations, such as those having to do with patient beliefs and treatment models, as we move toward a further understanding of how to best provide treatment for this very destructive illness. It is important to remember, however, that the research of the last 40 years has yielded a clear understanding of the areas of symptomatology that must be investigated in order to arrive at a reasonably precise understanding of alcoholism and its course in any specific patient. At the same time, it has demonstrated at least one major dichotomy with profound implications for the course of the illness and treatment: the alcoholic with and the alcoholic without pre-existing sociopathy or major mental illness. These nosologic gains have been responsible, in large part, for the continued development of research in alcoholism over the past 15 years, since the formation of the National Institute on Alcohol Abuse and Alcoholism. As our knowledge of the specific characteristics of patient subgroups continues, we look forward to an increasingly useful, if pluralistic, nosology that may be applied flexibly in evaluating and selecting treatment for specific patients in specific settings. We look forward to the enlightenment that new understanding will bring.

REFERENCES

Annis, HN, Chan, D, 1983. Differential treatment models: empirical evidence from a personality typology of adult offenders. Crim Justice and Behav, 10: 159-173.

Brower, KB, Blow, FC, Beresford, TB, 1989. Treatment models of alcoholism, manuscript.

Cahalan, D, 1970. Problem Drinkers: A National Survey. San Francisco: Jossey-Bass.

Cloninger, RA, 1987. Neurogenetic adaptive mechanisms in alcoholism. Science, 236: 410-416.

Diagnostic and Statistical Manual, Third Edition, Revised, 1987. Washington, D.C.: American Psychiatric Press, Inc.

Emrick, CD, 1975. A review of psychologically oriented treatment of alcoholism, II: the relative effectiveness of different treatment approaches and the effectiveness of treatment versus no treatment. J Stud Alcohol, 36: 88-109.

Glueck, S and E, 1950. Unraveling Juvenile Delinquency. New York: Commonwealth Fund.

———, 1968. Delinquents and Non-delinquents In Perspective. Cambridge, Mass.: Harvard University Press.

Gomberg, E, 1980. Drinking and Problem Drinking Among the Elderly. Ann Arbor, Mich.: Institute of Gerontology, University of Michigan.

______, 1985. Gerontology and alcohol studies, in Gottheil, E, Druley, KA, Skoloda, TE et al., eds., The Combined Problems of Alcoholism, Drug Addiction and Aging. Springfield, Ill.: Charles C Thomas.

Jellinek, EM, 1960. The Disease Concept of Alcoholism. New Haven: College and University Press.

Schuckit, MA, 1984. Drug and Alcohol Abuse, 2nd ed. New York: Plenum Press.

Vaillant, GE, 1983. The Natural History of Alcoholism. Cambridge, Mass.: Harvard University Press.

______, 1966. A twelve-year follow-up of New York narcotic addicts: IV. Some characteristics and determinants of abstinence. Am J Psychiatry, 123: 573-584.

______, 1978. Alcoholism and drug dependence, in A.M. Nicholi, ed., The Harvard Guide to Modern Psychiatry. Cambridge, Mass.: Harvard University Press.

Vaillant, GE, Schnur, P, 1988. What Is a Case? A 45 year study of psychiatric impairment within a college sample selected for mental health. Arch Gen Psychiatry, 45: 313-318.

On Terms Used and Abused: The Concept of "Codependency"

Edith S. Lisansky Gomberg, PhD

As with any biopsychosocial disorder, the language used by researchers and clinicians presents problems. There are other manifestations of disordered behavior (neurosis, anxiety, etc.) in which problems of definition are critical, but is there any like alcohol and drug abuse which produces both dictionaries of "the alcohol language" (Keller & Seeley, 1958; Keller & McCormick, 1968; Keller, McCormick & Efron, 1982) and a compendium of slang or "street" terms for the reinforcers and the processes (Johnson et al., 1988)? The unending squabble over whether alcoholism is to be defined as a disease or not defined as a *disease* (Jellinek, 1960; DeLint, 1971; Finn & Clancy, 1972; Keller, 1976; Rocm, 1981; Keller, 1982; National Council on Alcoholism, 1988; Fingarette, 1988) is not resolved. The World Health Organization has struggled with and changed its definition of drug dependence and alcohol dependence over the years (World Health Organization, 1954; Eddy et al., 1965; World Health Organization, 1980).

Definition of the terms used by practitioners, diagnosticians and researchers are so fluid that the Diagnostic and Statistical Manual of the American Psychiatric Association (DSM-III, 1980) required revision within a few years of publication (DSM-IIIR, 1987); the re-

Edith S. Lisansky Gomberg, is Professor of Psychology, Alcohol Research Center, Department of Psychiatry, and Professor of Social Work, University of Michigan, Ann Arbor, MI 48104.

This work was aided in part by grant 1P50 AA07378, National Institute on Alcohol Abuse and Alcoholism.

moval of a distinction between "substance abuse" and "substance dependence" is one among many revisions. And the definition and diagnostic criteria are under review again.

In the 1970s and 1980s, both research and clinical facilities for alcohol and drug abusing persons expanded very rapidly. The expansion of research created a need for more journals so that research results could be communicated. The number of journals increased. The expansion of detoxification, treatment and rehabilitation facilities for substance abusers created a demand for training in relevant skills. A surfeit of trainers, institutes, visiting "experts" and consultants developed to meet this demand. As a byproduct, a number of rather simple-minded conceptualizations developed. These were, for the most part, insider terms like "enabler" "ACOA" (adult children of alcoholics), "coalcoholic," "chemical dependency," "codependent," etc. Some would argue that "chemical dependency" makes no sense as a description of drug abuse because we are dependent on oxygen, water, food and other chemicals for survival. Perhaps "chemical dependency" grew out of the trend toward integration of services for problem drinkers and persons involved with other drugs, which began in the 1960s. Perhaps "chemical dependency" was a term which originated in the recognition of multiple drug abuse; while drug dependent people may have a favorite substance, most appear to use more than a single drug (Gomberg, 1982a; Gomberg, 1982b; Gomberg, forthcoming; Johnston, 1973; Stimmel et al., 1972).

Another interesting term which has surfaced is "coalcoholic." To me, the term suggests the alcoholic's drinking companions but as used by insiders, it means someone who, in a sense, conspires with the alcoholic to maintain his/her drinking, presumably a family member or spouse who is therefore also an "enabler."

We will examine the origins and development of one of these invented terms, "codependency," the popularization of which has proceeded apace, totally out of touch with rich research developments in family processes, the impact of alcoholism on the family, and systems theory. Our discussion of "codependency" will present three theses:

1. The impact of a deviant member of a family, whether that member is alcoholic, depressed, schizophrenic, phobic, brain damaged, mentally retarded, delinquent or symptomatic in any way, has *long* been recognized as a major source of stress and distress within the family.
2. There are *no* data at all which justify diagnosing family members in any family in which substance abuse occurs, as manifesting personality disorder, solely on the basis of their family membership.
3. The term, "codependency," has been expanded without any consideration of its meaningfulness or its contribution to theory and practice, so that it encompasses virtually the entire population of the United States.

WHAT IS "CODEPENDENCY"?

Larsen (1983) described as a codependent, ". . . anyone affected . . . " by a substance abuser, and Wegscheider-Cruse (1984) elaborated the concept so that it included not only spouse, lover or children of alcoholics, but anyone who "..grew up in an emotionally repressive family." Cermak (1984, 1986a, 1986b) defined the diagnosis of "codependence" so that substance abuse professionals might find, diagnose and treat these "codependents":

> . . . Co-dependence is a recognizable pattern of personality traits, predictably found within most members of chemically dependent families, which are capable of creating sufficient dysfunction to warrant the diagnosis of Mixed Personality Disorder as outlined in DSM III . . . (Cermak, 1986a)

The diagnosis having been made, the next step is treatment:

> . . . In response to a rapidly growing need as more and more people identify themselves as codependents or adult children from dysfunctional families, an increasing number of treatment centers and individual therapists are offering codependency treatment . . . (Cruse & Johnson, 1988)

The concept probably reaches its full flowering in a recent book by Schaef (1986) which describes "codependency" as an addiction and a disease. With the belief that "codependency," addiction and other "diseases" are fostered by the lack of moral and spiritual values in American society, it emerges finally that *the whole society* is in the grip of "the addictive process." So we have moved with this concept from the impact of a substance abusing member on other family members to anyone who grew up in an "emotionally repressive family," to psychiatric diagnosis and treatment of the family member, to a sick society!!

THESIS 1

The impact of a deviant member of a family, whether that member is alcoholic, depressed, schizophrenic, phobic, brain damaged, mentally retarded, delinquent or deviant in any way, has *long* been recognized as a major source of stress and distress within the family.

In midcentury urban America, the state of theory and practices relating to causes and treatment of mental disorders, was heavily influenced by psychoanalysis. In retrospect, it is interesting to note the extent to which the therapist's full attention was focussed on the patient. Among most practicing psychoanalysts, for example, the idea of contact—even a single interview with a family member of a patient—was looked upon as questionable. The assumption was that such contact would disturb the delicate balance of transference effects and should, therefore be avoided. The psychoanalytic theory viewed the disorder as a product of the patient's interaction with others, primarily parents, and the history obtained by the therapist was self-report, i.e., the family history as perceived and reported by the patient. Preoccupied with the unconscious, the effect of the patient on people around him was given short shrift.

During the same time period, the redefinition of alcoholism as a psychosocial problem, rather than a moral issue, was taking hold. It is of interest that in the volume of lectures delivered in the 1944 Yale Summer School of Alcohol Studies, one sociological lecture was given on "excessive drinking and the institution of the family" (Bacon, 1945), and another, more clinically-oriented lecture was delivered on "social case work with inebriates" (Baker, 1945). Baker noted that,

> . . . the social case worker seldom sees the alcoholic as an isolated person but rather as an integral part of the world he lives in. Others in that world must gain insight into his problem and their reaction to it in order to help him become a well-adjusted person like themselves . . .

A long way from the view of those who are, ". . . an integral part of the world (the alcoholic) lives in," as personality disordered and pathological!

Early studies reported the wife of the alcoholic to be a frustrated, dependent woman whose hostility often generated the husband's drinking bouts (Price, 1945). It was argued that the wives had married alcoholics to deal with needs of their own, and such wives were described as, ". . . Suffering Susan . . . Controlling Catherine . . . Wavering Winifred . . . Punitive Polly . . . " (Whalen, 1953). Furthermore, as the alcoholic recovered, the wife "decompensated" (Futterman, 1953; Kalashian, 1969). These early works may be seen as the ancestors of "codependency": the nonalcoholic wife is indeed described as "dysfunctional."

A classic paper appeared in 1954 which dealt not only with the *reactions of family members to an alcoholic in the family*, but went much further in recognizing that such reactions were dynamic and *changed with the duration of the problem* (Jackson, 1954). Jackson, using participant-observer methods, described the stages in family adjustment to alcoholism. Families began with attempts to minimize and deny during the early incidents of intoxication, and ended with reorganization after the husband/father achieved sobriety.

At about the same time, family treatment approaches in alcoholism began to develop. Gliedman and co-workers (1956) used concurrent group meetings of male alcoholics and their wives. Ewing and his collaborators (1961) evaluated concurrent group therapy, and found that the likelihood of engaging and keeping an alcoholic in treatment was greatly increased by the group therapy approach. There are several early reviews of the literature on alcoholism and marriage (e.g., Bailey, 1961). By 1975, twelve distinct family therapeutic approaches were being used (Bowen, 1975) which included working with alcoholics in conjoint family therapy (Meeks & Kelly, 1970), multiple couples therapy (Cadogan, 1973) and others. A recent review of work on marital and family therapy (O'Farrell, 1987) distinguishes among approaches to motivate into treatment, to produce "short-term changes," and to prevent relapse, i.e., maintain the changes.

The impact of the alcoholic member of a family on family life has been recognized, studied, reported from the beginning of recognition and treatment of alcoholism. The first thesis, that the impact of a deviant member of the family on others in the family, has *long* been recognized, is demonstrated. Q.E.D. What is needed at this time is recognition of the impact of *all* deviant, disordered or stressful behavior on family life. A parent, child or sibling who is depressed or who is handicapped or who is chronically ill, produces marked effects and a need for adjustment within the family system. While alcoholism or other drug dependence may have *unique* effects on family members, this remains to be demonstrated.

THESIS 2

There are *no* data at all which justify diagnosing family members in any family in which substance abuse occurs, as manifesting personality disorder solely on the basis of their family membership.

Most of the work in family therapy in alcoholism has been focused on the male alcoholic *and the wife*. In a comprehensive critical review of the literature, Edwards et al. (1973) organized the foci into three categories: the disturbed personality theory, the stress theory, and the psychosocial theory. Wives who had separated from the alcoholic husband and wives living with the husband were compared in several studies, and the question of the uniqueness of personality disturbance among alcoholics' wives was raised. There were many methods of coping, e.g., safeguarding the family's interests, withdrawal, attacking, acting out, protecting the alcoholic husband (Orford & Guthrie, 1968). *The evidence did not support the view of the alcoholic's wife* as pathological, but rather suggested that there was a wide range of personalities and a wide range of adjustments. Where problems occur, they appear to be related to the stresses, and Edwards et al. concluded that, " . . . the only tenable hypothesis is that these wives are not unique."

While the believers in "codependency" do not limit themselves to wives of alcoholics, problem behavior and pathology in the non-alcoholic family members is the resurfacing of an old viewpoint. Such conceptualization ignores the recency and duration of the drinking problem (e.g., Jackson, 1962), the different family effects of daily versus binge drinkers (Jacob, 1987), differing family patterns of response (e.g., Kaufman & Pattison, 1981; Stanton & Landau, 1985; Steinglass, 1981; Vannicelli, Gingerich & Ryback, 1983; Wolin et al,, 1980; Fichter & Postpischil, 1988). There is a wide range of behaviors, adaptive and maladaptive, which is manifested by individual members and by families in which there is an alcohol or drug abusing person. Labeling family members pathological, i.e., mixed personality disorder, ignores the individual differences and myriad coping mechanisms with which people and families continue to function.

If it is true that in "chemically dependent families," there is a recognizable pattern of personality traits found among most family members which creates sufficient dysfunction to warrant a psychiatric diagnosis, the burden of proof rests on those who posit this state of affairs. Indeed there are some family members who show serious disturbance when confronted with the problem of an alcoholic family member and this will vary with the age of the family member, the relationship, presence or absence from the home, and other variables. That some family members will be disturbed is a long way from the assumption that, ". . . most members" of the family show dysfunction. Where are the data? There are no surveys, no clinical research, no evaluations only descriptive, impressionistic statements. There are lists of "codependency" characteristics, like adult-children-of-alcoholic traits, and there are "dysfunctional family rules." One need not be a relative:

> . . . Any relationship in which one of the partners is chemically dependent is likely to manifest at least some degree of dysfunction . . . Parents, children, marital partners and even co-workers can be affected. (Jenkins, 1988)

All the hypotheses about "chemically dependent families" and the dysfunctional nature of relationships with a "chemically dependent" person may be true, but where is the evidence? Our second thesis, then, that there are *no* data to justify the descriptions of "codependency" with added stigma of psychopathology and personality disorder, is demonstrated. Q.E.D. Quod erat demonstrandum.

THESIS 3

The term "codependency" has been expanded without any consideration of its meaningfulness or its contribution to theory and practice, so that it encompasses virtually the entire population of the United States.

In the increasing recognition of alcoholism as a distressing personal and social problem, and with increasing third-party payments for treatment available, inevitably, facilities to treat alcoholics and other kinds of drug abusers have increased. These include detoxification units, hospital wards, outpatient clinics, residential facilities. With this growth of services, the demand for useful ideas and for skill training has also increased. Unfortunately, this has *not* led to a notable increase in knowledge base training. This is true not only for "two hatters" and nonprofessional people with interest in substance abuse, it is also true in medical education, social work and nursing training, and the education of psychologists.

Is a knowledge base useful or essential for those who would help the individual alcoholic and the family, or—for that matter—those who seek to influence policy? It is of historical interest to note Jellinek's discussion, in 1945, of the curriculum of the first Yale Summer School of Alcohol Studies:

> . . . I know that the lecture program may disappoint many of you. The disappointment of the different members of this group may lie in different directions. Those who are interested primarily in the question of what to do with the alcoholic may find it a bore to have to listen to such lectures as, let us say, the philosophy of the temperance movement or the economic aspect of alcohol in modern society . . . those who are interested

> in alcoholism primarily as a national manifestation may be impatient with the lectures which are devoted to the individual problems of the alcoholic and to the treatment of the alcoholic. But I can assure you that unless those interested in the public care and therapy of the alcoholic learn about the economic and social involvements which have led their patients to the need for treatment, efforts at rehabilitation will be frustrated. And those who are interested in alcoholism as a national phenomenon will never be successful until they have realized the importance of those individual problems whose aggregate forms the national manifestation. (Jellinek, 1945, pp. 6-7)

Whether it was the Keep-It-Simple-Stupid attitude of some members of Alcoholics Anonymous, the influx of many recovering alcoholics into the treatment field, the anti-intellectualism and anti-science of the last decades, or simply the wish for quick, easy solutions to problems of need for training, Jellinek's view has gone by the board. Most summer schools, institutes, workshops emphasize skill training and there is very little communication between the researchers who hold their own meetings, and the practitioners.

In the demand for skill training, the concept of "codependency" expanded. Starting from its original application to members of the alcoholic's or drug abuser's family, it has gone far afield. The family, of course, may include one's parents, grandparents, aunts and uncles, children, cousins, spouses, siblings, nieces, nephews, etc. (Miller W.R., 1987), but these are all familially related to the alcoholic. One expansion of the term "codependent" is the application to *co-workers* and *friends* of the alcoholic or drug abusing person. The term is, in fact, applied to ". . . any relationship" (Jenkins, 1988). *Any* relationship! Still another expansion moves the term to include not only human beings; "codependency" then becomes ". . . an unhealthy preoccupation or dependence" on:

> . . . someone or something. The dependency may be on *work* such as with one who is labeled a workaholic. It might be dependence on *food* as in the compulsive overeater, the bulimic or anorexic. The dependence might be on *religion* . . . (Williams, 1988) [italics added]

Ms. Williams adds that "... codependency, like alcoholism, is a progressive and sometimes fatal disease."

Expansion of the concept of "codependency" has gone as far as "... codependence among helping professionals" (Murck, 1988), described as a major cause of on-the-job professional problems among helping professionals. A historical note: among practitioners in the earlier days of alcoholism treatment (the 1940s to the 1970s), there was a good deal of concern about "burnout," usually attributed to the difficulties of working with the alcoholic client who was resistive, denying, and tended to relapse. There is a sharp contrast between contemporary behavioral treatment strategies sometimes described as "relapse prevention" and the "codependency" view which attributes professional problems and difficulties in treating the drug dependent client to the professional therapist's own shortcomings and disturbances. Commenting on the apparently disproportionately large number of therapists with family histories of alcohol or other substance abuse, it is argued that for persons with such a history, entering the help profession increases "..the risk of activating codependence tendencies" (Murck, 1988). Instead of blaming the victim, this becomes an exercise in blaming the therapist.

It may be true that there is a disproportionately large number of substance abuse therapists with positive family histories. That is a testable hypothesis, although one of the research issues might be to question what is the optimal proportion of therapists with positive family history working in *any* mental health area. It may also be true that the reported "..codependence among helping professionals," is attributable to the large number of therapists and counselors who are themselves recovered alcoholics or drug abusers. Once again, the question is: what is a *large* number? Again, this is a researchable, testable hypothesis: are there significantly more recovered alcoholics and/or drug abusers among counselors and therapists working in substance abuse than there are recovered individuals in other areas of mental health work? Are recovery rates for patients the same, better, or worse for counselors and therapists who come from alcoholic or drug abusing families as for those who do not? From these research questions, one may proceed to others: are there differences in first choice of treatment modality, in interactional style, in patient rapport, between therapists with positive personal or family history of substance abuse and therapists with no personal or family history of substance abuse?

Perhaps the conceptualization and expansion of "codependency" is most understandable in historical perspective. Public interest and governmental interest in alcohol and drug problems have been intensifying for two decades, and in the 1988 election, drug abuse and the call for more treatment resources was a campaign issue. A decade earlier, the competition between ". . . degreed and nondegreed counselors" (Ottenberg, 1974; Valle, 1977) intensified, and while the rivalry and negative feelings of professionally trained and the recovered alcoholic therapists became less with time (or at least less overt), the acceptable standards for a counselor or therapist in substance abuse have been defined only recently and in response to a chaotic situation. Both professionally trained and "nondegreed counselors" required additional training. Inevitably, the demand was met by entrepreneurs who supplied such training and many of them established training businesses, consultantships, and traveling presentations. Jellinek's idea that a knowledge base about alcohol was useful, even necessary, for the development of treatment skills, went by the board, and the chasm between researchers and scholars on the one hand, and the treatment community on the other, grew larger. Services directed by physicians, usually within hospitals, went their own way. Perhaps inevitably, simplistic concepts like "codependency" expanded to include not only family members but co-workers, friends, any relationships, "workaholics," dependence on food or religion, "helping professionals," and so on.

The third thesis, that the concept of "codependency" has been expanded and extended without consideration of its meaningfulness or of its contribution to theory and practice, is demonstrated. Q.E.D. Quod erat demonstrandum.

RECENT CRITICISM OF "CODEPENDENCY"

In the same journal issue in which Cermak outlined his diagnostic criteria (1986), there appeared a critical review of the concept of "codependency" (Gierymski & Williams, 1986). The authors described "codependency" as being used to diagnose ". . . a primary disease (and) a treatable diagnostic entity," in spite of the fact that it was a concept not based on data but rather on intuition, assertion and anecdotes. Gierymski and Williams, affiliated with the Hazelden Foundation in Minnesota, commented on the heterogeneity of response of those who live with an alcoholic person and the remarkable variety of inner resources and personal strategies for coping such people display. The conclusion: while family members in alcoholic families, as a group, manifest more emotional problems than comparable family members in nonalcoholic families, the degree and kinds of emotional problems vary but, " . . . no clear-cut clinical entity, corresponding uniquely to the concept of codependency has emerged."

This was followed by an announcement by the Hazelden Foundation (Professional Update, 1987) that it would no longer use the diagnosis of "codependency." Challenging the validity of the concept elicited a response which may say a great deal about reasons for the popularity of "codependency" (Miller, M.E., 1987):

> . . . But what's wrong with calling a co-dependent just that? For many, the term has become a guiding light in the dark despair that has shrouded their lives for years. It is a word that connotes a sense of belonging so often lacking in their lives.

There are at this moment, at least two constructive, parallel, independent lines of inquiry which involve alcoholism and the family. One is current research on family interactions, the role of family rituals and the disruption of such rituals as an important factor in the intergenerational transmission of alcoholism (e.g., Wolin et al., 1980). Another fruitful line of inquiry is the family interaction study of Jacob and his colleagues (1987) which reports significant differences in marital satisfaction measures when binge drinkers and steady drinkers are compared. It is anticipated that such research, using the methods of the experimental laboratory and the ethnography of the family, will yield results which could be utilized by practitioners. A second line of constructive development is practitioner-oriented and consists of a beginning revolt against the narrow definition of a family member in an alcoholic family as "codependent." This revolt comes from practitioners who are sensitive to the heterogeneity of human response to stress and will not fit their client into neat, predetermined pigeonholes.

A NOTE ON THE TERM "ADDICTION"

There are so many definitions of addiction, it has become a word which, " . . . eludes precise definition" (Ray & Ksir, 1987). In fact, most definitions of addiction include: tolerance, physiological and psychological dependence, the abstinence syndrome, and addiction-related human problems.

In 1957, the World Health Organization Expert Committee on Addiction-Producing Drugs tried to distinguish between definitions of "addiction" and "habituation." The definition of "addiction" included tolerance, psychological and physiological dependence, individual and societal problems, and compulsion or craving. Unfortunately, what this produced was uncertainty and,

> . . . confusion in the use of the terms addiction and habituation, and particularly misuse of the former. (Eddy et al., 1965)

A commonsense, dictionary definition of addiction says nothing about tolerance, drug dependence or addiction-related problems but it forthrightly sets down a concept of craving. The word *addiction* is defined as,

> . . . the compulsive uncontrolled use of habit-forming drugs beyond the period of medical need or under conditions harmful to society. (Webster's, 1964)

The concept of craving or compulsion has been a touchy point in discussions of addiction. In the ill-fated 1957 attempt to differentiate between addiction and habituation (World Health Organization, 1957), *habituation* was defined as including, ". . . a desire (but not a compulsion) to continue taking the drug." Addiction, then was defined as involving *compulsion* or *craving*, whereas habituation was defined as involving *desire* but not compulsion. In the subsequent confusion, it is small wonder that drug experts argued for decades about whether cocaine was an addicting substance!

In the 1980s, there have been a number of works looking for definitions and models of addiction (e.g., Miller, 1980; Orford, 1985; Peele, 1988). Some behaviorists omit the concept. Marlatt and Baer (1988), summarizing recent experimental work on addictive behaviors, define addiction behavior as,

. . . a repetitive habit pattern that increases the risk of disease and/or associated personal and social problems. (Marlatt et al., 1988)

Other behaviors, however, do struggle with theoretical processes and treatment issues involved in the concept of craving (Baker et al., 1987).

In spite of the generally agreed upon core of addiction as including tolerance, dependence and personal/social consequences, the whole problem of defining addiction is neatly set aside by the American Psychiatric Association. In both the Diagnostic and Statistical Manual of Mental Disorders, 3rd edition (1980), and the Diagnostic and Statistical Manual of Mental Disorders, 3rd edition-Revised (1987), the word does not appear. Perhaps the committees which assembled the Manuals agree with Ray and Ksir (1987) that addiction is ". . . a muddy term."

There has been one use of the term, *addicted*, which should be noted. That is the popular description of infants born to alcohol or drug abusing mothers with evidence of the drug's presence in the infant, as "addicted babies." Obviously the effects of drug use by a pregnant woman will have both short-term and long-term effects on the developing fetus, but the infant, born with clinical signs of the presence of the drug, is described both by the media and, often by professional personnel, as "addicted." Is the infant "addicted"? An interesting legal question has arisen recently in the case of a cocaine-abusing mother; she is charged with violation of the drug laws because of her baby's "cocaine addiction" (*New York Times*, 1988).

FROM ALCOHOLIC TO LOTTOHOLIC

It is the term *alcoholic* which has inspired an astonishing proliferation. One early extension was a description of driving, hard-working people as "workaholics." People fond of chocolate became "chocaholics," and there are, ". . . confessions of a lottoholic" (Firestein, 1989).

In these popular extensions, one may become addicted to almost anything. There are "religious addicts," complete with a support group called Fundamentalists Anonymous. There is a ". . . hidden addiction" to sugar (Phelps & Nourse, 1986). There is "exercise addiction," (Health in the Workplace, 1988), "romantic and sexual addictions" (Diamond, 1988) and, ultimately, addictions to relationships or "women who love too much" (Norwood, 1986). One may become addicted to shopping, addicted to video games, addicted to playing lotto games.

Along with the new categories of addiction, has come a new term, a new kind of practitioners: an "addictionologist," one who can presumably treat addiction to anything. Modeled on the assumptions of Alcoholics Anonymous, it appears that the prevailing viewpoint posits any addiction, whatever it involves, as "a disease." Staying with the Alcoholics Anonymous model, the addiction is a "disease" which cannot be cured although it can be arrested (this is the rationale by which members of Alcoholics Anonymous may argue that they are not to be called "recovered" alcoholics but only "recovering" alcoholics). Treatment is modeled on Alcoholics Anonymous too, and there are self-help groups called variously Sexual Compulsives Anonymous, Workaholics Anonymous, Gamblers Anonymous, Co-Dependents Anonymous, etc. Members of such groups, interviewed by journalists, often assert that membership in the group has helped them. It probably has, and it is a commentary on the lonely crowd.

One may wonder if this phenomenon has run its course or if it will expand further. A few recent media articles have asked questions like, "Is America becoming hooked on addictions?" (Hall, 1988). Amusingly, *Utne Reader*, an "alternative press" magazine, featured a recent article, "Are you addicted to addictions?" (1988). The magazine cover has a picture of Opus, speaking at a meeting of "Herringholics Anonymous,"

> . . . Hi. My name is Opus, and I am a herringholic. I admit I am powerless over fish innards and that my life has become unmanageable.

DISCUSSION

We have discussed the concept of "codependency," and the extension of the term *addiction* to cover a very wide range of behaviors. Both phenomena have similar origins: popularizers write books and give workshops and lectures about the invented terms, and the response of the book-buying public and the training-skills-seeking practitioner is positive and supportive. In both instances, there is a neglected parallel development, a rich body of research literature and clinical reports. There is a burgeoning development of research on family processes and family therapy, and there is also an increasing, challenging professional literature on conceptions of addiction.

Perhaps these popularizations and the support they receive is not a controversial issue at all, but a kind of Gresham's law in which there is need, on the one hand, and an offer of easy, simple answers. Easy, simple answers apparently tend to drive out of the marketplace more complex ideas which take more energy and time to master.

What are the needs these simplistic concepts speak to? In the case of "codependency," we have suggested that the need is related to substance abuse treatment as a growth industry, an expanding number of facilities, and the need for education and training in substance abuse treatment. In the case of the expansion of the conception of addiction, it is more difficult to say. Perhaps a kind of trendy fashion, keeping in style: a "shrink" or a psychoanalyst for one generation, an Addiction Anonymous group for another? Perhaps a need for belonging and a substitution for religious belief? Perhaps a true *cri de coeur*?

REFERENCES

Bailey, M.B. (1961) Alcoholism in marriage: a review of research and professional literature. *Quarterly Journal of Studies on Alcohol*, *22*, 81-97.

Baker, L.H., Cooney, N.L. & Pomerleau, O.F. (1987) Craving for alcohol: theoretical processes and treatment procedures. In: W.M. Cox (Ed.) *Treatment and prevention of alcohol problems*. (pp. 184-202). Orlando: Academic Press.

Baker, S.M. (1945) Social case work with inebriates. In: *Alcohol, science and society*. (pp. 419-436). New Haven: Quarterly Journal of Studies on Alcohol.

Bowen, M. (1975) Family therapy after twenty years. In: S, Ariete (Ed.) *American handbook of psychiatry*. New York: Basic Books.

Cadogan, D. (1973) Marital group therapy in the treatment of alcoholism. *Quarterly Journal of Studies on Alcohol*, *34*, 1187-1194.

Cermak, T.L. (1984) Children of alcoholics and the case for a new diagnostic category of codependency. *Alcohol Health and Research World*, *8*, 38-42.

Cermak, T.L. (1986a) *Diagnosing and treating co-dependence*. Minneapolis: Johnson Institute.

Cermak, T.L. (1986b) Diagnostic criteria for codependency. *Journal of Psychoactive Drugs*, *18*, 15-20.

Cruse, J.R. & Johnson, K.A. (1988) Codependency treatment strategies. *Professional Counselor*, 48-54.

DeLint, J. (1971) The status of alcoholism as a disease: A brief comment. *British Journal of Addiction*, *66*, 108-109.

Diagnostic and Statistical Manual of Mental Disorders, 3rd edition (1980). Washington, D.C.: American Psychiatric Association.

Diagnostic and Statistical Manual of Mental Disorders, 3rd edition-Revised (1987). Washington, D.C.: American Psychiatric Association.

Diamond, J. (1988) *Looking for Love in All the Wrong Places: Overcoming Romantic and Sexual Addictions*. New York: G.P. Putnam's Sons.

Eddy, N.B., Halbach, H., Isbell, H. & Seevers, M.H. (1965) Drug dependence: its significance and characteristics. *Bulletin of the World Health Organization*, *32*, 721-733.

Edwards, P., Harvey, C. & Whitehead, P.C. (1973) Wives of alcoholics: A critical review and analysis. *Quarterly Journal of Studies on Alcohol*, *34*, 112-132.

Ewing, J.A., Long, Z. & Wenzel, G.G. (1961) Concurrent group psychotherapy of alcoholic patients and their wives. *International Journal of Group Psychotherapy*, *11*, 329-338.

Fichter, M.M. & Postpischil, F. (1988) Alcoholism. In: I.R.H. Falloon (Ed.) *Handbook of behavioral family therapy*. (pp. 350-371). New York: Guilford.

Fingarette, H. (1988) *Heavy Drinking: The Myth of Alcoholism as a Disease*. Berkeley: University of California Press.

Finn, R. & Clancy, J. (1972) Alcoholism, dilemma or disease: A recurring problem for the physician. *Comprehensive Psychiatry*, *13*, 133-138.

Firestein, L. (1989) Confessions of a lottoholic. *New York Times*, January 6, 1989.

Futterman, S. (1953) Personality trends in wives of alcoholics. *Journal of Psychiatric Social Work*, *23*, 37-41.

Gierymski, T. & Williams, T. (1986) Codependency. *Journal of Psychoactive Drugs*, *18*, 7-13.

Gliedman, L.H., Rosenthal, D., Frank, J.D. & Nash, H.G. (1956) Group therapy of alcoholics with concurrent group meetings with their wives. *Quarterly Journal of Studies on Alcohol*, *17*, 650-670.

Gomberg, E.S.L.(1982a) Historical and political perspectives: women and drug use. *Journal of Social Issues*, *38*, 153-167.

Gomberg, E.S.L. (1982b) The young male alcoholic: A pilot study. *Journal of Studies on Alcohol, 43*, 683-701.

Gomberg, E.S.L. (forthcoming) Alcoholic women in treatment: Early alcohol and drug experience and adult use of drugs other than alcohol.

Hall, T. (1988) Is America becoming hooked on addictions? *New York Times*, October 7, 1988.

Health in the Workplace (1988) Workers Assistance Program of Texas, Inc. Exercise addiction: When healthy habits become harmful. September, 1988, 1-3.

Jackson, J.K. (1954) The adjustment of the family to the crisis of alcoholism. *Quarterly Journal of Studies on Alcohol, 15*, 562-586.

Jackson, J.K. (1962) Alcoholism and the family. In: D.J. Pittman & C.R. Snyder (Eds.) *Society, Culture, and Drinking Patterns*. (pp. 472-492). New York: John Wiley & Sons, Inc.

Jacob, T. (1987) Alcoholism: a family interaction perspective. In: P.C. Rivers (Ed.) *Alcohol and addictive behavior. Nebraska Symposium on Motivation 1986*. (pp. 159-206). Lincoln: University of Nebraska Press.

Jellinek, E.M. (1945) Introduction to the curriculum. In: *Alcohol, Science and Society*. (pp. 1-12). New Haven: Quarterly Journal of Studies on Alcohol.

Jellinek, E.M. (1960) *The disease concept of alcoholism*. New Haven: Hillhouse Press.

Jenkins, G. (1988) Co-dependency. Health in the Workplace, Workers Assistance Program of Texas, March 1988, pp. 1-2; April 1988, pp. 1-2; May 1988, pp. 1-2.

Johnson, N.P., Davis, C.W. & Michels, P.J. (1988) *Dictionary of street alcohol and drug terms*, 3rd edition. Columbia, SC: School of Medicine, University of South Carolina.

Johnston, L.D. (1973) *Drugs and American youth*. Ann Arbor, MI: Institute for Social Research, University of Michigan.

Kalashian, M.M. (1959) Working with the wives of alcoholics in an outpatient clinic. *Marriage and Family, 21*, 130-133.

Kaufman, E. & Pattison, E.M. (1981) Differential methods of family therapy in the treatment of alcoholism. *Journal of Studies on Alcohol, 42*, 951-971.

Keller, M. (1976) The disease concept of alcoholism revisited. *Journal of Studies on Alcohol, 37*, 1694-1717.

Keller, M. (1982) Perspective on medicine and alcoholism. *Alcoholism: Clinical and Experimental research, 6*, 327-332.

Keller, M. & McCormick, M.A. (1968) *A dictionary of words about alcohol*. New Brunswick, NJ: Rutgers Center of Alcohol Studies Publication.

Keller, M., McCormick, M.A. & Efron, V. (1982) *A dictionary of words about alcohol, 2nd edition*. New Brunswick, NJ: Rutgers Center of Alcohol Studies Publications.

Keller, M. & Seeley, J.R. (1958) The alcohol language: with a selected vocabulary. Toronto: University of Toronto Press.

Larsen, E. (1983) *Basics of co-dependency* Brooklyn Park, MN: Larsen Enterprises.

Marlatt, G.A., Baer, J.S., Donovan, D.M. & Kivlahan, D.R. (1988) Addictive behaviors: etiology and treatment. *Annual Review of Psychology*, *39*, 223-252.

Meeks, D.E. & Kelly, C. (1970) Family therapy with the families of recovering alcoholics. *Quarterly Journal of Studies on Alcohol*, *31*, 499-413.

Miller, M.E. (1987) Co-dependent contradictions? *The U.S. Journal of Drug and Alcohol Dependence*, *11*, May 1987.

Miller, W.R. (Ed.) (1980) *The addictive behaviors: treatment of alcoholism, drug abuse, smoking and obesity*. Oxford: Pergamon.

Miller, W.R. (1987) Adult cousins of alcoholics. *Psychology of Addictive Behaviors*, *1*, 74-76.

Murck, M.W. (1988) Co-dependence among helping professionals. *Observer*, *10*, 4-5.

National Council on Alcoholism (1988) *Who says alcoholism is a disease*?

New York Times (1988) *Infant addicted, mother charged*. *New York Times*, December 16, 1988.

Norwood, R. (1986) *Women who love too much*. Pocket Books.

O'Farrell, T.J. (1987) Marital and family therapy for alcohol problems. In: W.M. Cox (Ed.) *Treatment and prevention of alcohol problems*. (pp. 205-234). New York: Academic Press.

Orford, J. (1985) *Excessive appetites: a psychological view of addiction*. Somerset, NJ: John Wiley & Sons.

Orford, J. & Guthrie, S. (1968) Coping behavior used by waves of alcoholics: a preliminary investigation. *28th International Congress on Alcohol and Alcoholism* (abstract), p. 97.

Ottenberg, D.J. (1974) Traditional and non-traditional credentials in addictive problems—A dispatch from the battlefield. *7th Annual Eagleville Conference Proceedings*.

Peele, S. (1988) (Ed.) *Visions of addiction: major contemporary perspectives on addiction and alcoholism*. Lexington, MA: Lexington.

Phelps, J.K. & Nourse, A.E. (1986) *The hidden addiction and how to get free*. Boston: Little, Brown and Company.

Price, G.M. (1945) A study of the wives of twenty alcoholics. *Quarterly Journal of Studies on Alcohol*, *5*, 620-627.

Professional Update, Hazelden Foundation (1987). Editorial.

Ray, O. & Ksir, C. (1987) *Drugs, society and human behavior, 4th edition*. St. Louis: Mosby.

Room, R. (1981) A farewell to alcoholism? A commentary on the WHO 1980 Expert Committee Report. *British Journal of Addiction*, *76*, 115-123.

Schaef, A.W. (1986) *Co-dependence: misunderstood, mistreated*. San Francisco: Harper and Row.

Stanton, M.D. & Landau, J. (1985) The family and substance abuse. In: S. Henao & N.P. Grose (Eds.) *Principles of family systems in family medicine*. (pp. 195-212). New York: Brunner/Mazel.

Steinglass, P. (1981) The alcoholic family at home. *Archives of General Psychiatry*, *38*, 578-584.

Steinglass, P. (1982) Alcoholism and the family. In: E.L. Gomberg, H.R. White

& J.A. Carpenter (Eds.) *Alcohol, science and society revisited*. (pp. 306-321). Ann Arbor, MI: Univ. of Michigan Press.

Stimmel, B., Vernace, S. & Tobias, H. (1972) Hepatic dysfunction in heroin addicts: the role of alcohol. *Journal of the American Medical Association, 222*: 811-812.

Utne Reader (1988) Are you addicted to addiction? A skeptical look at AA and other 12-step programs. No. 30, November/December 1988.

Valle, S.K. (1977) The relative effectiveness of degreed and non-degreed alcoholism counselors. *Maryland State Medical Journal*, 1977.

Vannicelli, M., Gingerich, S. & Ryback, R. (1983) Family problems related to the treatment and outcome of alcoholic patients. *British Journal of Addiction*, *78*, 193-204.

Webster's Third New International Dictionary of the English Language, Unabridged (1964). Springfield, MA: G. & C. Merriam Company.

Wegscheider-Cruse, S. (1984) *Co-dependency: an emerging issue*. Pompano Beach, FL: Health Communications, Inc.

Whalen, T. (1953) Wives of alcoholics: four types observed in a family service agency. *Quarterly Journal of Studies on Alcohol*, *14*: 632-641.

Williams, M.W. (1988) Identifying and treating codependency. Michigan Alcohol and Addiction Association Dispatch, August 1988 Newsletter, pp. 1, 3.

Wolin, S.J., Bennett, L.A., Noonan, D.L. & Teitelbaum, M.A. (1980) Disrupted family rituals. A factor in the intergenerational transmission of alcoholism. *Journal of Studies on Alcohol*, *41*, 199-214.

World Health Organization Expert Committee on Alcohol (1954). First report. *World Health Organization Technical Reports Series*, *No. 84*.

World Health Organization Expert Committee on Addiction-Producing Drugs (1957).

World Health Organization Expert Committee on Problems related to Alcohol and Consumption (1980). Problems related to alcohol consumption. *World Health Organization Technical Report Series, No. 650*.

Adult Children of Alcoholics: Is It Really a Separate Field for Study?

Robert J. Beidler, DSW

During the past few years adult children of alcoholics has emerged as a field of study. As such, this field has produced a large body of literature, which generally attempts to define difficulties in adult human functioning and/or adjustment as rooted in having had an alcoholic parent.

Indeed, this is a new field of study, and much of the work remains primarily anecdotal (e.g., Ackerman, 1983; Wegscheider, 1981; Woititz, 1983). However, a small body of recent empirical studies does exist (e.g., Black et al., 1986; Clair and Genest, 1987). In addition to work which is focused directly on the adult child of the alcoholic, there is relevant empirical work on the effects of alcoholism on the family (e.g., Moos and Billings, 1982) and more general grounded theory on adult adjustment and coping (e.g., Lazarus and Folkman, 1984; Seltzer, 1982; Vaillant, 1977) which cannot be ignored in the discussion of adult children of alcoholics.

The focus of this article will be to delineate a number of the core issues involved in understanding the process of adjustment of adult children of alcoholics. In doing so it will draw upon representative work in the field as well as relevant work in related fields. No attempt will be made to provide a complete critical review of the literature. The focus will be on identifying a number of core issues. Thus, this article deals with knowledge development and theory and

---

Dr. Beidler is Director of Quality Assurance and Staff Development, Department of Social Work and Community Health Services, Hospital of the University of Pennsylvania, and Lecturer at the University of Pennsylvania School of Social Work, Philadelphia, PA 18104.

includes the following sections: (1) children of alcoholics, a diagnostic label or category for study?; (2) adult children of alcoholics and individual adjustment; (3) the family, alcoholism, and the adult child; (4) general theory on adult adjustment and the adult children of alcoholics; and (5) the interaction of alcoholism and sociopathy and its possible relationship to adjustment.

CHILDREN OF ALCOHOLICS, DIAGNOSTIC LABEL OR CATEGORY FOR STUDY?

Perhaps the major issue with regard to adult children of alcoholics is the way the term is used. There is a tendency to treat all adult children of alcoholics as if they represent a diagnostic category. Within some of the anecdotal literature, group membership is viewed as predictive of a variety of clearly definable dysfunctional behaviors in adults who are children of alcoholics (e.g., Wegscheider, 1981; Woititz, 1983). According to Woititz, adult children of alcoholics must be labelled as such if they are truly to be understood (1983); for Wegscheider virtually every individual from an "alcoholic" family takes on one or more of five basic roles which then continue as the basis for adult dysfunction (1981). Many authors do not account for the diversity of adult functioning in children of alcoholics (Clair and Genest, 1987) or the effects of other environmental, personality, and/or biological factors in the formation of the complement of adult coping strategies. What often is presented is a simple relationship between *having an alcoholic parent* and *possessing a set of characteristics as an adult*. The use of the label, adult children of alcoholics, may support this simplistic view even when not intended (e.g., Ackerman, 1983). Whether intended or not it appears that a set of dysfunctional characteristics are the *explained* variable and the label, adult children of alcoholics, is the *explaining* variable. All of this is not to argue that alcoholism in the family does not contribute to the probability of adult functioning problems. There is empirical evidence that suggests that having an alcoholic parent may contribute to adult functioning difficulties for *some* adults (Black et al., 1986: Clair and Genest, 1987; Vaillant, 1983). There is evidence that alcoholism adversely affects the family system (Jackson, 1954; Moos and Billings, 1982) and that family of origin problems predict difficulties in lifelong adaptation (Vaillant, 1977) and sociopathy (Vaillant, 1983). None of this however, suggests a clearly defined, unique syndrome. Better to move away from the labelling of individuals as adult children of alcoholics to the study of how individuals' behaviors associated with alcoholism affect both the family and individuals within it. Since adult individual coping is a result of a myriad of systems (Lazarus and Folkman, 1983) it is important that the study be multifaceted in order to describe the interaction of many variables which contribute to risk or which strengthen the individual against vulnerabilities associated with being a child of an alcoholic.

ADULT CHILDREN OF ALCOHOLICS AND INDIVIDUAL MALADJUSTMENT

Closely associated with the labelling issues is the question of whether adult children of alcoholics are more likely to be impaired by being the offspring of an alcoholic, and if so are they impaired in a manner which constitutes a separate, identifiable group with a unique set of characteristics? The meager evidence available on the first questions suggest that children of alcoholics are more likely to have adult functioning difficulties (e.g., Black et al., 1986; Clair and Genest, 1987; Vaillant, 1983; Werner, 1986). None of these studies suggest *uniform* difficulties. Black suggests a greater frequency of adult difficulties but not the presence of a specific set of difficulties present in adult children of alcoholics. Even more important is work such as that of Werner (1986) which not only documents the variability of adjustment in children of alcoholics, but also identifies certain characteristics of both the individual and the environment which distinguish those who have difficulties in adjustment from those who do not. Thus, individual characteristics such as (1) belief in self-help; (2) more internal locus of control; (3) positive self-concept; (4) achievement orientation and (5) at least average intelligence and adequate communication skills, and early environmental factors such as (1) a high level of attention from the primary caretaker during infancy; (2) no long separations; (3) no new births within two years of life; (4) low family conflict first two years of life, predict children of alcoholics probably not developing serious coping problems in childhood or adolescence. Though longitudinal work on the effects of family alcoholism on childhood and adolescence neither confirms nor rejects hypotheses about ongoing adult difficulties, it does clearly question any model which reports that children of alcoholics *inevitably* develop maladjusted behaviors as children which then are carried throughout life,

> . . . Indeed children of alcoholics were more likely to have difficulties in coping, but it was the difference in both the environment and the individual which predicted who would have difficulties and who would not, and not the presence/non-presence of alcoholism per se (Werner, 1986).

THE FAMILY ALCOHOLISM AND THE ADULT CHILD

A small body of empirical work does provide direction for testing hypotheses on relationships between alcoholism, the family, and the effects on children raised in families of alcoholics (e.g., Jackson, 1954; Moos and Billings, 1982). If we put aside the issue of alcoholism and sociopathy for a moment there is empirical support for the following contentions: (1) that alcoholism leads to personality/behavioral changes in the individual who is alcoholic (Vaillant, 1983); (2) that active alcoholism increases conflict, and decreases cohesiveness and expressiveness in families (Moos and Billings, 1981); and (3) that families, or at least spouses, go through phases in an attempt to adapt/cope with the alcoholic's behavior (Jackson, 1954). However given these data, a number of questions remain. *How* are adult children affected by family difficulties related to alcoholism? Are they affected in the same way? What factors in the alcoholic's behavior, the altered family system, and the patterns of adaptation can be linked with ongoing difficulties of adult human functioning?

In answering these questions a number of authors take a simplistic view, often drawing conclusions without reference to any data and/or empirical literature. For example, Wegscheider (1981) defines a number of rules which govern chemically dependent families and maintain its maladjustment. She further claims to have identified five basic roles which are taken on by individual family members. In her work these roles are worked out in great detail. The roles are then viewed as ongoing "cages" which continue to control the incumbents throughout their lives in a pattern of maladjustment. Typically, little effort is made to connect these theories with the findings of empirical studies on the effects of alcoholism on the family, family attempts at adaptation and/or on individual functioning (e.g., Woititz, 1983).

In a recent article, Clair and Genest (1987), do draw on existing empirical knowledge on the effects of alcoholism on the family and on grounded theory about human coping mechanisms in order to establish and test hypotheses about the effect of alcoholism on adult children. In their findings, not all adult children reported difficulties. They also found that though adult children of alcoholics did report greater family conflict, the levels of family conflict did not necessarily lead to adult difficulties. Instead, the study found that cohesiveness, expressiveness, and encouragement of the child's independence were associated with adult adjustment, suggesting that a family can maintain stable functions despite conflict generated by the presence of an alcoholic in the family. In a word, the simplistic view that adult adjustment difficulties *directly* accrue from alcoholism in the family was not supported. The assumption that any level of conflict necessarily causes the family to be maladjusted and thus produces maladjusted adults was not supported. If the family is able to reorganize functionally, maladjustment may be less likely. Interestingly this research suggests a lack of uniqueness in families of alcoholics by identifying family functioning patterns as the predictors of adjustment as opposed to the alcoholism per se and/or conflict associated with alcoholism. In a word, the empirical work suggests linkage to general family theory and the effects of family functioning on adult adjustment, rather than a conceptualization of "alcoholic " families as causing specific adult adjustment problems.

GENERAL THEORY ON ADULT ADJUSTMENT AND ADULT CHILDREN OF ALCOHOLICS

The previous sections on individual maladjustment, family maladjustment and adult children of alcoholics alluded to the discrepancies between some of the literature on adult children of alcoholics and more general findings on adult adjustment. A comprehensive analysis of the literature on adult children of alcoholics and the more general findings on adult adaption and coping is beyond the scope of this article. However, some observations about more general findings on adult behavior and the adult children of alcoholics is in order. First of all, the one prospective study on adult adjustment available does support the notion that poor family environment predicts poor adult adjustment (Vaillant, 1977). This is a basic premise of much of the adult children of alcoholics literature (e.g., Wegscheider, 1981; Ackerman, 1983; Woititz, 1983). Family environment however, in and of itself was not supported in Vaillant's work as the strongest predictor of adult adjustment. Subjects who took jobs after school or during vacation, helped with chores at home, participated in extracurricular activities at school, had school grades at their intelligence level, who had good peer relationships, and who made a good adjustment to home life were *not* negatively influenced by a poor home environment. Note the importance of *both* individual adjustment factors and performance outside the home in predicting life long adjustment rather than the family environment alone (Vaillant, 1977).

In Seltzer's work on adolescent development, the primary emphasis in identity development moves away from the nuclear family to interaction with peers. Inadequate development of adult identity is linked to deficits in opportunity or ability to participate fully In such interactions (Seltzer, 1982). Seltzer's work does not deny the importance of early family experience but rather points to the importance of other variables, indeed, to the importance of the shift of focus from the family to peer group during adolescence.

Existing data on adult adjustment support the hypotheses which connect childhood family environment with adult behavior but emphasize other factors of equal importance, e.g., peer relations and competent performance of tasks outside the home. These more general findings on adjustment (Vaillant, 1977; Seltzer, 1982) are important in considering any relationship between early life experience and adult behavior.

SOCIOPATHY, ALCOHOLISM, AND ADULT CHILDREN OF ALCOHOLICS

An issue which has not been discussed in the literature on the adult children of alcoholics, is that of the possible interaction between alcoholism and sociopathy. Indeed this issue of sociopathy and alcoholism has been much debated (McCord and McCord, 1960; Robins, 1966; Vaillant, 1983; Workman-Daniels and Hesselbrook, 1987). Yet, even with the view that alcoholism and sociopathy are not necessarily related, there is evidence that sociopaths are more likely to abuse alcohol, that there is a subset of alcoholics who are sociopathic and that early onset of alcoholism is associated with sociopathy among men (Vaillant, 1983). Furthermore, a recent study has identified the presence of specific brain malfunction as possibly predictive of the combination alcoholism and sociopathy in some individuals, of alcoholism without sociopathy in others, and sociopathy without alcoholism in a third group (Workman-Daniels and Hesselbrook, 1987). There is evidence that some alcoholics are sociopathic and some are not. The question is whether the presence of sociopathy in an alcoholic differentially affects the family environment and the adjustment of children of alcoholics.

This issue is more complicated than the relationship of alcoholism, family and adjustment of offspring of alcoholics because of the number of questions to be considered. The first question is whether family environments of children of alcoholics who are sociopathic are more likely to be disturbed than the family environments of children of alcoholics who are not sociopathic. The next question is whether individual dysfunction is more related to the age of onset of parental alcoholism than to sociopathy per se; in the prospective study on alcoholism, sociopaths who became alcoholics became alcoholic in their twenties while non-sociopaths became alcoholic in their thirties and forties (Vaillant, 1983). The presence of a sociopath in a family is likely to be disruptive, whether the individual is alcoholic or not. How does a sociopath influence family environment with, without, or before alcoholism? The question of the adjustment of children of alcoholics would remain less complicated if the relationship of alcoholism and sociopathy is set aside, but this is an issue which cannot be ignored.

CONCLUSION

A number of years ago, Bacon noted that in the field of alcoholism, "conceptual confusion in thinking. . . . is related to a problem orientation as contrasted with a phenomenological orientation." He further notes, "that an intellectual art of any given field may be characterized as moving toward maturity as it applies itself primarily to phenomena of a given class rather than to the 'problem' or 'pathology' aspects of a class" (Bacon, 1976, p. 60). Though Bacon was concerned about the whole field of alcohol studies, his comments seem especially apropos to a discussion of adult children of alcoholics. Indeed, much of this article has focused on the discrepancies between a problem/pathology orientation and a phenomenological orientation. The pathology/problem model, in its simplest form explains a series of adult problems/pathologies as the consequence of having had an alcoholic parent. The task of building models for understanding becomes harder when explanation moves away from simplistic problem/pathology orientations toward understanding which views alcoholism in a parent as only one factor which may influence subsequent behaviors. When the more recent empirical literature is reviewed, the findings consistently move away from problem orientation toward broader understanding of the phenomena of individual and family functioning, even when the empirical literature is presented within a problem/pathology orientation (Clair and Genest, 1987; Werner, 1986). As knowledge development matures, the focus needs to move away from the problem/pathology mode of conceptualizing to one in which alcoholism-in-a-parent is considered in its relationship to a broader understanding of *all* diverse systems which affect individual development.

As the focus moves away from the simple problem/pathology model, the need to consider children of alcoholics as a special field of study also seems to evaporate. Indeed, as the focus moves to a more phenomenological orientation alcoholism in the family would seem to take its place as one factor to be considered. Children of alcoholics should not be considered a separate field of study.

REFERENCES

Ackerman, R.J. *Children of Alcoholics*. New York: A Learning Publications/ Finesille Book (Simon & Schuster, Inc.), 1983.

Bacon, S. "Concepts" in *Alcohol and Alcohol Problems: New Thinking and New Directions*. Cambridge, MA: Ballinger Publishing Company, p. 57-133, 1976.

Black, C., Bucky, S.F., and Wilder-Padilla, S. The Interpersonal and Emotional Consequences of Being an Adult Child of an Alcoholic. International Journal of the Addictions, 21(2):213-231, 1986.

Clair, D. and Genest, M. Variables Associated with Adjustment of Offspring of Alcoholic Fathers. JSA, 48(4):345, 1987.

Jackson, J.K. The Adjustment of the Family to the Crisis of Alcoholism. QJSA, 15:562-586, 1954.

Lazarus, R. and Folkman, S.F. *Stress, Appraisal and Coping*. New York: Springer Publishing Co., 1984.

McCord, W. and McCord, J. *Origins of Alcoholism*. Stamford: Stamford University Press, 1960.

Moos, R. and Billings, A. Children of Alcoholics During the Recovering Process. Addictive Behaviors, 7:155-163, 1982.

Robins, L.N. *Deviant Children Grown Up: A Sociological and Psychiatric Study of Sociopathic Personality*. Baltimore: Williams and Wilkins, 1966.

Seltzer, V.C. *Adolescent Social Development: Dynamic Functional Interaction*. Lexington, MA and Toronto: Lexington Books, 1982.

Vaillant, G.E. *The Natural History of Alcoholism*. Cambridge, MA and London: Harvard University Press, 1983.

Vaillant, G.E. *Adaption to Life*. Boston: Little Brown, 1977.

Wegscheider, S. *Another Chance–Hope and Health for the Alcoholic Family*. Science and Behavior Books, Inc., Palo Alto, CA, p. 191.

Werner, E.E. Resilient Offspring of Alcoholics: A Longitudinal Study from Birth to Age 18. JSA, 47(1), 1986.

Woititz, J.G. *Adult Children of Alcoholics*. Pompano Beach, FL: Health Communications, Inc., 1983.

Workman-Daniels, K.L. and Hesselbrook, V.M. Childhood Problem Behavior and Neuropsychological Functioning in Persons at Risk for Alcoholism. JSA, 48(3):187-192, 1987.

The New Temperance Movement: Through the Looking-Glass

Dwight B. Heath, PhD

SUMMARY. A long-term rise in drinking by Americans slowed in the 1970s and then reversed; several interest-groups pressed for higher taxes on alcohol, server-liability, severe penalties for drunk-drivers, a higher purchase-age, and many other legislative and regulatory restrictions. Several similar changes are occurring in other countries. A quasi-scientific rationale for reducing alcohol consumption links quantity directly to a wide range of social and individual problems, although the correlation often varies, both cross-culturally and over time in the U.S. The new temperance movement holds out the false promise of a quick and easy solution to drinking problems, and provides a socially acceptable outlet that allows people to blame alcohol and wrongdoers in a Neo-Victorian complacency.

In any discussion about current controversies in the drug field, one of the most pervasive and visible ones has to do with increasing pressures to reduce the consumption of alcoholic beverages among all populations. Ironically, it is also a controversy that is perceived as such by few other than those who have taken a strong stand on one side or the other. Many of the principal spokespersons are academicians and other scientists whose writings often are scrupu-

---

Dr. Heath is Professor of Anthropology, and Director of the Center for Latin American Studies, Brown University, Providence, RI 02912.

Correspondence and requests for reprints should be addressed to: Dr. Dwight B. Heath, Anthropology, Box 1921, Brown University, Providence, RI 02912, USA.

The author is grateful to his long-term friend and colleague, A.M. Cooper, for suggesting the title and providing other kinds of intellectual and moral support for this paper, including the loan of the term "Neo-Victorian."

lously phrased in order to minimize controversy, and much that is written on the subject is interpreted as scientifically based and, therefore, straightforward and objective. Besides which, who could be so hard-hearted as to take issue with the World Health Organization's prescriptions for achieving "Health for all in the year 2000"? Unfortunately, much of what is said along these lines constitutes what many refer to as "the new temperance movement," and it has more to do with politics and emotion than it does with science.

Writing about "the new temperance movement" is in many ways like following Alice's adventures through the looking-glass in Lewis Carroll's classic story which some read as nonsense, others as childish adventure, and yet others as profound allegory. Things are not always as they first appear, and relationships among them are especially problematic. For that matter, some might even question whether there is any such movement, suggesting perhaps it's simply a figment of the imagination of a few among those who hold different views.

In a paradoxical way, it could be said that "the new temperance movement" is hardly new, has a questionable association with temperance, and lacks the degree of formal organization that most people associate with a movement in which the N, T, and M are most often capitalized. Nevertheless, it is firmly imbedded in the journalistic literature, and appears to be real from the points of view of many people who are engaged in various aspects of alcohol studies, public health, business and industry, as well as policy-making. This paper is an effort briefly to sort out who, what, where and when the movement can be discerned, and some speculations about why such a pattern should have emerged at this point in history, following almost half a century in which the consumption of virtually all kinds of alcoholic beverages climbed rapidly and progressively throughout most of the world.

Like "the military-industrial complex," "the Eastern liberal establishment," and many other sociological phenomena, "the new temperance movement" appears to be a construct, a label that is most often applied by observers who are not necessarily in or of it. There is no formal entity with that name, and there is probably no organization by any other name of which all members would be comfortable accepting the label. Furthermore, there are probably few individuals who would volunteer the information that they consider themselves "members" or otherwise affiliated with or engaged in the movement. (A dramatic exception will be noted below.) Nevertheless, it is apparent that the 1970s and 80s have witnessed a widespread and increasing series of actions that are clearly directed toward progressively restricting the consumption of alcoholic beverages in the United States and abroad. It is such actions that have prompted many social scientists and other observers to refer, in various contexts, to "the new temperance movement" (often, but not always, with key words capitalized); a few illustrative examples include Beauchamp (1984b), Danovitch (1984), and Musto (1984).

I will leave it to a future historian or lexicographer to play the game of attempting to identify the initial use of the term. I once credited it to Dan Beauchamp (1984a), but he recently (personal communication) suggested that it might have been David Musto, and that he (Beauchamp) had for some time rejected the label before championing it. Musto, in turn, told me (personal communication) that he doubted that he had originated the term, and suggested that it may have been "someone in the [alcoholic beverage] industry." Queries to Jack Blocker, Mark Keller, Harry Levine, David Pittman, and other colleagues who are interested in the social history of alcohol studies were similarly indecisive about the specific etymology of "the new temperance movement." The important point in all of this has to do with the sociocultural ambience, what many would call "the climate of the times." The adoption of a linguistic innovation such as "the new temperance movement," and its continuing vitality attest to its immediate relevance regardless of its origin. It followed a brief period in which there had been criticism directed toward "the Neo-Prohibitionists" in some journalistic writings. The "Neo-Prohibitionist" label may have first been used in a public forum by Boche (1977), while he was stepping down from the presidency of the Alcohol and Drug Problems Association. But the label was rejected by those who saw it as a threat to their professed concern for public health (e.g., Beauchamp, 1984a), and they were quick to deny that they were aiming for reinstatement of prohibition, emphasizing that their concern was with fostering temperance. The construct of a "new temperance movement" is clearly a sociocultural invention which would almost certainly not have gained any currency if there were not some referents, real or imagined, that fit with it.

Even when we give up on the quest for origins of the name, some key questions remain about the semiotic qualities of that label. It is not at all clear whether it refers to a movement that is committed to a *new kind* of temperance, or whether the word "new" refers instead to *this* particular temperance movement, in contradistinction to earlier temperance movements, which may (or may not) have been very different in their aims. There is some evidence in support of both interpretations.

ANTECEDENTS IN U.S. HISTORY

Regardless of which of those emphases or interpretations is put on this "new temperance movement," it is apparent that there are significant analogues in earlier American history. Recent efforts at tracing the history of thought have contributed substantially to our understanding of social dynamics and their relation to other aspects of culture; this is especially true with respect to alcohol which has only lately been the focus of considerable synthesis and some penetrating analysis (see, e.g., Social History of Alcohol Review, 1985-).

One striking revelation of such studies has been the large role that alcoholic beverages played in American culture from early times. It is ironic that the native populations of North America, long stereotyped as "the drunken Indian" (Westermeyer, 1974), were among the few indigenous peoples who did not have alcoholic beverages until the coming of Europeans. Shortly after the arrival of Whites, alcohol was widely adopted by many but by no means all tribes (Heath, 1983) and quickly became an important tool in commerce and political manipulation. Earlier generations' mistaken imagery of Puritanism obscured popular understanding of many aspects of the immigrants' culture during the early colonial period, but it is now widely recognized that beer, cider, and various distilled drinks ("ardent waters") were used by men, women, and children, as normal foods, energizers, restoratives, and for medicinal purposes (Lender & Martin, 1986). Some historians have gone so far as to suggest that beer predominated because the early settlers were afraid of drinking water (Rorabaugh, 1979) but that appears to be an overstatement based on inappropriate projection of contemporary thinking. Certainly the day-by-day account of the Mayflower voyage that brought the first Pilgrims to New England was positive enough about water (Heath, 1986, pp. 20-21, 39). And even the dour pastor Increase Mather affirmed that "Drink is in itself a Creature of God, and to be received with thankfulness," dangerous only if carelessly misused (Mather, 1673, pp. 3-4).

Per capita consumption appears to have climbed steeply until the beginning of the 19th century, but drinking was viewed as an integral part of daily life rather than problematic behavior. Beer and hard cider were normal beverages with meals, with rum a common drink for sociability, shared with those who helped in reciprocal labor-exchange such as barn-raising or cornhusking, at funerals, and so forth. Taverns were important centers of civic action as well as providing food and lodging for travelers, and there were few restrictions on the sale of alcoholic beverages except to Indians, slaves, indentured servants, and "habitual drunkards." Those who did drink too much or too often were viewed as personally weak, but not sinful, addicted, nor diseased. Although such a person might not support his family well, there was no categorization of him or her as vicious, socially dangerous, or in need of recuperative treatment.

With the War of Independence, rum distilled from Caribbean molasses was displaced by whiskey from domestic grains. The newly popular drink, often produced by Scotch-Irish farmers on the westward-moving frontier, became an important commodity in the Appalachians and beyond, where it provided high value in small volume, unbreakable, easy to transport, not subject to spoilage, and easy to divide almost infinitely. Its importance is reflected in the Whiskey Rebellion which flared in 1794 in response to imposition of the first federal excise tax in U.S. history, and which was quickly quelled by the first commitment of federal troops.

With the coming of the 19th century, there was enormous geographic mobility. All kinds of production and consumption increased dramatically. Cities grew haphazardly, and an urban proletariat appeared, at the same time that the stability of small communities was eroded and a more individualistic social order was not only accepted but idealized by many. The "Great Revival" in religious fervor swept westward from northern Europe. A distinguished American physician, Benjamin Rush, came out against distilled liquor as harmful, and temperance societies like those that were springing up in Europe at the time gained popularity. By the late 1830s, a dominant faction of the temperance movement publicly called for prohibition. There was a flurry of regulatory activity and by 1855, 13 states had gone officially dry. In a brief reaction against the abuses of teetotalism, however, 7 of them voted wet by 1863. The nationwide Prohibition Party stated in 1869, and the Women's Christian Temperance Movement began with a strikingly progressive agenda in 1874. During the '80s, another 6 states enacted prohibition. An interpretation that fits the data well is that "The prohibition movement in the late 19th century involved an attempt by 'the decent classes' to create a morally coherent national culture" (Aaron & Musto 1981, p. 152), at a time when large-scale culturally different immigration threatened to eclipse much of what had been viewed as typically good about America.

By 1919, fully 14 percent of the U.S. population lived in dry states, and nationwide prohibition was enacted, partly in the hope of quieting rampant social unrest. The era of Prohibition (1920-1933) provided a vivid demonstration of the fact that legal controls, even when backed by extremely strict enforcement measures such as the Volstead Act, diminished apparent consumption only briefly. It was not long before bootlegging (illegal importation) and moonshining (illicit production) proliferated on an enormous scale. These new sources combined with a new pattern of consumption, in large-scale popular defiance of the law. "The Roaring Twenties" have been described as a virtual orgy of drinking, often by individuals who might not have turned to alcoholic beverages if it weren't for the titillation provided by the fashionable risk-taking that was associated with bathtub gin, speakeasys, and an illusion of participating on the fringes of the underworld, while simultaneously thumbing one's nose at "the Establishment" and its puritanical conventions. Ironically, we do not yet have the kind of solid quantitative data that would allow us to confirm or refute that image, but there is broad consensus that "the noble experiment" of prohibition was a failure in terms of protecting the American people from what had been vividly portrayed as "the evils of drink."

Joseph Gusfield very effectively made the point that Prohibition may not have been such a failure in other terms. He suggests that the architects of the law may not really have been surprised or even particularly disappointed to find that it was unenforceable. In a remarkably perceptive analysis, he called it a "symbolic crusade" (Gusfield, 1963), perhaps intended less to revolutionize popular attitudes and behavior than to demonstrate that the Anglo-Saxon middle-class values of those who had long held power in this country were not yet displaced by other norms that had been brought by recently arrived waves of immigrants from different cultural backgrounds.

Although prohibition appears to have been well received by many Americans at the outset, the ensuing era of infamous lawlessness and corruption disenchanted many. Although officially dry, the era was anything but, and drinking became fashionable as never before. Economic collapse in 1929 aggravated social unrest to an unprecedented level that threatened domestic order, and many viewed repeal as an easy way to restore both jobs and taxes that had been lost with curtailment of the drink industry. This country's ambivalence about alcohol is epitomized in the fact that Prohibition, the first amendment to our long-standing Constitution that deals with workaday behavior of private people, later became the only amendment ever to be repealed.

In the half-century following repeal, the experience of prohibition had been largely forgotten, and there was a moratorium in the American pattern of ongoing public debate about drinking and its occasional ill-effects. In fact, a new kind of discourse came to predominate, which focused on the individual rather than social aspects of drinking problems. The so-called "Alcoholism Movement," summarily chronicled by Keller (1976), was itself a strange coalition of interests. The interdisciplinary team of scientists who pioneered in systematic research on the subject and laid a firm foundation for broad information-dissemination were best known at the Yale Center of Alcohol Studies. Their work gained notoriety at about the same time that Alcoholics Anonymous did. Marty Mann bridged the two, and founded the National Council on Alcoholism.

E.M. Jellinek, Selden Bacon, and several other key figures also recognized the value of linking their academic interests with the preventive and therapeutic interests that motivated others. One major point of convergence was "the disease concept of alcoholism," which served significantly to change the status of alcoholics and popular attitudes toward them. Victims of a disease are generally thought in this society to be blameless, and it is the medical community rather than police and correctional institutions that are invoked to deal with them. Such medicalization of alcoholism undoubtedly relieved many people of guilt or shame, and may have prompted some to seek treatment who might otherwise have avoided it. But it ignored a variety of other problematic behaviors that are sometimes associated with drinking, such as drunk-driving, rowdy behavior, and so forth.

Ever since repeal, and more rapidly since World War II, sales of all classes of alcoholic beverages increased. Laws and regulations restricting their sale or consumption were gradually loosened in many jurisdictions, with Mississippi the last state voting itself wet in 1966. During the 1960s, the fact that women and children often drink began to be taken into account by researchers, although laws still disallowed sales to minors, and women were expected to drink only in a decorous manner.

During the Vietnam War, the average age of combatants was only nineteen, raising again the fallacy that men old enough to fight and die for their country were being denied the right to drink. The federal voting age was lowered to 18, and several states reduced the minimum purchase-age from 21 in the 1960s. Meanwhile, much of the rest of the world was undergoing a similar long and uninterrupted rise in alcohol consumption since the 1930s, with rapid acceleration after 1945.

With all of these historical antecedents, one might well wonder how – or even whether – a new temperance movement might spring up in the world of the 1970s. There is abundant empirical evidence that the United States has been the scene of such a phenomenon, and many other countries show signs of something very similar.

EMPIRICAL EVIDENCE

Anthropologists are accustomed to dealing with witchcraft, possession, zombies, and a wide range of other phenomena that cannot easily be explained in terms of the simplistic view many people hold concerning the nature of scientific paradigms. We explicitly reject the proposition that "reality" refers only to qualities that can be weighed, measured, charted, graphed, and otherwise "objectively" quantified. It has become a truism in sociology and related fields of study that many things are "real" – that is, they participate in a social construction of reality (Berger & Luckmann, 1966) – precisely because so many people act *as if* they were real. It is in this sense that the phenomenon of a new temperance movement deserved to be recognized as an important source of controversy in thinking about drugs and society, even before Beauchamp (1984b) invited others to join him in it, with several clearly stated goals.

Another approach to the question of empirical evidence that may be more congenial and convincing to many readers is for me to point to a number of things that have happened, both in the United States and abroad, that are congruent with what one would expect in the context of a new temperance movement. Sales of alcoholic beverages have ceased to climb rapidly, and are falling in some areas. A number of legislative and regulatory controls are being imposed, after a long period of progressive liberalization. Taxes on alcohol have been increased in many jurisdictions, and there is strong lobbying for still higher taxes. The idea of indexing prices so that they will keep pace with inflation has been widely recommended. Minimum purchase-age has risen, and servers are increasingly being held liable for damages caused by others. Drunk-drivers are subject to new and heavy penalties and stigma. Young people are being coaxed to "Just Say No," and various jurisdictions have mandated warning-signs in places where drinks are sold. A variety of health warning-labels have been proposed, as have restrictions or outright bans on advertising. Government and international agencies have taken major policy stands in favor of curtailing alcohol consumption, and a number of private organizations are calling for further restrictions on availability. It is evident that the millions of dollars spent on advertising have not bought blind acceptance of drinking, and negative attitudes toward alcohol are, if not increasing, at least increasingly being translated into action. Let us focus first on the United States as an important case-study of "the new temperance movement" in action, and then briefly note some similar and related happenings elsewhere in the world.

New Temperance in the United States

Regardless of exactly where and when it may have started, it is apparent that a new temperance movement can be discerned in terms of changes that have taken place during the past two decades. It is undoubtedly important that Beauchamp (1984b) overcame his initial resistance to the term and forcefully declared himself a major spokesman on behalf of the New Temperance Movement, spelling out the key aims that he felt the Movement should strive for. But it is not irrelevant that, for a decade or more before that, changes in the direction he called for had already begun. The changes were probably at a slower pace than he envisioned, and their scattered and sporadic quality suggest that they were not the work of an organized constituency.

One of the principal lines of evidence has to do with what those in alcohol studies call apparent consumption of alcoholic beverages in terms of gallons of ethanol per capita of the drinking-age population. ("Apparent consumption" refers to taxed sales, and so does not include moonshine or other home-production; "gallons of ethanol" allow easy comparability of various kinds of beverages by expressing each in terms of alcohol-per-volume, so that the large overall volume of beer or wine not obscure comparisons with higher-proof spirits; and "drinking age" meant 15 years and over through 1969, but was lowered to 14 and over in 1970.) From the repeal of prohibition in 1934 until about 1970, these figures increased almost every year with respect to beer (including ale, malt liquors, stout, and other brewed drinks), wine, and spirits (distilled beverages) (NIAAA, 1981, p. 17). Although the shift in population-base on which figures were calculated makes it difficult to pinpoint the exact year, the early 1970s saw the end of that long-term rise with respect to spirits, and consumption began to fall in the

1980s, after having briefly stayed on a plateau. Consumption of wine and beer continued to climb slowly, but the mid-1980s have seen a levelling-off of them as well, and, although it is too early to call it a trend, wine-consumption appears also to have begun to decline.

There are many reasons why consumption may have declined, even in the absence of any planning or organization, and it seems likely that individuals have made their choices in this connection on the basis of diverse motivations. In the popular press, much has been made of the pervasive concern with general health that spread through much of the population at that time. Others suggest that the tight labor market prompted those who are concerned about achieving financial success to guard any advantage they may have over others, in effect drinking less to assure that they not lose any competitive edge. Satiety with permissiveness of the 1960s' so-called "Age of Aquarius" is another glib quasi-sociological justification for increasing moderation in terms of sexual activity, dress, haircare, and a number of behaviors as well as drinking. It is also possible that cumulative and increasing educational emphasis on the potential risks of drinking have had some impact. It was in 1970 that Public Law 91-616, the "Comprehensive Alcohol Abuse and Alcoholism Prevention, Treatment and Rehabilitation Act," was passed unanimously by both Houses of Congress, and the National Institute on Alcohol Abuse and Alcoholism (NIAAA) was established within the Department of Health, Education, and Welfare (subsequently: Health and Human Services).

That federal agency provided a new focus and impetus for the study of alcohol use and its outcomes, which had been an underfunded and little recognized enterprise on the part of a small and scattered constituency for only a few decades. NIAAA's involvement rapidly resulted in large-scale funding for research, information-dissemination, and education about alcohol, as well as support for various kinds of prevention and treatment programs with respect to alcoholism and problem drinking. Under its founding director, Morris Chafetz, a major theme was the promotion of "responsible drinking," emphasizing knowledge about ethanol and its effects, decision-making skills, and the ability to withstand adverse social pressures that might prompt one to drink too much (NIAAA, 1971).

The second director, Ernest Noble, explicitly rejected his predecessor's educational approach, declaring "responsible drinking" a vague and inoperable concept. He opted instead to strive to "stabilize per capita consumption" as the best way to ameliorate alcohol-related problems (NIAAA, 1978). The shift from trying to understand ethanol as a natural and pleasurable substance that has been enjoyed in moderation by a majority of the world's population for centuries, to trying to curb it as a dangerous drug, was a major new direction. Under strong influence from Europeans who favor formal institutional mechanisms of control, rather than trusting informal individual and social controls, an increasing number of researchers and policymakers embraced "the control model" of prevention. It calls for a variety of legislative and regulatory restrictions that would make it more difficult for people to get and drink alcohol, and is often contrasted with "the sociocultural model," which favors educating people in ways that would tend to foster moderate drinking, thereby lessening problems in the long run.

Some members of the beverage alcohol industry felt threatened by the official shift toward "the control model," and many scholars and researchers were concerned about what they viewed as an unwarranted and potentially counterproductive change in outlook and emphasis. There was a brief flurry of allusions to "neo-prohibitionists" and "the new prohibitionism" (e.g., Boche 1977), alarmist overstatements that were quickly and easily countered with renewed emphasis by the people so labelled, on the fact that their aim was to curb increases and not necessarily to achieve a decrease in consumption.

During the same period, the United States witnessed a rapid proliferation of groups that called for increasing legislative and regulatory controls on alcohol and its use. Remove Intoxicated Drivers (RID) began in upstate New York in 1979; perhaps more widely known is Mothers against Drunk Drivers (MADD), begun in California in 1980. Unlike some self-help groups that do little beyond providing social support among individuals who feel they share a given problem, these groups speak out strongly for tougher sanctions against drunk-drivers, campaigned vigorously for raising the minimum purchase-age, and support a variety of other measures that they think will significantly diminish the consumption of alcoholic beverages. A young constituency has been enlisted in Students against Driving Drunk (SADD), and various parents' groups (such as National Congress of Parents and Teachers, National Federation of Parents for Drug-Free Youth). The National Council on Alcoholism recently adopted a militantly control-oriented temperance stance. The American Assembly focused on the subject for a year (West, 1984), and a committee within the American Public Health Association has become increasingly outspoken in favor of controls. Many of the publications and lectures by members of various federally funded Alcohol Research Centers around the country, and even those of NIAAA, emphasize increased restrictions on availability as the surest way to prevent alcohol-related problems.

Many of the organizations appear to be grass-roots movements, and are presumably thought to be so by many of their members. Close inspection reveals, however, that elaborate nationwide networks link many of them together, and overlapping directorates suggest that Beauchamp's (1984b) aim of building a major coalition may already have been achieved. It is also noteworthy that such organizations are active in many ways. Their advocacy is not limited to letter-writing, but includes long-term monitoring of court-trials, forceful lobbying among legislators, testifying before Congressional committees, and so forth. Rightly or wrongly, they are credited by many with having played a major role in raising the minimum purchase-age, increasing liquor taxes, pushing for warning-labels, and increasing server-liability.

Like the alcoholism movement of preceding decades, this new temperance movement comprises a loose association of scientists and laypersons, with frequent emphasis on the cachet of academic research lending a different kind of strength to what are basically moral pronouncements and appeals. Although it has not been affiliated with Ralph Nader for several years, Center for Science in the Public Interest enjoys the favorable consumer-protection image that derives from earlier association. Their publications are more pamphlets than scientific papers, but they are widely cited by journalists who treat them as authoritative (e.g., Hacker, Collins & Jacobson, 1987; Jacobson, Hacker & Atkins, 1983). It was CSPI that organized Project SMART, a campaign to *S*top *M*arketing *A*lcohol on *R*adio and *T*elevision, and that got nationwide media attention recently by pointing out that some children could name more brands of beer than they could former presidents.

After the U.S. withdrew its troops from southeast Asia, it became popular to deplore traffic fatalities as a tragic and preventable loss, half of which were "associated with" alcohol. The fallacy of confusing "associated with" and "caused by" has been discussed in critical detail by knowledgeable specialists, but the distinction is ignored, whether wittingly or not, by most who write or talk about traffic safety and/or the need to curtail drinking. A flood of reports appeared to show that alcohol-related traffic deaths had increased disproportionately in those states that had recently lowered the minimum purchase-age; some studies that showed no effect, or the opposite effect, tended to be ignored. No one suggested raising the driving-age to 21, as is the case in many other countries throughout the world, but the concerted application of energy and political know-how were so strong that states began to raise the purchase-age, some abruptly and others incrementally. By 1984, the U.S. Congress virtually mandated 21 as the minimum, and by 1988, Wyoming was the last to comply. This was achieved indirectly, with states' rights being made moot in the face of the threat of withholding federal highway safety funds.

The drive to "get the killer-drunk off the road" has already been insightfully analyzed by sociologist Joseph Gusfield (1981), but it deserves some closer inspection in the context of a new temperance movement. Much of the rhetoric used by those who monitor court-cases and ask for more stringent laws is couched in terms of retribution for harm done to innocent victims. Zealous police departments have repeatedly run afoul of Constitutional guarantees of privacy when they stop cars and check drivers for alcohol, and some polls suggest that a majority of respondents would forego some civil rights in the interest of assuring that wrongdoers be caught and punished. Mandatory jail sentences were invoked as a way of proving the gravity of driving while intoxicated, but few judicial systems could carry such heavy case-loads. Local newspapers often publish lists of those who have been convicted of DWI, although they do so for no other crime, and some even list the names and addresses of those who declined to submit to a test measuring blood-alcohol level. These moves all reflect attempts at branding anyone who drinks and drives as both a criminal and a social pariah, far different from the earlier pattern of permissiveness that often dismissed such "tipsy" behavior as vaguely humorous.

Even during the Reagan administration when most federal taxes were drastically reduced, those on distilled spirits were markedly increased (19% in 1985). Many politicians appear ready to increase further what are often publicly referred to as "sin taxes" (excise levies on alcohol and tobacco), a label that is strongly reminiscent of 19th-century temperance movements. Another measure that is often proposed is to adjust taxes so that they be proportionate to the absolute-alcohol content of each beverage, by raising levies on beer and wine rather than lowering those on spirits.

NIAAA's major push (under Noble) to publicize fetal alcohol syndrome (FAS) succeeded to the point that repeated national polls have found over 80% of respondents aware of the risk that a mother's heavy drinking can pose. Despite that apparently widespread awareness, there was a flurry of activity in 1983 to get localities to require that warning-posters about FAS be posted in all places where alcohol is sold. New York City is one of about a dozen jurisdictions that passed such an ordinance; similar laws have been rejected in many other places.

A related effort has been the push to require warning-labels on all alcoholic beverage containers. Repeatedly proposed at the federal level by Sen. Strom Thurmond since 1967, it repeatedly lost. He most recently called for five labels, to be rotated over time, warning against mental retardation and birth-defects; impaired ability to drive a car or operate machinery; hazards in combination with other drugs; increased risk of hypertension, liver disease or cancer; and possible addiction. Testimony each time included affirmations that such labels would prevent alcohol-related problems by educating users, but no substantive evidence was presented in support of that view. In 1986, Congress called on the Public Health Service to conduct a search of the literature on this controversial subject. The project was contracted to Macro Systems, Inc., and results were promptly published. The empirical finding that there was a total "absence of national experience with warning labels on alcoholic beverages" has been virtually ignored, whereas subsequent conjectures about how "health warning labels *can* have an impact on the consumer *if* . . . " (USDHHS, 1987, p.3) have been construed by many as proof of the value of such warnings. With no fanfare, a limited warning-label provision was included in the Omnibus Drug Act of 1988 (P.L. 100-610: Title VIII), comprising a dual warning from the Surgeon General about possible fetal damage and risk while driving or operating machinery.

Presumably no one believes that a warning-label would deter an alcoholic from continuing to drink, but some believe that it might prevent a young person from starting. Our national experience with tobacco, ladders, cleaning fluids, sugar-substitutes, all-terrain vehicles, and a variety of other products that can be harmful if misused raises doubts about the efficacy of labeling as a risk-prevention strategy, but there appears to be a widespread belief that "it won't do any harm, so why not hope it may do some good." By contrast, a few see this as another form of the traditional scare-tactic that has long proven ineffective in keeping young people from any "forbidden fruit." Presumably a similar logic prompted HHS Secretary Bowen (1987) recently to insist that people in his agency no longer refer to "substance abuse" but pointedly to "alcohol and other drugs."

Another line of evidence that "the new temperance movement" has been successful is the resurrection in recent decades of a variety of long-ignored "dram-shop laws" and consequent proliferation of litigation that holds the server responsible for harm done by an intoxicated individual. Many laypersons were happy enough to see server-liability judgments brought and won against bartenders, restauranteurs, and other commercial servers, but are having second thoughts when it comes to their own liability as hosts at private parties, and so forth.

Court cases are currently pending in the State of Washington, charging that producers and sellers of alcoholic beverages were negligent in not warning consumers of the potential risk to a fetus when a mother drinks. Another case (in Texas) seeks damages because there was not a warning against a young man's consuming liquor so rapidly that he died of alcohol poisoning. The fact that the U.S. has recently been characterized as "litigation-prone" does not in itself account for the large number and variety of unprecedented cases that have a new temperance thrust.

It is evident that a new temperance movement can be discerned in terms of many cultural changes in the United States, regardless of what portion of those changes can be attributed to any organized or self-styled New Temperance Movement. It also deserves to be noted that some analogous changes are underway in many other nations now.

Analogues Throughout the World

Earlier temperance movements in various parts of the world have met with uneven success. "The great Jewish drink mystery" cited by Keller (1970) relates to a shift from the stereotypically drunken behavior of the Canaanites to the stereotypically sober demeanor of Jews, following the establishment of the Second Temple, around 500 B.C. The questions raised about drinking in the Koran have generally been interpreted as constituting a prohibition for Muslims, and, like most religious prohibitions (but unlike most secular ones), it appears to have been generally effective.

Finland, Iceland, and Sweden all experimented with nationwide prohibition around World War I, but all found it unenforceable and went instead to a state monopoly system. One Mexican state had prohibition briefly in the 1920s, and India in the 1940s. Rationing was tried in Scandinavia, and some countries also experimented with restrictions on the strength of alcoholic beverages sold in various areas, hours of sale, numbers of sales outlets, and so forth. None of those control measures appears to have been particularly efficacious in preventing a wide range of alcohol-related problems. In fact, the experience of viticultural peoples around the Mediterranean suggests that teaching children early to drink, using alcohol as an adjunct to food and sociability rather than for psychoactive effect, and treating drinks as a normal part of everyday living may do even more to protect people from developing drinking problems.

A distinctive feature of this new temperance movement is its international quality. To be sure, there are few other nations in the world where someone, like Beauchamp (1984b), has publicly declared himself an adherent and activist in the New Temperance Movement. Nevertheless, there are many people who have gone on record as supporting the same legislative and regulatory changes. A number of such changes have taken place and others have been proposed but not yet enacted. In much of the world, there has been considerable movement in the direction of increasing temperance in recent years. In fact, it may be that the intellectual roots of "the new temperance movement" are at least as deep in Europe as they are in the United States.

According to a sociologist who has paid close attention to what various key people around the world have said and done with respect to alcohol policies throughout this century (Room, 1984), the major redirection of NIAAA's efforts (from "responsible drinking" to "stabilized consumption") was strongly influenced by a book that grew out of collaboration among delegates from Finland, Canada, Denmark, and the United States. That book, *Alcohol Control Policies in Public Health Perspective* (Brunn et al., 1975), served as a milestone in publicizing and lending credence to "the control model" (sometimes called "the single distribution model" or "the distribution of consumption model") as a means of preventing alcohol-related problems (Schmidt & Popham, 1978). Based on Ledermann's (1956) superficial transnational sampling, it is asserted that the distribution of consumption of alcoholic beverages in any population follows a lognormal distribution, so that any change in the mean will change the overall curve. Reducing average consumption, therefore, reduces virtually everyone's consumption. Linked with this is the premise that level of consumption is in virtually direct proportion to the incidence of various alcohol-related problems. The wording in the original is by no means so straightforward: ". . . changes in the overall consumption of alcoholic beverages have a bearing on the health of the people in any society. Alcohol control measures can be used to limit consumption: thus control of alcohol availability becomes a public health issue" (Bruun et al., 1975, p. 90). Although what "bearing" such changes have on health is not explicitly stated, the examples cited throughout the text are all couched in terms that imply that more drinking means more problems, and that less drinking means fewer problems.

However nuanced the writings of social scientists may have been in the original context (Room, 1988), the message received by policymakers and administrators was unambiguous. For example, the

Director General of WHO asserted unequivocally that "any reduction in per capita consumption will be attended by a significant decrease in alcohol related problems" (WHO, 1978, p. 4). Such a viewpoint may seem eminently logical, but it has often been challenged theoretically (deLint, 1988; Parker & Harman, 1978), and also contradicted by substantive evidence when researchers have paid attention to patterns over time (e.g., Peele, 1987; Mulford & Fitzgerald, 1986).

It is common enough for individual countries to undergo a sporadic ebb and flow of legal and regulatory controls on alcohol, but the 1970s and 80s have seen widespread tightening of policies, and a coordinated effort to foster restrictions even among nations where little thought had been given to them before. The World Health Organization of the United Nations has played an active role, by recommending the widespread adoption of a variety of measures that are collectively aimed at reducing alcohol consumption: significantly raising excise taxes on all kinds of alcoholic drinks, indexing prices to rise with inflation, raising minimum purchase-age, curtailing hours of sale, limiting places of sale, restricting or banning advertisements, and so forth (Grant, 1985; Moser, 1985).

Such recommendations are carefully phrased to emphasize that significant cultural differences are recognized, and that responsible persons should always feel free to choose among alternatives those that would be most appropriate to their own context. However, it is striking that legislative and regulatory controls are consistently favored whereas alternatives such as informal social controls are downplayed. Education is usually mentioned, but either negatively, with the implication that it is unlikely to be helpful in diminishing problems, or so summarily that an unsophisticated reader would have no reason to expect that it had any potential value.

Another striking feature of WHO's promotion of increasing legislative and regulatory controls is the extent to which it is couched in terms that many construe as scientific, but that often fall short of the criteria that are generally accepted among the international community of scientists (deLint, 1988). One example is the reliance on a so-called "consensus document" which purported to convey the conclusions of an international and multidisciplinary conference on alcohol use in Latin America, but that instead reiterated a litany of presumptions and truisms, some of which had never even been addressed during the conference (see Heath, 1988a,b; Levine, 1982,1984; and Selowsky, 1982). Another example is the volume in which the editor's control-oriented conclusions fit with only half of the case-studies that were reported in detail in the body of the book, but are contradicted by the other half of the same book (Grant, 1985).

Alcohol Control Policies . . . (Bruun et al., 1975) was only the first in a series of activities that underscored the same theme. A direct outgrowth of it was the International Study of Alcohol Control Experiences, a joint effort of the Addiction Research Foundation (of Ontario, Canada), Alcohol Research Group (of Berkeley, California), and the Finnish Foundation of Alcohol Studies, funded by NIAAA in cooperation with the World Health Organization. In seven Western nations, they traced changes in alcohol control policies (Mäkelä et al., 1981; Single et al., 1981).

> Between different cultures, we found considerable differences in the level of problems of any given kind that are attached to a given level of consumption. Even in a given cultural setting, the relationship between consumption and problems is by no means a simple one. (Mäkelä et al., 1981, p. 109)

Despite that equivocal conclusion, they affirmed in the very next sentence, "One of the basic findings of our study, however, is that the growth in alcohol consumption was accompanied by an increase in a broad variety of problems related to drinking" (Mäkelä et al., 1981, p. 109). A major review of the successes and shortcomings of various alcohol policies in dozens of countries does not support that generalization (Heath, 1989).

Using funds that came largely from the United States (through NIAAA), WHO conducted a multinational study of "Community Responses to Alcohol-Related Problems" (in Canada, Mexico, Scotland, USA, and Zambia), from 1976 to 1983. Some interesting insights have been gained concerning cultural variations in drinking patterns, attitudes toward alcohol, and the outcomes of drinking (e.g., Rootman & Moser, 1985), and several papers have appeared dealing with various aspects of alcohol in the participating countries. But the data collected by questionnaire-surveys virtually defy systematic analysis or comparison (Roizen, 1982), so the project has shed little light concerning correlates of consumption and other variables on the one hand, and drinking problems on the other.

The first country to mandate health warning-labels on alcoholic beverage containers was Mexico. A few countries have banned the advertising of alcoholic beverages on television, and many are considering broader or more limited bans. In Costa Rica, each ad must be approved by a review committee before it appears. Scandinavian countries have resumed an earlier pattern of experimenting with limiting hours of sale, and some areas of Oceania have instituted "local options," whereby individual communities may vote to be dry.

Even France, long the world's leader in per capita consumption has significantly reduced wine-drinking. In the Soviet Union, in an early experiment by Chairman Gorbachev, a number of restrictions were set in 1985, including penalties for absenteeism or for drinking during work-hours, sharp curtailment of production and sale of vodka, the closing of beer- and wine-bars, a ban on sales before 2 p.m. even in restaurants, among others. After three years of criticism, shortages of sugar (which are generally attributed to the increasingly popular home-distillation of *samogon*), and lost revenues, the Central Committee recently reversed many of those restrictions. If there is any country in which "the control model" might have been expected to work, the U.S.S.R. is one, but leaders there now admit that the restrictions caused more problems than they solved, and they are turning to education in the hope of changing the social norms that are *in*formal controls on behavior, as the most promising way of diminishing problems.

IMPLICATIONS

It is apparent that the New Temperance Movement is alive and active in the United States, and that at least a new temperance movement can be discerned in terms of recent changes that are occurring in many other parts of the world. Alcohol was widely viewed in the 1960s as something to be enjoyed, but during the 1970s it became something to be used in moderation, and during the

1980s it is increasingly characterized as something not to be used at all. Young people are exhorted to "Just Say No," and women, unsure about when they might be pregnant, are warned against drinking which could result in birth-defects. Increasing spot-checks on highways and drug-testing in the workplace are clear warnings that large categories of adults should not drink during significant portions of their daily round.

Public policy recommendations often emphasize the need for more stringent external controls on the availability of alcoholic beverages, rather than the value of developing internal controls whereby individual drinkers moderate their behavior and its outcomes.

The early findings by Cahalan and Room (1974) to the effect that many individuals drop in and out of the "problem drinker" category at various times has been replicated by many other researchers, notably Vaillant (1983); the literature on this topic was recently reviewed by Sadava (1985). At the societal level of analysis, the contrast between Irish (many abstainers but also many problems) and Jews (few abstainers and few problems) is well known (Bales, 1946). The case of the Bolivian Camba is especially salient, with the heaviest drinking population in the world virtually free of all of the problems that are usually associated with alcohol (Heath, 1958, 1965).

If Stein's imaginative psychoanalytic interpretation of alcohol as a metaphor is correct, then those who are associated with it make good scapegoats. The "bad" of society is siphoned off and vested in them "as containers for that badness." They then become like enemies, who can be "sacrificed to get rid of feelings of badness, guilt, and shame," thereby restoring to the surviving members of society their "feelings of well-being and order" (Stein, 1982).

The widespread call for increasing legislative and regulatory controls implies a correlative distrust of the individual and of one's ability appropriately to control his or her own behavior. Viewed in that light, "the new temperance movement" may be, among other things, a newly acceptable way of reacting to a world in which one feels unsure and vaguely threatened, symbolically shaking one's fist and invoking "law and order." Adherents to the New Temperance Movement may be less Neo-Prohibitionists than they are Neo-

Victorians. It remains to be seen whether this phenomenon, in combination with what some might see as merely a faddish fascination with Victorian dress, architecture, and other appurtenances, presages a major return of other values and aspects of culture that characterized that peculiar and restrictive interlude in history. If so, we may all feel, like Alice, as if we've passed to the other side of the looking-glass.

REFERENCES

Aaron, P. & Musto, D. (1981). Temperance and prohibition in America: an historical overview. In M.H. Moore & D.R. Gerstein (Eds.), *Alcohol and public policy: beyond the shadow of prohibition* (pp. 127-181). Washington: National Academy Press.

Bales, R.F. (1946). Cultural differences in rates of alcoholism. *Quarterly Journal of Studies on Alcohol*, *6*, 480-499.

Beauchamp, D.E. (1984a). Dilemmas in forging a national health policy. In H.D. Holder & J.B. Hallan (Eds.), *Control issues in alcohol abuse prevention: local, state and national designs for the '80s* (pp. 7-21). Charleston: Conference on Control Issues in Alcohol Abuse Prevention.

Beauchamp, D.E. (1984b). Keynote address to annual Conference on Control Issues in Alcohol Abuse Prevention, New York.

Berger, P.L., & Luckmann, T. (1966). *The social construction of reality: a treatise in the sociology of knowledge*. New York: Doubleday.

Boche, L. (1977). Presidential address to annual meeting of Alcohol and Drug Problems Association, Detroit.

Bowen, O.R. (1987). Remarks to National Conference on Alcohol Abuse and Alcoholism, Washington.

Bruun, K., Edwards, G., Lummio, M., Mäkelä, K., Pan, L., Popham, R.E., Room, R., Schmidt, W., Skog, O-J., Sulkunen, P., & Osterberg, E. (1975). *Alcohol control policies in public health perspective*. Helsinki: Finnish Foundation for Alcohol Studies.

Cahalan, D., & Room, R. (1974). *Problem drinking among American men*. New Brunswick, NJ: Rutgers Center of Alcohol Studies.

Danovitch, S. (1984). The New Temperance Movement: Americans set ground rules for drinking. *Policy Review*, *28*, 58-63.

de Lint, J. (1988). Alcohol data in longitudinal research. *Themes in Alcohol and Drug Problems*, *1*, 18-32.

Giesbrecht, N., Cahannes, M., Moskalevicz, J., Osterberg, E., & Room, R. (Eds.) (1983). *Consequences of drinking trends in alcohol problem statistics in seven countries*. Toronto: Addiction Research Foundation.

Grant, M. (Ed.) (1985). *Alcohol policies*. Copenhagen: World Health Organization European Regional Office.

Gusfield, J.R. (1963). *Symbolic crusade: status politics and the American temperance movement*. Urbana: University of Illinois Press.

Gusfield, J.R. (1981). *The culture of public problems: drinking-driving and the symbolic order*. Chicago: University of Chicago Press.

Hacker, G., Collins, R., & Jacobson, M. (1987). *Selling booze to Blacks*. Washington: Center for Science in the Public Interest.

Heath, D.B. (1958). Drinking patterns of the Bolivian Camba. *Quarterly Journal of Studies on Alcohol*, *19*, 491-508.

Heath, D.B. (1965). Comments on David Mandelbaum's "Alcohol and culture." *Current Anthropology*, *6*, 289-290.

Heath, D.B. (1983). Alcohol use among North American Indians: a cross-cultural study of patterns and problems. In R.G. Smart, F.B. Glasser, Y. Israel, H. Kalant, R. Popham, & W. Schmidt (Eds.), *Research advances in drug and alcohol problems, vol. 7* (pp. 343-396). New York: Plenum Press.

Heath, D.B. (Ed.) (1986). *Mourt's relation: a journal of the Pilgrims at Plymouth*. Cambridge, MA: Applewood Books.

Heath, D.B. (1988a). Alcohol control policies and drinking patterns: an international game of politics against science. *Journal of Substance Abuse*, *1*, 109-115.

Heath, D.B. (1988b). Quasi-science and public policy: a reply to Robin Room about details and misrepresentations in science. *Journal of Substance Abuse*, *1*, 121-125.

Heath, D.B. (1989). *International handbook of alcohol policies* (2 vols.). Westport, CT: Greenwood Press.

Jacobson, M., Hacker, G., & Atkins, R. (1983). *The booze merchants: the inebriating of America*. Washington: Center for Science in the Public Interest.

Keller, M. (1970). The great Jewish drink mystery. *British Journal of Addiction*, *64*, 287-296.

Keller, M. (1976). Problems with alcohol: an historical perspective. In W.J. Filstead, J.J. Rossi, & M. Keller (Eds.), *Alcohol and alcohol problems: new thinking and new directions* (pp. 5-28). Cambridge, MA: Ballinger.

Ledermann, S. (1956). *Alcool, alcoolisme, alcoolisation: donées scientifiques de caractére physiologique, economique et social*. Travaux et documents de l'Institut d'Etudes Démographique 29. Paris: Institut d'Etudes Démographique.

Lender, M.E., & Martin, J.K. (1986). *Drinking in America: a social-historical explanation, 1620-1980* (rev. ed.). New York: Free Press.

Levine, H.G. (1982). Alternative non-consensus view. In Institute of Medicine, *Legislative approaches to prevention of alcohol-related problems* (pp. 279-281). Washington: National Academy Press.

Levine, H.G. (1984). What is an alcohol-related problem? (Or what are people talking about when they refer to alcohol problems?) *Journal of Drug issues*, *14*, 45-60.

Mäkelä, K., Room, R., Single, E., Sulkunen, P., & Walsh, B. (1981). *Alcohol, society and the state: vol. 1, a comparative study of alcohol control*. Toronto: Addiction Research Foundation.

Mather, I. (1673). *Wo to drunkards: two sermons testifying against the sin of drunkenness. . . .* Cambridge, MA: Marmaduke Johnson.

Moser, J. (1985). *Alcohol policies in national health and development planning.* WHO Offset Publication No. 89. Geneva: World Health Organization.

Mulford, H.A., & Fitzgerald, J.L. (1986). Per-capita alcohol sales, heavy drinker prevalence and alcohol problems in Iowa for 1958-1985. *British Journal of Addiction, 83*, 265-268.

Musto, D.F. (1984, Jun. 25). New temperance vs. neo-prohibition. *The Wall Street Journal.*

National Institute on Alcohol Abuse and Alcoholism (1971). *Alcohol and health: first special report to the U.S. Congress.* DHEW Publication No. HSM 73-9031. Rockville, MD: National Institute on Alcohol Abuse and Alcoholism.

National Institute on Alcohol Abuse and Alcoholism (1978). *Alcohol and health: third special report to the U.S. Congress.* DHEW Publication No. ADM 78-569. Rockville, MD: National Institute on Alcohol Abuse and Alcoholism.

National Institute on Alcohol Abuse and Alcoholism (1981). *Alcohol and health: fourth special report to the U.S. Congress.* DHHS Publication No. ADM 81-1080. Rockville, MD: National Institute on Alcohol Abuse and Alcoholism.

Parker, D.A., & Harman, M.S. (1978). The distribution of consumption model of prevention of alcohol problems: a critical assessment. *Journal of Studies on Alcohol, 39*, 377-399.

Peele, S. (1987). The limitations of control-of-supply models for explaining and preventing alcoholism and drug addiction. *Journal of Studies on Alcohol, 48*, 61-77.

Roizen, R. (1982). *The World Health Organization study of community responses to alcohol-related problems: a review of cross-cultural findings.* Alcohol Research Group Report No. C36. Berkeley, CA: Alcohol Research Group.

Room, R. (1984). Alcohol control and public health. *Annual Review of Public Health, 5*, 293-317.

Room, R. (1988). Science is in the details: towards a nuanced view of alcohol control studies. *Journal of Substance Abuse, 1*, 117-120.

Rootman, I., & Moser, J. (1985). *Community response to alcohol-related problems.* DHHS Publication No. ADM 85-1371. Rockville, MD: National Institute on Alcohol Abuse and Alcoholism.

Rorabaugh, W.J. (1979). *The alcoholic republic: an American tradition.* New York: Oxford University Press.

Sadava, S.W. (1985). Problem behavior theory and consumption and consequences of alcohol use. *Journal of Studies on Alcohol, 46*, 392-397.

Schmidt, W., & Popham, R.E. (1978). The single distribution theory of alcohol consumption: a rejoinder to the critique of Parker and Harman. *Journal of Studies on Alcohol, 39*, 400-419.

Selowsky, M. (1982). Alternative non-consensus view. In Institute of Medicine, *Legislative approaches to prevention of alcohol-related problems* (pp. 281-282). Washington: National Academy Press.

Single, E., Morgan, P., & de Lint, J. (1981). *Alcohol and the state: vol. 2, the social history of control policies in seven countries*. Toronto: Addiction Research Foundation.

Social History of Alcohol Review: Journal of the Alcohol and Temperance History Group. (1985-). (Formerly: *Alcohol in History: A Multidisciplinary Newsletter*, and *Alcohol and Temperance History News*.)

Stein, H. (1982). Ethanol and its discontents: paradoxes of inebriation and sobriety in American culture. *Journal of Psychoanalytic Anthropology*, *5*, 355-377.

United States, Department of Health and Human Services (1987). *Review of the research literature on the effects of health warning labels: a report to the U.S. Congress*. Washington: U.S. Government Printing Office.

Vaillant, G.E. (1983). *The natural history of alcoholism: causes, patterns and paths to recovery*. Cambridge, MA: Harvard University Press.

Westermeyer, J.J. (1974). The "drunken Indian": myths and realities. *Psychiatric Annuals*, *4*, 29 et ff.

World Health Organization (1978, Nov. 27). *Alcohol-related problems: the need to develop further the WHO Initiative*. Report by the Director-General, Executive Board, Sixty-third Session, Provisional Agenda Item 23, Attachment E. Geneva: World Health Organization.

Public Policy on Alcohol and Illicit Drugs

Don Cahalan, PhD

"Public policy" can have several meanings. It can mean the established laws or regulations concerning an issue, or it can mean the popular consensus on an issue, or it can mean the rules or principles which *ought* to prevail in an ideal world. This ambiguity is well-suited to issues concerning alcohol and other mood-altering drugs because of popular ambivalence about their use and control. On the one hand, drugs are much in demand because they are so immediately reinforcing in generating euphoria or blotting out pain and anxiety. On the other hand, their use results in heavy costs for treatment of addiction and in mortality, reduced productivity and lost employment, accidents, crime, and remedial welfare programs, estimated at more than $116 billion dollars for alcohol and about 60 billion dollars for other mood-altering drugs for 1983 (Harwood and others, 1984, p. G-16). While social and economic damage due to excessive use of alcohol has been a prominent public issue during much of our nation's history, and heavy criminal penalties apply for any use of most of the other mood-altering drugs, and while hundreds of millions of dollars have been spent within the last generation on treatment of alcoholism and billions are now being spent to combat the sale and use of other drugs, there are proportionately even more alcoholics now than a generation ago; and many authorities are lamenting that we are losing the war on drugs.

Clearly, there must be something wrong with either our public

Don Cahalan is Professor Emeritus, School of Public Health, University of California at Berkeley, Berkeley, CA.

Mailing address: Don Cahalan, 1338 Grizzly Peak Boulevard, Berkeley, CA 94708.

policies or the ways in which we apply them to alcohol and drug problems. Exactly what is wrong; and what if anything can be done about it?

Researchers always take risks when they depart from their role of describing human behavior to venture opinions on what public policy *should* be. In a recent paper, Heath (1988) warns against scientists' going overboard in advocating policies on the basis of insufficient and biased information. In a rejoinder, Room (1988) agrees, but contends that his own main contribution to the prevention policy debate has been to try to open up the scope of discussion of strategies for the prevention of alcohol problems without necessarily endorsing any specific strategy. In the following paper, I have tried to discuss public policy on alcohol and illicit drugs in ways congruent with the available scientific evidence; but, like Eric Single (1987), I maintain that researchers who have accumulated an intimate knowledge of the pros and cons of a controversial field should not be denied the right to express opinions on which policies and practices are most likely to be effective. Thus, at the risk of inaccurately being given the invidious label of "neo-prohibitionist" in describing some of the major public policy issues on alcohol and illicit drugs, I will occasionally express opinions on which policies and practices are most likely to work in the future.

ILLICIT DRUG ISSUES

As regards illicit drugs, Congress and the federal administration currently are vying with each other to pass even harsher punishments for selling or using drugs (including mandatory death penalties for drug-connected murders) and billions more to try to stop the flow of drugs into the country. However, many authorities are convinced that the flow of drugs will not be diminished unless more is done to reduce the demand for such drugs; and some observers believe that the problem of illicit drugs will become much worse—especially in ghetto areas—if more is not done immediately to deal with the root causes of illicit addictions. One writer, in a *New York Times* article (Kerr, 1988), featured the views of Prof. David Musto of Yale that there are essentially two drug problems—one in middle-class America which may be waning after a 20-year mass experiment with illegal drugs, and the other among the poor. Musto is quoted as saying,

> The question we must be asking now is not why people take drugs, but why do people stop. In the inner city, the factors that counterbalance drug use—family, employment, status within the community—often are not there. It is harder for people with nothing to say no to drugs.

Other points in Kerr's article about the vulnerability of the poor to addictions cited additional authorities' views on these points:

With the exception of heroin and the crack form of cocaine among the poor, the use of illegal drugs appears to have peaked. Crack's recent rise has had devastating effects on poor neighborhoods, but not in middle-class areas. "The most deadly impact of illegal drug use is probably yet to come, as tens of thousands of intravenous drug users, their sexual partners and their children contract acquired immune deficiency syndrome. Most of those people will be poor," (Kerr, 1988). Several drug experts voiced concern to Kerr that since the casualties of drug use are coming increasingly from the ghetto, the drug issue will become less visible and will therefore receive less governmental attention.

Readers of our leading metropolitan newspapers regularly see stories of how crack cocaine has become a particular menace in urban ghettos. There youthful gangs trade openly in crack, which has become the major glue holding such gangs together. Dealing in crack has become one of the quickest and easiest routes to local fame and fortune for school dropouts. It is far easier to carry around a thousand dollars in crack in one's pocket to peddle than it was to conceal a hundred dollars' worth of bootleg booze in prohibition days. Even children of eight to ten years old can make several hundred dollars a day by serving as lookouts for crack-dealing gangs. Competition between rival gangs for the crack market and meting out penalties to police informers or those welshing on payments has escalated in some cities to gun wars which have killed scores of innocent bystanders. A fair number of ghetto citizens who have protested neighborhood crack dealing have been killed or injured or have had their homes torched. At the moment the police in several major cities admit that they are unable to keep crack-related crime under control, when roving crack-high gangs even are shooting passing bus drivers because they are wearing blue uniforms like the police.

Musto's book, *The American Disease* (1987) reminds us that the waves of alternating heavier and lesser use of drugs throughout our history are especially true of cocaine. There was a wave of fairly heavy use of it 75 years ago, and then usage dropped off after the passage of the Harrison Act of 1914. Musto is quoted in a *Washington Post* column (Raspberry, 1988) as seeing any number of parallels between the earlier epidemic and the situation today, especially the perception that cocaine abuse is an uniquely black disease. Musto is reported as contending that the middle-class is the first to pick up an addictive drug and the first to lay it down. While he is optimistic that the tide of middle-class opinion is turning nationally against cocaine, he concedes that negative attitudes toward the drug are now being turned against the users among the poor, to the point that ". . . instead of doing the things that might really turn the users around—increasing their educational and economic opportunities, for instance—we tend to turn toward stricter sanctions."

Musto was optimistic about our being able to control cocaine:

> . . . the main thing is that there is no reason for the pessimism that has taken hold, unless you expect to beat this thing by the next election. The thing to remember, though it may take a few years, is that we did beat this problem before, and we can do it again.

However, in a subsequent discussion in New Haven (personal communication, August 19, 1988), he agreed with me that the crack situation in our major cities may be much harder to deal with than past drug situations because the crack trade is becoming more and more a self-sustaining closed circle enmeshing more and more ghetto youth, serving as it does as a short-term antidote to failure and despair while it is also a means of upward mobility within the peer group and an enforcer of gang solidarity. We agreed that one probably effective way to deal with the crack problem in inner cities is through peer group sanctions and reinforcements, probably through organizations such as the Nations of Islam (Black Muslims) and the Guardian Angels, which patrol drug-ridden areas and help to organize both youths and adults to develop a different way of life. However, we agreed that unless city, county, state, and federal governments become willing to expend vast amounts of money over many years in job training and expanding employment opportunities in the inner cities, the crack trade will continue to be the employer of last resort. As it stands, a year and a half after President Reagan signed a bill he termed a "major victory" in the war on drugs, local governments had spent only 42 per cent of the more than half a billion dollars in block grants designated for curbing narcotic use, evidently because of turf wars between local jurisdictions as well as difficulty in deciding what programs might work (*San Francisco Chronicle*, 1988).

Certainly the imposition of harsher and harsher penalties is no more likely to diminish the illicit drug trade in the future than it has in the past, because already there are too few jail cells to hold those arrested for dealing or using. For example, the Alameda County juvenile justice system has been crippled by a 2,200 per cent increase in juvenile drug cases in the last four years (*San Francisco Examiner*, 1988). Those who are caught up in the trade stay in it because they see no hope outside it. In response to this reality, there has been a wave of recent agitation to legalize all drugs on the grounds that if they were legal and readily available, prices would drop and the druglords would no longer find the business profitable. Yet if our experiences with slack control over the advertising and marketing of alcohol and tobacco are any criterion, legalization of traffic in drugs ultimately would result in heavy commercial pressure on the part of the drug industry to move such profitable goods through retail channels.

Thus it appears that the programs most likely to result in diminished drug use through all segments of the population would have to hold forth the promise of fairly immediate reinforcement of drug-free behavior through access to training and apprenticeship in decent jobs, as well as *realistic* avenues to better health and better family life. The current "Just Say No" campaigns may make politicians and middle-class dowagers think they are accomplishing something, but they are no more likely to be effective in eliminating deep-seated drug habits in the future than they have been in the past.

ALCOHOLISM PREVENTION PROGRAMS

Alcohol and other mood-altering drugs vary in their addictiveness, but most of them are highly addictive because of their capability to increase the user's self-esteem and to drown out pain and sorrow temporarily. Getting users to stop using such reinforcing drugs or to reduce their consumption is very difficult and expensive once the habit has become firmly established (Cahalan, 1988). Thus *prevention* of heavy or otherwise potentially harmful consumption is the only real solution in the long run.

However, many obstacles to cooperation in prevention programs have prevailed within the American culture for many generations. One is the strong individualism of the average citizen, which helped to conquer our frontiers but which get in the way of going along with more stringent controls on handguns, fireworks, pollution, heavy drinking, and illicit drug use. In keeping with the life-style of our relatively new country is our optimism that we can find simplistic, quick solutions to deep-seated problems, with consequent disillusionment when immediate results are not forthcoming from new programs. Another problem is the politicians' passage of toothless or impractical laws for the purpose of looking good or to avoid the application of constraints which would offend the campaign-contributing alcohol industry. Further, social controls over excessive use of alcohol and drugs have been weakened within the last generation because of the decline of parental and religious influence and increases in geographical and cultural mobility.

In order to understand how to cope with alcohol and drug problems, we must get away from our nation's primary emphasis upon the individual's behavior, and recognize, in our research and action programs, that social problems require two levels of analysis other than that of the individual – the structural or general environmental level, and the situational or immediate environmental level (Pettigrew, 1988, p. 209). Many authorities are now beginning to recognize that in order to prevent or to change deep-seated addictive behaviors, in the long run the general environment (at home, at work, and in public) must become less supportive of such addictions, and in the short run the individual's risk of becoming or remaining addicted must be reduced by increasing realistic types of incentives for remaining drug-free and reducing the opportunities and incentives for addictive behavior. Otherwise, as Wallack has said (1984, p. 79), people will continue to fall into the river of addiction faster than we can pull them out and rehabilitate them through expensive or draconian temporizing measures.

Fundamental changes in the way preventive and treatment services are organized and reinforced must take place before the present level of alcohol and illicit drug problems can be reduced materially:

> As regards alcohol problems, while the widespread adoption of the disease model of addiction has had beneficial effects since the 1960s in that many more chronic alcoholics have been getting more humane treatment, it has put the medical profession in the driver's seat even though the profession has not been noteworthy for expertise or incentives to develop effective programs for primary prevention of addictions. Because of the high prestige of the medical profession in dealing with disease and disabilities, and the general public's overoptimism that the profession could find magic cures for alcoholism, most of the money and other resources that have been poured into alcohol programs since the 1960s have gone into treatment rather than prevention. As soon as the treatment funding mechanisms became established, the treatment fraternity adapted to optimize their financial and power rewards. Increasing numbers of physicians have become specialists in treating alcoholism. Hospitals have learned that they can keep more of their hospital beds full if they emphasize expensive inpatient alcoholism treatment. Biomedical laboratories emphasizing the medical aspects of alcoholism have drawn the lion's share of available research funds. (Cahalan, 1988)

As medical treatment of alcoholism became more and more expensive, there arose more of a demand for prepaid or insured treatment of alcoholism; and corporate America found it had to get on the medical-treatment bandwagon through employee assistance programs. Insurance companies in turn were induced to provide coverage almost exclusively for medically-administered programs because they were less likely to be criticized or sued if they chose to put the responsibility for treatment on the prestigious medical profession. Thus we have seen the spiraling of the costs of alcoholism treatment through an emphasis on expensive 28-day in-patient treatments even though (as discussed later) longer-term (but less expensive) outpatient programs have been found more effective in many instances.

Thus throughout the 20 years since the National Institute on Alcohol Abuse and Alcoholism was founded, virtually all the incentives have operated to reward expensive treatment programs and to discourage effective primary prevention programs. The brutal fact is that professional people can make money out of relatively ineffective treatment programs, but it is hard to make a profitable career out of primary prevention programs.

As discussed in detail in Chapters 5, 6, and 9-11 of my 1987 book, primary prevention must get the cooperation of several major power groups or they will not cooperate.

To be supportive of preventive efforts, the general public must get enough short-term benefits and must not have to put up with too many harassing constraints. Governmental administrators and congressmen must be induced to push for adequate legislation and sufficient budgets, most difficult because of intensive lobbying and campaign contributions on the part of the alcohol beverage industry. Means must be found to reward the treatment industry sufficiently for cooperating in prevention programs designed to reduce the need for expensive treatment programs for far-gone alcoholics and other addicts. The print and broadcast media should be provided with incentives to cooperate in remedial public education and information programs in ways which offset their loss of advertising revenue from the alcohol and tobacco industries. And the alcohol industry itself might well be induced, through tax reductions or other financial incentives, to cooperate with restraints on production and marketing.

For some years after the repeal of prohibition, alcohol marketing and advertising was relatively low-key, being limited primarily to announcements of availability and assurances of product quality. However, after years of intensive lobbying and popular demand for relaxation of state controls, alcohol marketing evolved into a multi-billion-dollar operation, with alcoholic beverages being pushed on the basis of sex appeal, macho sports, and appeals to under-age potential consumers and special market segments such as minority groups and women.

The story of the post-prohibition burgeoning of the alcohol beverage industry and the case for introducing more restraints on alcohol marketing have been set forth dramatically in *The Booze Merchants* (Jacobson, Hacker, and Atkins, 1983) and *Alcohol and Public Policy: Beyond the Shadow of Prohibition* (Moore and Gerstein, eds., 1981) and many other publications. The general consensus which appears to be emerging among public health and welfare specialists as to potentially helpful constraints on alcohol marketing and conditions of service is well-summarized in a compilation by Mosher and Jernigan (forthcoming 1989). In it they advance the public health case for increased controls over alcohol occasioned by conceptual shifts in public health thinking in the last twenty years, as discussed by Room (1984), especially the change in focus from "alcoholism" (with its emphasis on disease rather than behavioral factors) to "alcohol-related problems" and increased knowledge on the adverse health consequences of alcohol use. They go on to discuss the potential merits of the following controls over alcohol:

Tax policies. Alcohol prices have fallen 28 per cent relative to inflation since 1967; and the authors advance arguments that this trend is contrary to public health goals, as are tax deductions for business purposes. They advance arguments that a rise in alcohol taxes might be expected to lower the general levels of alcohol consumption and of drinking problems.

Alcohol advertising and other promotional practices. They cite research showing that the multibillion-dollar promotional efforts of the alcohol industry is deceptive, is being directed toward high-risk groups, and is promoting denial of problems. Arguments are advanced for constraints on false or misleading advertising.

Availability of alcohol. Research is cited which shows a direct link between the physical availability of alcohol and the level of alcohol problems. The authors recommend that local communities should be encouraged to develop regulations on hours and conditions of availability and alcohol service so as to reduce the risk of drunken driving and alcohol-related accidents.

Special protections for young people. The authors make the case that minimum age driving laws reduce alcohol-related accidents among young people, and that efforts should be exerted to regulate industry promotional campaigns directed toward under-age students on college campuses.

Other institutional targets for prevention cited by Mosher and Jernigan include corporations, the military, educational and medical institutions, professional sports, the insurance industry, and private foundations—particularly as regards the development of needed employee assistance programs to help those with alcohol problems, and toning down practices in the organizational environment that may foster heavy drinking (such as "happy hour" incentives for heavier drinking or the charging off of alcohol as a business expense).

The alcohol industry has mounted a vigorous campaign against such constraints on alcohol marketing (Distilled Spirits Council of the United States, 1985). In the light of their lobbying and campaign contributions to potentially sympathetic state and national legislators, it may be a long time before there are any notable increases in controls. However, the successful campaign waged by Mothers Against Drunk Driving and their friends to raise the national minimum drinking age to 21 (Cahalan, 1987a, 78-80) does illustrate how well-funded legislative lobbying campaigns by strong-willed pro-control groups may be able to prevail in the long run. But again, considering the backlash occasioned by national prohibition, any attempts at strengthening controls over alcohol marketing and conditions of service must get the long-term cooperation of not only legislators but the media, state and federal administrators, the courts, and the general public if they are to be successful over the long run.

ISSUES CONCERNING ALCOHOLISM TREATMENT

The disease concept of alcoholism has been getting the primary emphasis since the 1940s, and the vast majority of Americans now agree that alcoholism is a disease. One recent Gallup Poll found that 60 per cent labeled it a disease or illness, although 31 per cent termed it a mental problem, 23 per cent blamed lack of will power, and 16 per cent a moral weakness (George and Alex Gallup, 1988, p. A 8). While many writers, notably Fingarette (1988), have criticized the disease concept as being counterproductive in that it does not fit many types of destructive drinking, the disease model has persisted widely because, by reducing alcoholics' feelings of guilt, it has helped to bring many alcoholics in for treatment who might otherwise have been neglected, and also because the medical profession—whose stock-in-trade is treating diseases—has been put in primary charge of alcoholism treatment. The issue of whether to continue to treat alcoholics exclusively under the disease model or whether to rely more on the primarily nonmedical reinforcement model, continues to be a most controversial one. However, some of the current writings of recognized authorities on alcoholism treatment indicates that there is a growing desire to set this ancient controversy aside for the sake of amity in following a pragmatic course of accepting as legitimate *any* treatment which seems to work with a substantial number of problem drinkers.

In my discussion of "How Well Do Alcohol Treatment Programs Work?" (Cahalan, 1987a, Chapt. 7), I note that most run-of-the-mill alcoholism treatment programs in America are quite similar, first entailing a few days of medical detoxification and then turning the patient over to primarily nonmedical personnel, especially Alcoholics Anonymous, for counseling and moral support. As Miller (1986) has pointed out, most alcoholism treatment in America entails the following assumptions, *none* of which has been proved: that alcoholism is an irreversible disease; that the only hope for an alcoholic is total and permanent abstinence; and that the most effective treatment is through AA, although other group therapy and the use of disulfiram (Antabuse) are also assumed to be helpful. In a more recent paper offered in testimony to the U.S. Senate Committee on Governmental affairs, Miller (1988) says that his extensive review of treatment effectiveness shows that there is no one outstandingly effective treatment, although some work better than others—particularly those emphasizing: advice with feedback intervention, community reinforcement of sobriety, marital behavioral therapy, self-control training, and training in social skills and stress management. It will be noted that all of these more effective therapies entail personal interaction between the client and therapists or change-agents in which the client is required to take an active role in his own improvement, rather than passively relying on medical treatment or exhortations by authority figures.

As to the effectiveness of treatments in hospital settings, Miller says (1988, p. 6),

> . . . This question has been addressed in 20 controlled studies. In the typical study, alcoholics who would otherwise have been eligible for inpatient admission were assigned at random to be treated in residential versus nonresidential settings. Other studies have compared the effectiveness of longer versus shorter residential stays, again with random assignment. The findings of these studies have been strikingly consistent. Of 20 studies, 19 found no overall advantage for residential over nonresidential treatment, or for longer versus shorter residential stays. That is, *all else being equal*, the success rate of a treatment program does not appear to be increased by making it longer or offering it within a residential setting.

Closer scrutiny should be given to abuse of alcoholism treatment programs through conflicts of interest, not only outright fraud—such as financial kickbacks to alcohol or drug agency personnel in order to get referrals of alcoholics to one's clinic (Dalen, undated)—but also through the temptation to assign alcoholics to the most costly treatments allowable under current insurance coverage plans. Hospital-based treatment programs (especially in for-profit hospitals) are especially susceptible to such conflicts of interest in comparison to nonprofit social model recovery programs in which both the client and the community take responsibility for reduction of alcohol-related problems.

"Social model" alcoholism services should not be thought of merely in terms of the utilization of a non-hospital recovery situation. The full social model concept, as set forth in a paper for the National Academy of Sciences' Institute of Medicine (Reynolds and Ryan, 1988) emphasizes a range of activities blending together treatment with primary and secondary community prevention programs. A variety of agencies may be involved, including medical detoxification as needed, a length of stay in a halfway house or recovery home dependent upon the client's available outside social supports for continued sobriety, availability of professional psychological and social work counseling in a group setting as needed, resort to Alcoholics Anonymous or other mutual moral support groups on a long-term basis, and the existence of ongoing community prevention activities designed to make it easier for the susceptible drinker to maintain sobriety. Above all else, social model recovery programs are based on the premise that at all times the recovering alcoholic is an *active* participant in his or her *own* recovery process rather than the passive recipient of "expert" medical or psychiatric services.

The social model, with its emphasis upon joint involvement of the community and the client in the recovery process, is completely congruent with the types of treatment Miller has described as being the most effective. As he points out (1986), the social model of treatment is much more common in Europe than in America; and it is likely to be more widely adopted fairly soon here when further studies of cost-effectiveness prove out its advantages as compared to more limited but more expensive hospital-based treatments. However, as Reynolds and Ryan warn (1988, p. 2), entrenched interests will put up a battle to continue systems which are based on payment considerations rather than appropriateness, and focusing on billable services provided only for insured individuals already in distress rather than on long-term social supports of a preventive character.

ORGANIZATIONAL ISSUES

The prevention of alcohol problems and the treatment of alcoholics has been hampered by years of indecision over whether to have more or less centralization of policy and administration of alcohol programs. In the 1970s, strong leadership on the part of Senator Hughes, the Johnson administration, and such treatment-oriented constituencies as the National Council on Alcoholism promoted federal dominance through established guidelines to be followed by the states in applying for grants through the NIAAA to fund treatment programs for specific purposes. But in the 1980s, the Reagan administration's emphasis upon decentralization has meant that much of the federal funding has been allocated under formula grants for the states to spend largely at their own discretion. This trend has caused the withering away of much support for a larger role for the NIAAA in treatment and prevention programs, because NIAAA no longer has the power or the funds to assist constituency groups such as the National Council on Alcoholism to meet their objectives. Thus NIAAA has been relegated to serving primarily as a research institute and a funding agency for external research grants, much along the lines of the National Institute of Mental Health. In fact, there is much current pressure toward turning the NIAAA into an exclusively research agency, to be absorbed as a unit under the National Institutes of Health.

States-rights advocates and the alcoholic beverage industry would much prefer to have any controls over alcohol largely in the hands of the individual states, so that any sweeping changes in the direction of more stringent controls would be easier to circumvent. They argue, plausibly, that states do differ considerably in their attitudes toward controls, and that under the repeal amendment the decision had been made to turn the responsibility over to the states. However, provided that the people of the United States really *want* a unified and consistent set of controls over alcohol problems, a strong case can be made for the establishment of a central federal authority—along the lines of those in Scandinavian countries (Osterberg, 1985)—which would administer not only research grants and establish guidelines for prevention and treatment, but would also oversee the administration of rules governing the marketing and service of alcoholic beverages.

The Scandinavian central federal authorities over alcohol, which were established to reduce the pressures for profit and the lobbying power of the alcohol industry and to maintain the primary emphasis upon promoting public health and limiting alcohol-related accidents and delinquency, have now been operating for many years. Perhaps these centralized agencies are generally successful because the Scandinavian countries have much more homogeneous cultures and a citizenry with greater respect for laws and regulations than in the

U.S. However, a case could be made that we might be better off with a single national alcohol control authority instead of the present welter of overlapping agencies with entrenched bureaucracies, not only on the state level but also in such federal departments as Treasury, Justice, Agriculture, Commerce, and Health and Human Services. A plausible case could be made for establishing the central agency as a division of the Food and Drug Administration. The FDA has had long experience in administering laws and regulations to protect the purity of foods and the safety and efficacy of drugs, including the monitoring of food and drug labeling and advertising. As an old-line agency, the FDA already has the respect of the general public and enjoys broad congressional support against yielding to commercial pressures.

In a paper at a recent NIAAA-sponsored Washington meeting to present policy recommendations on alcohol programs to the Secretary of Health and Human Services (Cahalan, 1987b), I recommended that such a centralized agency should have at least the following ten responsibilities:

1. To serve as coordinator of alcohol-related activities of other federal agencies.
2. To set standards for purity of alcoholic beverages and for adequacy of labeling—including additives, strength, and warning about overuse.
3. To administer constraints against alcohol advertising that is misleading or otherwise injurious to the public. Such an agency certainly should have little conflict of interest in exerting needed controls over alcohol advertising as compared to the Bureau of Alcohol, Tobacco, and Firearms, which has been more protective of the interests of the alcohol industry than of the general public.
4. To maintain liaison with state agencies to help bring about more uniform control over alcohol.
5. To continue to develop model statutes and regulations for states' decriminalization of alcoholism, the inclusion of alcoholism among treatable health conditions to be covered by insurance, and dram shop liability and rules for conditions of alcohol sales.

6. To expand NIAAA's present data-gathering on state laws and regulations concerning alcohol control and expenditures of federal, state, and local funds on alcoholism treatment and prevention. Such data should be collected at more frequent intervals and should include more information relevant to program effectiveness.
7. To continue to give a high priority to comparative studies of alcohol policies and practices in other countries, so as to get the benefit of others' experiences in controlling alcohol problems.
8. To resume some of NIAAA's pilot grant or contract arrangements for implementing and assessing alternative modes of alcoholism treatment. However, such pilot programs are necessarily expensive and time-consuming and thus should not be undertaken until there is established a clearer consensus on the criteria for what constitute "improvements" and appropriate standards for the components of treatment.
9. To develop more pilot programs to foster improvement of primary prevention of alcohol problems on a community level. Programs should range from ambitious multimedia campaigns coordinated with local enforcement programs designed to reduce alcohol problems, down to small-scale pilot studies of the effectiveness of such campaigns as the prevention of drinking-driving accidents after high school proms.
10. To strengthen NIAAA's information retrieval and exchange programs, which have been hampered by stringent funding limits and the recent forced merger with not-too-compatible drug information programs.

It should be emphasized that over the long haul, to be effective, alcohol control programs must have the informed consent of the general public. Prohibition and negative moral pressures did not work too well even with past generations when religious and family influences were more powerful than they are today. The most effective model for minimizing alcohol problems would appear to be a non-prohibitionist *public health* model, with a strong emphasis on practical pointers on how to avoid excessive consumption of alcohol, as well as reasonable rules on alcoholic beverage marketing and service which have been proved to be effective in reducing alcohol-related accidents and health hazards.

REFERENCES

Cahalan, D. *Understanding America's Drinking Problem: How to Combat the Hazards of Alcohol*. San Francisco: Jossey-Bass, 1987a.

Cahalan, D. "Federal Leadership for Alcohol-Related Activities." Paper presented during the National Conference on Alcohol Abuse and Alcoholism, Washington, November 12, 1987b.

Cahalan, D. "Implications of the Disease Concept of Alcoholism." *Drugs & Society*, 2(3/4), 1988.

Dalen, M. "Ethical Considerations in Evaluation and Treatment of Court-Referred Clients." Alcohol and Drug Services, Inc., Mission, Kans. (undated 1988).

Distilled Spirits Council of the United States. *Annual Statistical Review, 1984/85*. Washington, D. C.: Distilled Spirits Council, 1985.

Fingarette, H. *Heavy Drinking: The Myth of Alcoholism as a Disease*. University of California Press, 1988.

Gallup, G. and Gallup, A. "Most Feel Alcoholism Is Disease." *San Francisco Chronicle*, April 25, 1988, A-8.

Harwood, H. and others. *Economic Costs to Society of Alcohol and Drug Abuse and Mental Illness: 1980*. Research Triangle Park, NC: Research Triangle Institute, June 1984.

Heath, D. "Alcohol Control Policies and Drinking Patterns: An International Game of Politics Against Science." *Journal of Substance Abuse*, *1*, 1988, 109-115.

Jacobson, M., Atkins, R. and Hacker, G. *The Booze Merchants: The Inebriating of America*. Washington, D. C.: Center for Science in the Public Interest, 1983.

Kerr, P. "Rich vs. Poor: Drug Patterns are Diverging." *New York Times*, August 30, 1987, 1, 17.

Miller, W. "Haunted By the *Zeitgeist:* Reflections on Contemporary Treatment Goals and Concepts of Alcoholism in Europe and the United States." *Annals of the New York Academy of Sciences*, July 11, 1986, *472*, 110-129.

Miller, W. "The Effectiveness of Alcoholism Treatment Modalities." Testimony to the U. S. Senate Committee on Governmental Affairs, 16 June 1988, 1-15.

Moore, M., and Gerstein, D. *Alcohol and Public Policy: Beyond the Shadow of Prohibition*. Washington: National Academy Press, 1981.

Mosher, J. and Jernigan, D. "New Directions in Alcohol Policy." Submitted for publication in *Annual Review of Public Health* 10 (1989).

Musto, D. *The American Disease: Origins of Narcotic Control*. New York: Oxford University Press, 1987.

Musto, D. Personal communication, August 19, 1988.

O'Toole, K. "Alameda County Courts Crippled by Crack Cases." *San Francisco Examiner*, July 24, 1988, B-1.

Osterberg, E. "From Home Distillation to the State Alcohol Monopoly." *Contemporary Drug Problems*, Spring 1985, *12*, (1), 31-51.

Pettigrew, T. "Influencing Policy With Social Psychology." *Journal of Social Issues*, *44*, No. 2, 1988, 205-219.

Raspberry, W. "The Second Cocaine War." *Washington Post*, May 4, 1988, A-23.

Reynolds, R. and Ryan, B. *Policy Implications of Social Model Alcohol Recovery Services*. Paper prepared for the National Academy of Sciences, Institute of Medicine, San Diego, July 1988.

Room, R. "Alcohol Control and Public Health." *Annual Review of Public Health*, 1984, *5*, 38-42.

Room, R. "Science is in the Details: Toward a Nuanced View of Alcohol Control Studies." *Journal of Substance Abuse*, *1*, 1988, 117-120.

Single, E. "The Researcher as Policy Maker: Reflections on Recent Developments in Canadian Alcohol Policy." Colloquium presented to the Rutgers Center for Alcohol Studies, March 10, 1987.

"States, Cities Cautious: Anti-Drug Money that's Going Unspent." *San Francisco Chronicle*, September 6, 1988, A-10.

Wallack, L. "Television Programming, Advertising, and the Prevention of Alcohol-Related Problems." In : D. Gerstein (ed.), *Toward the Prevention of Alcohol Problems: Government, Business, and Community Action*. Washington, D. C.: National Academy Press, 1984.

THE GREAT DRUG DEBATE

Taking Drugs Seriously

John Kaplan

It would be difficult to deny that the efforts and resources expended in our attempt to prevent the production of heroin and cocaine in other countries, and to keep out of the United States those drugs that are produced, have passed the point of diminishing returns. The outcry over drugs in the newspapers and on the political hustings, and a look at what is occurring in many public-housing projects and in the large lower-class black and Hispanic neighborhoods of our central cities, should be enough to convince sober observers that our present drug policies have simply not been successful enough.

Of course, there are politicians who still argue that our drug problems can be substantially improved by further attempts to push the Colombian, Mexican, Burmese, and other governments toward greater efforts. But with the military and internal strength they have at their disposal, they are doing about as well as one could expect.

John Kaplan is Professor at the School of Law, Stanford University, Stanford, CA 94305.

Reprinted with permission of the author from: THE PUBLIC INTEREST, No. 92 (Summer, 1988), pp. 32-50. © 1988 by National Affairs, Inc.

1. See my *The Hardest Drug: Heroin and Public Policy* (University of Chicago Press, 1983).

Nor is the related demand to increase the use of our army or navy to stop drug smuggling a more likely source of improvement. The ingenuity of smugglers, the tremendous volume of legitimate trade, and the huge number of individuals crossing our borders make it impracticable to achieve the kind of increases in the interdiction rate that would make heroin and cocaine significantly less available or more expensive in the United States.

The problem, then, for those who realize that our present efforts have bogged down, is what to do. In this respect, drug policy must proceed by elimination. None of the policy options is attractive. All involve great costs—either in expenditures on law enforcement or in damage to public health. Since no option is without severe disadvantages, we can aim only to choose the policy that is least bad.

At one level, the simplest solution would be simply to get out of the way, legalize heroin and cocaine, and allow their sale as we do alcohol's. Until recently this was rarely advocated in print, though for years one would hear such recommendations in private conversation with intellectuals. Now, however, the legalization movement is becoming respectable, and even popular.

A REPEAL OF DRUG PROHIBITION?

Probably the central problem with the solution of legalization is that it ignores basic pharmacology. There is such a thing as a dangerous drug, and both heroin and cocaine undoubtedly fall into this category. It is here, of course, that the alcohol analogy is usually brought up. The analogy is indeed suggestive, because alcohol is by any standard a dangerous drug as well. And when we repealed Prohibition, we replaced a legal ban on alcohol similar to that now imposed on heroin and cocaine with a system of legal, controlled sale, presumably much like that contemplated for heroin and cocaine. There is no doubt that legalization has attractions. When Prohibition was repealed, the enormous inflow of profits to organized crime and the large-scale corruption of public officials caused by the illegal alcohol traffic dropped sharply. And the large number of civil-liberties violations by Prohibition agents ceased as well.

Several factors, however, made the repeal of Prohibition a much better social decision than would be the case with heroin or cocaine.

Hard as it is to believe, the social cost of maintaining Prohibition was not only greater than that which heroin and cocaine currently impose upon us, it was even greater than that imposed by what is now our greatest drug problem—alcohol. Although the addict criminality caused by the high price of heroin and cocaine seems to have had no counterpart in the case of alcohol, the strain on our institutions was far greater. Corruption in the United States during Prohibition approximated that which we now associate with many Third World countries. It is true that the heroin and cocaine trades have corrupted many local police, some prosecutors, and a few local judges. During Prohibition, however, things were much worse. Federal judges, federal and state prosecutors, and countless politicians—from congressmen and state governors to mayors, city councilmen, and chiefs of police—were in the pay of bootleggers.

Part of the difference is due to the passage of time. Wave upon wave of reform has made our government a far more honest one in the last fifty years. Perhaps more important is the fact that both before and during Prohibition, alcohol use was common among all social classes and in virtually every area of the nation, and had a much better "image" than heroin and cocaine do today. A society where many people in all walks of life considered themselves drinkers made this activity far more respectable than the use of "hard drugs" is today. And, of course, when an activity is more socially acceptable, it becomes easier for government agents to accept bribes and favors to allow it to continue.

The strain and social costs attributed to Prohibition were not the only factors justifying the legalization of alcohol. The majority of drinkers enjoyed the use of alcohol without any harm to themselves or society. In a sense, the legalization of alcohol represented the willingness of these drinkers to shoulder their share of the social costs of legalized alcohol.

Nonetheless, the example of alcohol control illustrates a basic rule concerning all attempts to minimize the damage caused by habit-forming and destructive drugs. The principle also applies to a number of consensual (somewhat inaccurately called "victimless") crimes, such as gambling and prostitution. When one of these behaviors is made criminal, its enforcement is not particularly effective; it saddles the criminal-justice system with huge costs; it feeds organized criminal gangs; it causes official corruption; and it leads to large numbers of violations of civil liberties. Finally, the law does not really solve the problems of those engaging in the activity.

On the other hand, the legalization of the behavior produces an increase in the behavior, which can produce a public-health problem of enormous magnitude. Prohibition, for example, despite its faults—including the fact that it was not strictly enforced—did lower the amount of drinking in the United States. The comparative figures for cirrhosis of the liver demonstrate this clearly. With the repeal of Prohibition, both the number of drinkers and their per capita consumption of alcohol gradually but substantially increased, leading eventually to one of our major public-health problems—alcoholism. According to most estimates, alcoholism results in somewhere between 50,000 and 200,000 deaths per year. And regardless of whether the yearly social cost of alcoholism amounts to forty billion dollars or one hundred and ten billion dollars (two frequently cited figures), no one would deny that the social cost of alcohol use far exceeds that of all illegal drugs together. The issue then is not whether we were correct in legalizing alcohol or tobacco (I would strongly argue that we were), but what we should do about the drugs that are currently illegal.

A PRESCRIPTION SYSTEM?

Of course, criminalization and legalization are not the only possibilities. We are probably correct in using a prescription system for valium, for example, which is quite a dangerous drug—but also a useful one. When heroin addicts in England consisted overwhelmingly of middle-aged, middle-class men and women who had become addicted during the course of medical treatment, a prescription system was successfully used to dispense the drug. (Sale without a prescription was a rather serious crime.) However, when an increasingly higher percentage of those addicted came to be more like American addicts—lower-class, criminal, and thrill-seeking—the "British system" was abandoned. England stopped using the prescription system for more than a tiny and diminishing number of addicts, adopting instead a legal-control method much like that used in the United States.

In any event, no one seems to be arguing for a prescription system to control our major illegal drugs. If marijuana, cocaine, and heroin have legitimate medical uses (and the possibility that heroin is better than morphine at relieving intractable pain is the subject of heated debate, with most of the evidence apparently arguing against its superiority), then a prescription system seems most suitable. In fact, this is already being done: we allow prescriptions for medical use of cocaine and THC, the major active ingredient in marijuana.

Though we can regard heroin addiction itself as a disease, and hence a possible candidate for a prescription system, the problems in making such a system work seem insurmountable, as the British have discovered. The sizable pool of non-addicted heroin users forms a ready market for diverted prescribed heroin; the ranks of the addicted would thus swell. (It is impossible for a physician to determine how much heroin an addict really "needs," since this amount varies enormously over time.) Moreover, another drug—methadone—that is available by prescription (although only under certain conditions) is seen, both in the United States and in Britain, as much preferable to heroin for the medical treatment of heroin addiction.

The most important reason, however, why a prescription system for marijuana, cocaine, or heroin is just as inappropriate as it would be for alcohol and tobacco is that people generally use these drugs because they want to, and not to cure their ailments. We may be able to treat them and convince them not to use these drugs, but providing these drugs through prescription is not the way to do it.

If the choice for each of the "recreational" drugs is between criminalization and some kind of legalization, then it must be made on a drug-by-drug basis, as was the case with alcohol and tobacco (and coffee, for that matter), taking into account such variables as the pharmacological makeup of each drug and the cost of attempting to suppress it.

This is not an issue to be decided by John Stuart Mill's "simple principle"—that is, by letting each person decide for himself. No nation in the world follows his rule regarding self-harming conduct, and the rule is probably unworkable in a complex, industrial society—particularly one that is a welfare state. Mill's principle, moreover, seems singularly inappropriate when it is applied to a habit-forming, psychoactive drug that alters the user's perspective as to postponement of gratification and his desire for the drug itself.

NO SURRENDER?

On the other hand, certain arguments against legalization are even less impressive. Mill's principle, after all, is on the whole a rather sensible injunction to government, which tends—almost by reflex—to attempt to forbid any activity that it regards as harmful, immoral, or deviant. Far less sensible is the idea, advanced by Jesse Jackson and echoed by A. M. Rosenthal of the *New York Times*, that "you do not win a war by surrendering." Obviously, surrender is sometimes the better course. We did it with alcohol, and, if we go back further, we did it in many states with tobacco. (And in the international arena both we, in Vietnam, and the Soviet Union, in Afghanistan, seem to have improved our respective positions by abandoning a war.)

The non-pragmatic, no-surrender arguments are often coupled with warnings about the consequences of legalization. Such arguments, however, are insubstantial—particularly when compared with the serious arguments with which we should be grappling. Take Rosenthal's *Times* argument: "How can we continue to fight against alcoholism and tobacco addiction," asks Rosenthal, "if we suddenly say that other drugs—even more dangerous—should be made available?" This is not persuasive. First, virtually every scientist who has looked at the issue would acknowledge that one of the illegal drugs—marijuana—is certainly no more dangerous than alcohol. Second, the argument is a *non sequitur*. Legalizing drugs thought to be more dangerous than alcohol and tobacco might well make it even easier to convince alcohol and tobacco users that legalization does not guarantee that these drugs are safe. The educational message of treating what are patently dangerous drugs the same way we treat alcohol might be valuable for yet another reason. Many people still fail to understand that, by virtually any definition, alcohol is a drug. Treating alcohol the same way we treat cocaine and heroin might help drive this point home to many drinkers.

A similar fallacy lies behind a more common and somewhat more general argument—that legalization of a formerly illegal drug "sends the wrong message" to the public, implying that the drug is safe. The fact is that when Prohibition was enacted alcohol was regarded as dangerous, and Prohibition was not repealed because we changed our minds and decided that alcohol was safe. We all grew up believing that tobacco was habit-forming and stunted one's growth, at the very least. People who chose to drink and smoke did not do so because they believed that no one could be hurt by such behavior or that the government gave them its blessing. The simple increase in availability seems to account for all the increase in drug use when a drug is legalized. After all, those who use dangerous drugs that the public condemns tend not to be highly aware of the nuances of governmental messages.

As a result, the issue boils down to a careful weighing of the costs of criminalization of each drug against the public-health costs we could expect if that drug were to become legally available.

I will not consider the case of marijuana. It is the most used of the three major illegal drugs (although its use has decreased considerably in the last decade); but at present marijuana is also the least socially costly of the illegal drugs, in addition to being the drug that has been most effectively interdicted (because of its relatively large bulk). Finally, marijuana is the drug that promises the lowest public-health costs if legalized.

Various commentators have considered the social costs of marijuana's criminalization and the projected public-health costs of legalization. And though they have been shouted down by parent groups and those who seek their votes, these commentators, by and large, have leaned toward legalization. The report of the National Academy of Sciences Committee on Substance Abuse and Habitual Behavior made a rather conservative recommendation: it merely asserted that "the current policies directed at controlling the supply of marijuana should be seriously reconsidered."

Nor need we devote any attention to LSD, mescaline, PCP, or any number of other illegal drugs here; for the illegal status of these drugs has not created a significant social problem.

Needless to say, this is not the case with heroin and cocaine. The costs of restricting supply of these drugs are substantial. Since space does not permit discussions of both heroin and cocaine, I will discuss only the anticipated costs of legalizing cocaine. First, a reasonable calculation of the public-health costs of heroin legalization, based on our admittedly inadequate information, already exists.[1] Second, since cocaine is far more prevalent than heroin, it imposes greater social costs upon us—from the amount of money flowing into criminal syndicates to the number of users arrested for predatory crimes. Third, there seems to be a widespread public agreement—although it is probably mistaken—that cocaine is the more benign of the two drugs.

THE CASE OF COCAINE

At a minimum, it is clear that anyone advocating the legalization of cocaine would have to make a serious estimate of how many more people would use the drug after it was legalized; how many of these users would become dependent on the drug; and how much harm this would cause them and society. Instead, there has been no serious discussion of all this. Moreover, no one has seriously considered the impact of a "new" drug upon a culture that has yet to develop patterns of self-control with respect to its use; by contrast, we should recall that over many generations our culture has developed a variety of informal controls over alcohol use, which allow most people to lessen the harm that alcohol does both to them in particular and society in general. Societies not accustomed to alcohol, however, such as England prior to the "gin epidemic" of the late seventeenth and early eighteenth centuries, and many Native American and Eskimo cultures, have experienced a public-health catastrophe of huge proportions as a result of the introduction of distilled spirits.

Nor have the advocates of the legalization of cocaine considered how we would be able to prevent teenagers from gaining access to the now legal drug. Many people assume that legalization of a drug would affect only adults, since, as with alcohol, we would make it illegal to sell the drug to minors. The problem, however, is that legal access for adults makes a drug *de facto* available to the young. This has been the experience with alcohol and tobacco. Cocaine is far less bulky and more concealable than alcohol, and its use does not leave the telltale aroma of smoke; thus it would be even more difficult to keep away from minors.

Yet another problem is the possibility of changes in public consciousness and values. Such changes can make use of a drug less dangerous, but they can also greatly augment its dangers. There are many examples of changes in public consciousness, entirely apart from governmental action, that have influenced drug use. The use of tobacco, alcohol, and marijuana seems to have dropped in the last several years, just as jogging and low-fat diets have increased, all as a consequence of the nation's greater fixation on health. Unfortunately, we cannot guarantee that such cultural trends will continue, or even that they will not be reversed, as has often happened in the past.

Youth culture, moreover, seems to be subject to dramatic fluctuations. The rapid changes in styles of dress, hair, music, and entertainment among the young have bewildered their elders for generations; and the appearance of a charismatic proselytizer for cocaine (as Timothy Leary was for LSD and marijuana) could change youth attitudes toward cocaine. Such a cultural change, even if only temporary, could present us with a permanent problem of large numbers of young people who became drug-dependent during the period of the drug's "window of acceptability."

Consider the case of heroin. Though most people have not noticed, the epidemic of heroin use stopped about ten years ago. Each year, the average age of heroin addicts goes up by about a year. Nevertheless, the last heroin epidemic has left us with an endemic problem of about 500,000 addicts who impose large social costs upon us.

THE DANGERS OF COCAINE

This is not to say that problems like these cannot be solved, or that more careful thought and research might not satisfy us. As far as we now know, however, there is no particular cause for comfort. The pharmacological nature of cocaine, in fact, is especially worrisome. We need not list all the serious negative effects cocaine may have on its users, since an impressive list of such effects can be drawn up for any of the psychoactive drugs. The problem is to determine just how prevalent these effects would be if the drug were legalized.

With cocaine, we do not have to consider the relatively rare stoppages of the heart muscle or the incidence of strokes; the common effects of cocaine are the most appropriate reasons for concern. The most important fact about cocaine is that it is an extremely attractive drug. In the 1950s a double-blind experiment on the "enjoyability" of a number of injected drugs was undertaken with twenty normal volunteers. Although fewer than half of the subjects found heroin or morphine euphoric, fully 90 percent liked an amphetamine (which is a pharmocological relative of cocaine), giving it by far the highest "pleasure score."

Probably related to its "pleasure score" is the fact that cocaine is the most "reinforcing" drug known to us. Animal studies corroborate the reports of many human users. Over the past four decades, self-administration equipment has been developed that permits animals to "work" for supplies of a drug and to administer all they want. It turns out that opiates such as heroin lie somewhere between alcohol and cocaine in their reinforcing power. Alcohol seems relatively unattractive; it is quite difficult to get most animals to drink alcohol, and unless they are already addicted, monkeys and many other animals will go to some length to avoid ingesting alcohol. Virtually all monkeys, however, will continue injecting themselves with opiates until they become addicted, and even non-addicted animals will perform considerable amounts of work to "earn" their injections. But cocaine is the most impressive drug in this respect: animals will do enormous amounts of work to earn their cocaine shots. Indeed, if permitted, they will hit at their levers again and again to gain their reward of cocaine, neglecting food or rest until they die of debilitation.

This problem is exacerbated by several other properties of cocaine. Along with amphetamines, it is one of the few drugs that can improve one's mental and physical performance of a task. In fact, this improvement is limited to performance under conditions of fatigue, and the improvement is only temporary. Nonetheless, there will be many occasions during work, athletics, or studies when an individual will be willing to mortgage his future for a little more energy and mental clarity. Moreover – and in this respect unlike amphetamines – cocaine not only produces an alert high, but also subsequently causes a noticeable low, a kind of depression after its relatively short-term course has been run. This rather unusual effect results in the urge to use the drug again, both to re-create the past enjoyable high and to fight off the present dysphoric low.

The damage wrought by heavy cocaine use in terms of psychiatric symptoms and general debilitation is now widely known. What is less appreciated are the more subtle changes that regular cocaine use can cause. Unlike alcohol and heroin, cocaine use can easily be integrated with everyday activities. Its use can be quite inconspicuous, and, like cigarette smoking, can accompany a host of everyday activities. Cocaine use makes one feel good, then highly competent, then nearly omnipotent. It is easy to see why the use of such a drug would be damaging in a complex, mechanized, and interdependent society such as ours.

Nor should we take much comfort from the fact that most of those who use cocaine today have not become dependent upon the drug. As long as the drug is expensive and relatively difficult to procure, most of its users will be able to avoid dependence. When the drug is easily available, however, we can expect the temptations toward use to increase considerably.

We can see this by doing a quick calculation. Once the non-financial cost of cocaine (that is, inconvenience and criminal danger to the user) is greatly reduced by legalization, the drug's financial cost looms as the dominating one. At present, a gram of cocaine sells for about $80-$100. Its cost of production is certainly less than three dollars. Presumably, legalized cocaine would be taxed as heavily as possible, though the cost including tax would have to be sufficiently low, so as to make bootlegging unprofitable. Profits in today's cocaine trade are so huge, though, that it is hard to believe that we could keep the retail price of a gram of cocaine above $20. (Keep in mind that the bootlegger, who tries only to cheat the government out of its tax receipts, is treated much more leniently by both the criminal-justice system and society than is the universally maligned drug pusher.) When one considers that there are about fifty "hits" of cocaine in a gram, one is startled by the realization that at $20 per gram the cost of a hit will be only forty cents—a figure well within the budget of almost all grade-school children. Nor is the specter of very young children destroyed by the use of cocaine in any way unrealistic; there are ten-year-old cocaine addicts on the streets of Bogota today.

It is true that if the number of those dependent upon cocaine merely doubled, we would arguably be well ahead of the game, considering the large costs imposed by treating those users as criminals. But what if there were a fifty-fold increase in the number of those dependent on cocaine? We simply cannot guarantee that such a situation would not come to pass; since we cannot do so, it is the height of irresponsibility to advocate risking the future of the nation.

If all this is not enough to convince reasonably prudent people that legalizing cocaine is too risky a course, we can also consider the consequences of taking the risk and being wrong. After all, if we had legalized cocaine five years ago, we would not have known how easy it is to make cocaine into "crack," universally considered to be a much more habit-forming and dangerous form of the drug. If we legalize cocaine now, how long should we wait before deciding whether we made a mistake? And if we decided that we had, how would we go about recriminalizing the drug? By then, substantial inventories of legal cocaine would have been built up in private hands, and large numbers of new users would have been introduced to the drug. And once a drug has been made legally available, it is very difficult to prohibit it. This consideration helps to explain why Prohibition failed, and also explains why almost no one advocates the criminalization of tobacco.

FINDING A SOLUTION

The problem, then, is what we can do about the present situation. Several factors have made our drug policy politically tolerable up to now. First, it has protected most of middle-class America from the kind of continuous exposure to the use of drugs (and encouragement favoring their use) that are most likely to lead to the problems of drug abuse; such exposure and encouragement characterize the underclass areas in which drug use is endemic. Second, although drug enforcement has been expensive, it would have been even more expensive to do more. Third, we have continued to entertain hopes that we could solve our drug problem on the cheap, either by pressuring other nations to prevent the production of illegal drugs or by keeping drugs from being smuggled into the United States.

If we were to choose to take our drug problem more seriously, it is not clear what we could do. According to public-opinion polls, education is currently the most popular method for dealing with our drug problem. A recent Gallup Poll showed that 47 percent of Americans believe it is the best antidrug strategy. (Thirty-six percent favor interdiction, and 6 percent favor drug treatment.)

Our research shows that it is doubtful that education can do much to lower the level of drug abuse, however. Newspaper advertising campaigns to discourage alcohol abuse and drug use have been shown to be ineffective. We have had experience with temperance campaigns, but as far as we can tell, most young people do not appear to pay much attention to them. Nor do school-based programs seem to be able to reduce alcohol and drug abuse.

This is predictable. Young people are notoriously resistant to their elders' efforts to get them to live less risky, more forward-looking lives. Well into adolescence, they tend to retain what psychiatrists refer to as "remnants of infantile omnipotence." Moreover, entirely apart from the question of risk, young people often take pleasure in things that adults tell them are bad. They are constantly told that they should avoid things (like sex or junk food) that they enjoy. At best they tend to disregard such advice—when they do not actually seek out occasions to disobey their elders' counsel. Indeed, the real mystery is how we have managed to convince significant numbers of youths in inner-city school systems—more than 50 percent of whose students drop out of school, despite a massive publicity campaign to the contrary—to avoid taking drugs, since at least in the beginning they would find drug use so enjoyable.

Nevertheless, one kind of drug education does show some promise. Several small-scale experiments have attempted to use peers to teach young students techniques by which they can refuse cigarettes if they want to. They learn, for instance, what to say when others offer them cigarettes or even exert social pressure on them to smoke; this approach has produced significant decreases in the initiation of cigarette use. Such programs are still quite rare, however, and whether we can duplicate them on a large scale with respect to cocaine and heroin, in the neighborhoods that most need them, is by no means clear. At the very least, we need years of research before we can develop programs that can be trusted to do more good than harm.

The charm of education, nonetheless, is seductive. Compared with other means of coping with illegal drugs, it is cheap and seems humane, because it does not require the coercion of our fellow citizens. In this regard, it is similar to bringing pressure upon foreign nations to prevent the production of illegal drugs. Indeed, education may well become the "crop substitution" of the nineties—that is, the supposed panacea for all drug problems.

Conceivably, we will decide simply to continue our present policies. We can spend a great deal on education programs; we can assign the military the task of sealing our borders against drugs; we can seize yachts or fishing boats when passengers or workers have abandoned marijuana cigarettes on them; we can legislate capital punishment for drug-related killings (as when drug dealers murder one another). But by adopting such a course of action, we would only be making an emphatic statement that we were taking the drug problem seriously; we would not really be acting seriously. For to act in this manner would in effect be to choose to keep putting up with our problem.

For most middle-class Americans, the use of heroin and cocaine is not a major threat. Heroin never was a threat; and although cocaine was very popular with some wealthy users—the conventional wisdom held that they were heavily overrepresented in advertising, entertainment, and professional sports—and its use significantly harmed the lives of many middle-class youths, much of the damage has already been done. Today, cocaine—especially in the form of "crack"—is increasingly becoming a drug of the lower classes. It is true that all of us suffer from the intimate connection between these drugs and predatory crime, and in more indirect ways from the enormous dislocation and damage done to lower-class neighborhoods by the sale and use of these drugs. Nonetheless, we learned to live with problems like these many years ago. Indeed, it seems that the public gets really excited about the drug problem only when someone from the middle class is killed in a gang shoot-out.

In an ideal world, the best way to reduce the damage done by illegal drugs would be to convince everyone not to use them. In this world, however, we will probably have to reconcile ourselves to using some coercion. On the other hand, once we give up on finding an inexpensive solution, we may take the problem seriously and apply more careful thought and more resources to the job.

SUPPLY-SIDE ENFORCEMENT

So long as we are unable to suppress the sale of drugs, we will be remitting large parts of our cities to the terrorization of innocent people, drug-related killings, and the brutalization that comes from constant exposure to the use of drugs. Perhaps equally demoralizing is the sight of the large number of teenage drug lords who own Jaguars or Ferraris before they are old enough to have driver's licenses. Nonetheless, we can accomplish much more than we have in the past.

Apart from our efforts in other countries and at the borders, the major thrust of enforcement within the United States has been the attempt to break up large-scale drug rings, arrest small-scale dealers when they sell drugs outside the areas in which drug use is endemic, and punish users when they commit other crimes. In recent years local police have stepped up their efforts to restrain street-level selling, and private employers have exerted greater efforts to apprehend their workers' "connection," and to weed out illegal drug users from their work force. The result has been a slow but steady loss of ground for law-enforcement agencies.

One cannot say that careful thought and greatly augmented law-enforcement resources will solve our drug problem. There are large numbers of sellers arranged hierarchically within the United States as part of loose but fairly sizable organizations, taking the drug from its importation into the United States through smaller wholesalers down to the small-scale sellers who provide the drug to users. Unfortunately, we cannot expect to achieve much of a reduction in the number of drug suppliers, even if we jail a sizable percentage of them. The high profits at every level of the drug trade guarantee a huge reservoir of individuals prepared to take the places of those who have been imprisoned. At each level in the distribution scheme there are more than enough competitors; and even at the lowest ranks, those who do minor jobs for the sellers (such as acting as lookouts for the police) seem ready to enter the business.

On the other hand, pressure upon the retailing of heroin and cocaine is not necessarily an unattractive option. In fact, it is probably the major governmental means of restraining drug use in the United States today. The number of locations in which an ordinary middle-class individual can buy heroin and cocaine is not very large. In most of the country, cocaine is not widely available to most people. Heroin is less so. A major task of law-enforcement resources is to increase that area of drug unavailability. At the very least, the police should act immediately to suppress the open-air drug markets that spring up whenever the police are distracted by other duties. In most of our urban areas, greater efforts could drive much of the dealing indoors, where a large percentage of potential customers are afraid to go.

At least for the foreseeable future, it is hard to imagine the police being able to do more than gradually drive the dealing back into the public-housing projects and other relatively small areas in which the police are unable to maintain a presence. Nonetheless, increases in law-enforcement efforts at the retail level may lower the availability of heroin and cocaine to large numbers of people without creating a need to involve ourselves in the most hard-core drug-trafficking areas, in which the police would have to maintain a virtual army of occupation.

Apart from the difficulty of policing the hard-core drug areas, the most important constraint upon our ability to suppress the sale of drugs is the cost of incarceration space. Our prisons and jails are full, and despite a massive and continuing effort to provide the infrastructure to imprison more and more lawbreakers, the demand threatens to permanently outrun the supply. Drug sales, moreover, are especially difficult and expensive to restrain through imprisonment. The deterrence we expect from the legal threat is in large part neutralized by the high profits at all levels of the drug trade. And incapacitation, the other major restraint provided by imprisonment, is weakened by the fact that the skills necessary to participate in the drug trade are not at all scarce.

Although we must allocate a large percentage of prison space to the incarceration of drug dealers if we are to make headway, there are other methods that can help. At the higher levels of the drug trade, the forfeiture of assets has proven quite successful. We cannot show that the threat has caused any drug dealers to get out of the business, but at the margin it should have that effect; depriving sellers of working capital makes their reentry into the industry more difficult. At the very least, it assuages our sense of justice, as well as providing additional resources with which to further enforcement. It is likely that we can go a great deal lower in the drug-trade hierarchy before forfeiture is no longer worthwhile. It will require a little more ingenuity by the police and cooperation from the agencies of the criminal-justice system before we can strike at the pocketbook of the small-scale seller, but it can be done—and to good effect.

DEMAND-SIDE ENFORCEMENT

While pressure on the small-scale sale of drugs represents an attempt to influence drug supply, it also has an impact on drug demand—perhaps a greater one. The buyer who does not reside in an area of heavy drug sales must not only come up with the money to pay for the drugs; he may also have to search longer to make a purchase and worry more about the danger of being robbed or assaulted. He may also be more conspicuous to the police. To some extent, we can take advantage of this problem faced by drug buyers by using a relatively inexpensive means of lessening the number of those who are willing to obtain their supplies from the areas of heavy drug dealing. On a few occasions police have seized the automobiles of those who drove them to purchase drugs. This is not only inexpensive, but also far less brutal than imprisoning otherwise law-abiding drug users—and it may have more of an impact. This should be a regular feature of all drug enforcement.

Probably the most important aspect of the attack on drugs is the attempt to lower the amount of predatory crime that drug use engenders. We know, for example, that those who use illegal drugs commit a substantial proportion of our urban burglaries, robberies, and thefts. A number of studies have demonstrated that the criminality rate of those using heroin daily—that is, those who were addicted—was about seven times as great as the criminality rate of the same people when they were using the drug only sporadically or temporarily not using it at all.

Newer studies have shown an even higher correlation between criminality and drug use, and have implicated cocaine as well. Urinalysis of those arrested for crimes in 1986 has revealed that a staggering percentage of those apprehended had recently used cocaine or heroin. In the District of Columbia, 74 percent of non-drug-felony arrestees tested positive for at least one illegal drug other than marijuana. (No one has alleged that marijuana use helps to cause predatory crime, in part because the drug is cheap, in part because it has a tranquilizing effect.) In New York City the figure was 72 percent; in Chicago, 60 percent; and in Los Angeles, 58 percent. It turns out that in large cities about 70 percent of those arrested for robbery, weapons offenses, and larceny tested positive for heroin, cocaine, or (in the few cities where use is common) PCP.

The data on urinalysis suggest an obvious course of action. We must institutionalize routine urinalysis for those arrested for any of the typical crimes arising out of drug use. Then we must act on this information by making maintenance of a urine clean of cocaine, heroin and PCP a requirement for all those who are released on bail or, after conviction, are placed on probation or released on parole.

A positive urine sample must reliably and immediately mean a return to jail. It is far more important that the enforcement of these rules be consistent than that the jail terms be long. We do not have the jail space that would be needed to provide long terms for this type of offense. And if we try, our efforts will backfire: we will deprive the system of the consistency necessary to get the message through to drug users. But a properly implemented system of imprisonment can make possible a more lasting cure for drug dependency.

This kind of regimen is not without disadvantages. There will inevitably be a dispute over whether we can demand "clean" urine before releasing someone on bail. On the one hand, our jurisprudence tells us that bail is to be used only to guarantee the presence of the accused at judicial proceedings, and there is no firm evidence that drug users are less likely than others to show up in court. On the other hand, more recent precedent seems to allow consideration of the danger to the community if an arrestee is released on bail, and those who use illegal drugs are, on average, much more likely to commit crimes after they have been freed.

Such a system of mandatory urinalysis will also require more money. Parts of the criminal-justice system will simply not give up – even temporarily – the funds they already have and need, even though doing so may help to save money in the long run. The jails are already full, and in many cases under court order not to exceed their present population. Even at two days per failed urinalysis, the increased demand upon those institutions will be substantial. And the maintenance of such a system will require the police to go looking for those who miss urinalysis appointments, a burden that may initially be only partially compensated for by the lower criminality of those now compelled to be drug-free.

Furthermore, the inexpensive urine test, which costs only about $5, but is less than completely accurate, will have to be supplemented by a system in which an arrestee who was confident that he had not used an illegal drug could simply file an affidavit to that effect and be tested by a more expensive but foolproof method (costing about $70). Although there will have to be some sanction for a false affidavit, expensive prosecutions for perjury will not be necessary to deter such conduct (though it is hard to imagine a simpler case to prosecute). The judge, in revoking bail or probation, can simply revoke it for longer.

Then there are the privacy concerns. It should be noted that urinalysis for those who have been arrested involves far fewer restraints on the citizen's right to privacy than the usual attempt to require urinalysis of government employees or members of other large groups, who, as individuals, give us no reason to suspect their drug use. (Nor is it nearly so expensive.) Our statistics on the drug use of those arrested for street crimes already single them out. And apart from the use of urinalysis in the bail decision, there are no real constitutional doubts. If there is a good reason, those arrested for drunken driving, for example, may constitutionally be subjected to blood, urine, or breath analysis, and those released on bail or, after conviction, on probation or parole, forfeit even more of their privacy. They are subject not only to intrusive searches but also to various restrictions on their autonomy. Very few of the restrictions on the privacy and autonomy of defendants in the criminal-justice system make as much practical sense as requiring urinalysis in order to monitor their drug use.

THE PROGNOSIS

What, then, could we expect from the institutionalization of such a regimen? Many of those using drugs will find themselves constantly in and out of jail. Some would simply decide that enough is enough and clean themselves up. We do know that this can occur when the consequences are immediate and certain enough. Nonetheless, in most cases we will have to rely upon drug treatment to prevent the urinalysis system from becoming a huge, inhumane, and expensive revolving-door operation. While it is true that the most reliable and cost-effective drug treatment—methadone maintenance—is helpful only with heroin addicts, there are other therapies that are more cost-effective than permitting the drug abuser to continue untreated; and it is likely that requiring urinalysis will help persuade drug users to undergo treatment.

Indeed, probably the most foolish aspect of our antidrug posture has been the starvation of drug treatment. In many cities there is a months-long wait for those who want to enter a drug-treatment program; this is a serious problem, considering that the desire to reform is often ephemeral, and disappears if it cannot be acted upon at once. Part of the reluctance to invest in drug treatment stems from the moralistic view that it is wrong to spend resources on making life better for criminals; part stems from the (incorrect) belief that treatment does not work. Treatment is difficult; it is frustrating; and it does not always work. But it is cost-effective—and far more so than its only substitute, imprisonment. A necessary component of any serious effort to lower the social costs of illegal drug use, therefore, is a massive increase in funds for drug treatment.

Another fact about drug treatment is also quite important. Although many believe that compulsory treatment is ineffective, this does not appear to be the case. Virtually everyone undergoing drug treatment is in one way or another forced to do so. Indeed, like many alcoholics, who simply want to become social drinkers again and escape the social, psychological, and physical effects of overindulgence, most drug users do not wish to be abstinent, but rather to return to the early days of their more casual drug use. Nonetheless, one of the effects that those dependent on cocaine and heroin may most wish to escape is the pressure of the criminal-justice system. And a criminal-justice system that makes use of urinalysis will be more effective in driving them into—and keeping them in—treatment.

The approach I am recommending may have another important effect. For years, the drug-producing nations have argued that the United States must share the blame for the drug problem: if they cannot control the production of illegal drugs, neither can we control our consumption. We may now be able to have some success. Those users who are both criminals and drug consumers appear to be not merely a random selection of drug users; they tend, rather, to be the heaviest users. Thus it is likely that these heavy users consume a disproportionate percentage of the illegal drug supply. This should not be surprising: the heaviest-drinking 10 percent of all drinkers drink well over half the total quantity of alcohol—and our evidence, though less conclusive, points in the same direction with regard to illegal drugs. Indeed, the "J curve" seems to be a constant in human behavior: 15 percent of health-insurance users use 90 percent of the resources; 6 percent of Philadelphia's youths commit over 50 percent of its crimes; and 10 percent of Stanford Law School's students file 90 percent of the petitions to be excused from one requirement or another.

As a result, those users we will be focusing on will be those who do the most to support the illegal market. On average, each seller is supported by three heavy users. If we can bring their use under control—in addition to decreasing the number of predatory crimes—we may finally be able to deal a major blow to the illegal retail-distribution networks. We may also create a sizable cohort of former drug users who can help discourage drug use. If the zeal of the convert in this area is as strong as it seems to be in others—think of ex-smokers, for example—we may reap unanticipated and sizable dividends from our efforts. For decades we have attempted to get at the sellers as a way of preventing use; now we may have the means to get at the users as a means of restraining sales.

I do not mean to suggest that we will be able to solve the problem easily. For the foreseeable future we will have a serious drug problem, but we can lessen it considerably if we have the will. Where will the money necessary to accomplish this come from? The additional resources we need for law enforcement and drug treatment will come from the federal government, or they will not come at all. Whether the resources will come is simply a question of whether we have finally begun to take our drug problem seriously. It will be interesting to find out.

Don't Legalize Drugs

Morton M. Kondracke

The next time you hear that a drunk driver has slammed into a school bus full of children or that a stoned railroad engineer has killed 16 people in a train wreck, think about this: if the advocates of legalized drugs have their way, there will be more of this, a lot more. There will also be more unpublicized fatal and maiming crashes, more job accidents, more child neglect, more of almost everything associated with substance abuse: babies born addicted or retarded, teenagers zonked out of their chance for an education, careers destroyed, families wrecked, and people dead of overdoses.

The proponents of drug legalization are right to say that some things will get better. Organized crime will be driven out of the drug business, and there will be a sharp drop in the amount of money (currently about $10 billion per year) that society spends to enforce the drug laws. There will be some reduction in the cost in theft and injury (now about $20 billion) by addicts to get the money to buy prohibited drugs. Internationally, Latin American governments presumably will stop being menaced by drug cartels and will peaceably export cocaine as they now do coffee.

However, this is virtually the limit of the social benefits to be derived from legalization, and they are far outweighed by the costs, which are always underplayed by legalization advocates such as the *Economist*, Princeton scholar Ethan A. Nadelmann (see "Shooting Up," TNR, June 13), economist Milton Friedman and other libertarians, columnists William F. Buckley and Richard Cohen, and

---

Morton M. Kondracke is Senior Editor, *The New Republic*, 1220 19th Street N.W., Washington, DC 20036.

Reprinted by permission of: THE NEW REPUBLIC, © 1988 by the New Republic, Inc. This article first appeared in *The New Republic*, Vol. 198, No. 26, Issue 3832 (June 27, 1988), pp. 16-19 (ISN 0028-6583).

Mayors Keith Schmoke of Baltimore and Marion Barry of Washington, D.C. In lives, money, and human woe, the costs are so high, in fact, that society has no alternative but to conduct a real war on the drug trade, although perhaps a smarter one than is currently being waged.

Advocates of legalization love to draw parallels between the drug war and Prohibition. Their point, of course, is that this crusade is as doomed to failure as the last one was, and that we ought to surrender now to the inevitable and stop wasting resources. But there are some important differences between drugs and alcohol. Alcohol has been part of Western culture for thousands of years; drugs have been the rage in America only since about 1962. Of the 115 million Americans who consume alcohol, 85 percent rarely become intoxicated; with drugs, intoxication is the whole idea. Alcohol is consistent chemically, even though it's dispensed in different strengths and forms as beer, wine, and "hard" liquor; with drugs there's no limit to the variations. Do we legalize crack along with snortable cocaine, PCPs as well as marijuana, and LSD and "Ecstasy" as well as heroin? If we don't—and almost certainly we won't—we have a black market, and some continued crime.

But Prohibition is a useful historical parallel for measuring the costs of legalization. Almost certainly doctors are not going to want to write prescriptions for recreational use of harmful substances, so if drugs ever are legalized they will be dispensed as alcohol now is—in government-regulated stores with restrictions on the age of buyers, warnings against abuse (and, probably, with added restrictions on amounts, though this also will create a black market).

In the decade before Prohibition went into effect in 1920, alcohol consumption in the United States averaged 2.6 gallons per person per year. It fell to 0.73 gallons during the Prohibition decade, then doubled to 1.5 gallons in the decade after repeal, and is now back to 2.6 gallons. So illegality suppressed usage to a third or a fourth of its former level. At the same time, incidence of cirrhosis of the liver fell by half.

So it seems fair to estimate that use of drugs will at least double, and possibly triple, if the price is cut, supplies are readily available, and society's sanction is lifted. It's widely accepted that there are now 16 million regular users of marijuana, six million of cocaine, a half million of heroin, and another half million of other drugs, totaling 23 million. Dr. Robert DuPont, former director of the National Institutes of Drug Abuse and an anti-legalization crusader, says that the instant pleasure afforded by drugs—superior to that available with alcohol—will increase the number of regular users of marijuana and cocaine to about 50 or 60 million and heroin users to ten million.

Between ten percent and 15 percent of all drinkers turn into alcoholics (ten million to 17 million), and these drinkers cost the economy an estimated $117 billion in 1983 ($15 billion for treatment, $89 billion in lost productivity, and $13 billion in accident-related costs). About 200,000 people died last year as a result of alcohol abuse, about 25,000 in auto accidents. How many drug users will turn into addicts, and what will this cost? According to President Reagan's drug abuse policy adviser, Dr. David I. McDonald, studies indicate that marijuana is about as habit-forming as alcohol, but for cocaine, 70 percent of users become addicted, as many as with nicotine.

So it seems reasonable to conclude that at least four to six million people will become potheads if marijuana is legal, and that coke addicts will number somewhere between 8.5 million (if regular usage doubles and 70 percent become addicted) and 42 million (if DuPont's high estimate of use is correct). An optimist would have to conclude that the number of people abusing legalized drugs will come close to those hooked on alcohol. A pessimist would figure the human damage as much greater.

Another way of figuring costs is this: the same study (by the Research Triangle Institute of North Carolina) that put the price of alcoholism at $117 billion in 1983 figured the cost of drug abuse then at $60 billion—$15 billion for law enforcement and crime, and $45 billion in lost productivity, damaged health, and other costs. The updated estimate for 1988 drug abuse is $100 billion. If legalizing drugs would save $30 billion now being spent on law enforcement and crime, a doubling of use and abuse means that other costs will rise to $140 billion or $210 billion. This is no bargain for society.

If 200,000 people die every year from alcohol abuse and 320,000 from tobacco smoking, how many will die from legal drugs? Government estimates are that 4,000 to 5,000 people a year are killed in drug-related auto crashes, but this is surely low because accident victims are not as routinely blood-tested for drugs as for alcohol. Legalization advocates frequently cite figures of 3,600 or 4,100 as the number of drug deaths each year reported by hospitals, but this number too is certainly an understatement, based on reports from only 75 big hospitals in 27 metropolitan areas.

If legalization pushed the total number of drug addicts to only half the number of alcoholics, 100,000 people a year would die. That's the figure cited by McDonald. DuPont guesses that, given the potency of drugs, the debilitating effects of cocaine, the carcinogenic effects of marijuana, and the AIDS potential of injecting legalized heroin, the number of deaths actually could go as high as 500,000 a year. That's a wide range, but it's clear that legalization of drugs will not benefit human life.

All studies show that those most likely to try drugs, get hooked, and die – as opposed to those who suffer from cirrhosis and lung cancer – are young people, who are susceptible to the lure of quick thrills and are terribly adaptable to messages provided by adult society. Under pressure of the current prohibition, the number of kids who use illegal drugs at least once a month has fallen from 39 percent in the late 1970s to 25 percent in 1987, according to the annual survey of high school seniors conducted by the University of Michigan. The same survey shows that attitudes toward drug use have turned sharply negative. But use of legal drugs is still strong. Thirty-eight percent of high school seniors reported getting drunk within the past two weeks, and 27 percent said they smoke cigarettes every day. Drug prohibition is working with kids; legalization would do them harm.

And, even though legalization would lower direct costs for drug law enforcement, it's unlikely that organized crime would disappear. It might well shift to other fields – prostitution, pornography, gambling or burglaries, extortion, and murders-for-hire – much as it did in the period between the end of Prohibition and the beginning of the drug era. As DuPont puts it, "Organized crime is in the business of giving people the things that society decides in its own interest to prohibit. The only way to get rid of organized crime is to make everything legal." Even legalization advocates such as Ethan

Nadelmann admit that some street crimes will continue to occur as a result of drug abuse—especially cocaine paranoia, PCP insanity, and the need of unemployable addicts to get money for drugs. Domestic crime, child abuse and neglect surely would increase.

Some legalization advocates suggest merely decriminalizing marijuana and retaining sanctions against other drugs. This would certainly be less costly than total legalization, but it would still be no favor to young people, would increase traffic accidents and productivity losses—and would do nothing to curtail the major drug cartels, which make most of their money trafficking in cocaine.

Legalizers also argue that the government could tax legal drug sales and use the money to pay for anti-drug education programs and treatment centers. But total taxes collected right now from alcohol sales at the local, state, and federal levels come to only $13.1 billion per year—which is a pittance compared with the damage done to society as a result of alcohol abuse. The same would have to be true for drugs—and any tax that resulted in an official drug price that was higher than the street price would open the way once again for black markets and organized crime.

So, in the name of health, economics, and morality, there seems no alternative but to keep drugs illegal and to fight the criminals who traffic in them. Regardless of what legalization advocates say, this is now the overwhelming opinion of the public, the Reagan administration, the prospective candidates for president, and the Congress—not one of whose members has introduced legislation to decriminalize any drug. Congress is on the verge of forcing the administration to raise anti-drug spending next year from $3 billion to $5.5 billion.

There is, though, room to debate how best to wage this war. A consensus is developing that it has to be done both on the supply side (at overseas points of origin, through interdiction at U.S. borders and criminal prosecution of traffickers) and on the demand side (by discouraging use of drugs through education and treatment and/or by arrest and urine testing at workplaces). However, there is a disagreement about which side to emphasize and how to spend resources. Members of Congress, especially Democrats, want to blame foreigners and the Reagan administration for the fact that increasing amounts of cocaine, heroin, and marijuana are entering the country. They want to spend more money on foreign aid, use the U.S. military to seal the borders, and found "nice" treatment and education programs, especially those that give ongoing support to professional social welfare agencies.

Conservatives, on the other hand, want to employ the military to help foreign countries stamp out drug laboratories, use widespread drug testing to identify—and, often, punish—drug users, and spend more on police and prisons. As Education Secretary William Bennett puts it, "How can we surrender when we've never actually fought the war?" Bennett wants to fight it across all fronts, and those who have seen drafts of a forthcoming report of the White House Conference for a Drug Free America say this will be the approach recommended by the administration, although with muted emphasis on use of the U.S. military, which is reluctant to get involved in what may be another thankless war.

However, DuPont and others, including Jeffrey Eisenach of the Heritage Foundation, make a strong case that primary emphasis ought to be put on the demand side—discouraging use in the United States rather than, almost literally, trying to become the world's policeman. Their argument, bolstered by a study conducted by Peter Reuter of the RAND Corporation, is that major profits in the drug trade are not made abroad (where the price of cocaine triples from farm to airstrip), but within the United States (where the markup from entry point to street corner is 12 times), and that foreign growing fields and processing laboratories are easily replaceable at low cost.

They say that prohibition policy should emphasize routine random urine testing in schools and places of employment, arrests for possession of drugs, and "coercive" treatment programs that compel continued enrollment as a condition of probation and employment. DuPont thinks that corporations have a right to demand that their employees be drug-free because users cause accidents and reduce productivity. He contends that urine testing is no more invasive than the use of metal detectors at airports.

"Liberals have a terrible time with this," says DuPont. "They want to solve every problem by giving people things. They want to love people out of their problems, while conservatives want to punish it out of them. What we want to do is take the profits out of drugs by drying up demand. You do that by raising the social cost of using them to the point where people say, 'I don't want to do this.' This isn't conservative. It's a way to save lives."

It is, and it's directly parallel to the way society is dealing with drunk driving and cigarette smoking—not merely through advertising campaigns and surgeon general's warnings, but through increased penalties, social strictures—and prohibitions. Random testing for every employee in America may be going too far, but testing those holding sensitive jobs or workers involved in accidents surely isn't, nor is arresting users, lifting driver's licenses, and requiring treatment. These are not nosy, moralistic intrusions on people's individual rights, but attempts by society to protect itself from danger.

In the end, they are also humane and moral. There is a chance, with the public and policy-makers aroused to action, that ten years from now drug abuse might be reduced to its pre-1960s levels. Were drugs to be legalized now, we would be establishing a new vice—one that, over time, would end or ruin millions of lives. Worse yet, we would be establishing a pattern of doing the easy thing, surrendering, whenever confronted with a difficult challenge.